Fast-moving

Currents in

Youth Culture

Fast-moving Currents in Youth Culture

Edited by Leslie J. Francis, William K. Kay,

Alan Kerby and Olaf Fogwill

LYNX

This edition copyright (c) 1995 Leslie Francis, William Kay, Alan Kerbey and Olaf Fogwill

The authors assert the moral right to be identified as the authors of this work

Published by Lynx Communications
Sandy Lane West, Oxford OX4 5HG, England
ISBN 0 7459 3062 X

Albatross Books Pty Ltd
PO Box 320, Sutherland
NSW 2232, Australia
ISBN 0 7324 1256 0

First edition 1995
All rights reserved

Printed and bound in Great Britain

Acknowledgments

Scripture quotations taken from the Holy Bible, New International Version. Copyright (c) 1973, 1978, 1984 by International Bible Society. Used by permission of Hodder & Stoughton Ltd, a member of the Hodder headline Group.

Illustrations by Howie Twiner

The Genesis of the research

Initial research on teenage beliefs and values was carried out by the Revd Professor L J Francis, who holds the D J James Chair of Pastoral Theology and the Mansel Jones Fellowship of the University of Wales, Lampeter, and Trinity College, Carmarthen. The research project was conducted in partnership with Crusaders and after securing funding from those to whom thanks are given below. Recognising the enormous value of this work to those involved in youth work, Crusaders suggested that various youth specialists should be invited to interpret the findings in a "user-friendly" manual and we are grateful to our publishers, Lynx, for the trouble they have taken in efficiently presenting this collaborative venture in the form we envisaged.

Acknowledgements and thanks

At the top of our list of acknowledgements come the headteachers, staff and pupils who responded so positively to the invitation to provide data. Without their time, co-operation and openness there would have been no information on which to base the statistics presented in this book. Secondly, we acknowledge the significant role of the Principal and Governors of Trinity College, Carmarthen, in actively seeking to promote such research initiatives through the newly established Centre for Theology and Education. Thirdly, we are indebted to several trusts and organisations which have sponsored specific parts of the survey: the Rank Foundation, the Hockerhill Education Foundation, the All Saints' Educational Trust and the Friends First Day Schools Trust. Finally we record our gratitude to Susan Jones who supervised the data management.

Contents

Contributors

John Allan
Senior Youthworker at Belmont Chapel, Exeter and Chairman of the Evangelical Alliance Youth Committee. Previously, John was Publishing Editor for World Evangelical Fellowship and Training Director of British Youth for Christ.

Colin Bennett
Director of Youth and Community Work Training at Moorlands College—a Christian Training Centre located in Dorset. Colin is married to Yvonne and they have three fantastic children: Ruth, Sarah and Daniel. The whole family are actively involved in New Covenant Church, Christchurch.

David Bruce
General Director of Scripture Union in Northern Ireland. David is an ordained Presbyterian minister and a former Travelling Secretary with UCCF.

John Buckeridge
Editor of *Youthwork* magazine and Assistant Editor of *Alpha* magazine. John is on the Executive Committee of Brainstormers, is a regular speaker at youth workers' conferences and seminars, and author of several books.

Michael Eastman
Secretary and Development Officer of Frontier Youth Trust, and Secretary of the Evangelical Coalition for Urban Mission. He also coordinates Scripture Union's Urban and Justice Ministries in England and Wales and their Specialist Cities Ministry internationally. Michael served as an advisor to the Archbishop's Commission on Urban Priority Areas, is on the board of YMCA National College and serves on the National Council for Voluntary Youth Services.

Sue Eccleston
Started in full-time youth work with Youth for Christ. Then South East Development Coordinator for Drugs and Alcohol with Band of Hope until recently. Now she wears four hats: work with a Christian charity for the homeless; at an alcohol advice centre; as a freelance drugs educator in schools; and as a youthworker in her church in Watford.

Heather Evans
Formerly Area Youth Worker with Oasis for London Baptist churches, she was involved in setting up the Oasis Youth Ministry Training Course. She currently divides her time between tutoring on this course and part-time study at the London Bible College.

Maggie Everett
Youth for Christ's Area Director for Central and Northern England. Additionally, Maggie regularly speaks at Spring Harvest, is part of the Brainstormers Executive Committee, and is a member of the Management Council for Wycliffe Bible Translators.

Dave Fenton
Youth and Children's Coordinator at Christ Church, Fulwood, Sheffield. Dave is committed to the idea that the church is the place for young people and that the Bible can be taught to all ages.

Olaf Fogwill

Olaf has many years of varied youth work experience and is now working with Crusaders as Public Relations and Support Manager. He formerly had a pastoral role with students, and lectured in Marketing and Business Studies.

Leslie J. Francis

D.J.James Professor of Pastoral Theology and Mansel Jones Fellow at Trinity College, Carmarthen and the University of Wales, Lampeter, and a prolific writer on theology, education and pastoral psychology.

Peter Gilbert

Pete is an evangelist working with the Pioneer network of churches in Great Britain and abroad. Part of the leadership team of Revelation Church; a member of Gerald Coates' Pioneer Team; involved in TV and radio work; and author of several books about teenagers and evangelism.

Nigel Hall

Holidays Manager with Crusaders, with responsibility for national holidays programme and the development of residential work within Crusaders. Nigel has extensive experience in youth work, including leadership of Scripture Union beach missions and local church youth work.

Andy Hickford

Youth Minister, Stopsley Baptist Church, Luton. He is an Executive Member of Brainstormers, and a Consultant Editor for Youthwork Magazine.

Bill Hogg

Director for British Youth for Christ in Scotland.

Rana Singh Johal

Area Development Worker with Crusaders, particularly working in Urban Priority Areas. Rana is deeply concerned with cross-cultural communication.

William K. Kay

Senior Research Fellow in the Centre for Theology and Education at Trinity College, Carmarthen.

Alan Kerbey

National Director of Crusaders. Prior to joining Crusaders, Alan pioneered a successful church-based youth ministry. Formerly Research Scientist at Oxford University and Lecturer in Biochemistry at Trinity College, Oxford.

Grahame Knox

A Senior Staffworker with British Youth for Christ, and Project Director of 2YO (2000 Years On), an RE resource for secondary education. Grahame has also written a number of books and resources for youthworkers and schools.

Phil Moon

A minister at Christ Church Lowestoft, Phil has worked with CYFA for the past seven years, training youth leaders and writing a variety of material. Formerly a curate in Sussex.

Russ Oliver

Russ works with the Pioneer network of churches and leads the 'Generation Epsom' Church. Work focuses on training, young people, church planting, evangelism and social action.

Sue Rinaldi

As a singer/songwriter/communicator, Sue travels the United Kingdom and abroad, as well as focusing on worship leading and speaking at seminars on a variety of issues, including youth-related issues. Sue is a member of the 'Pioneer People' church, where she is part of the schools team and works with the young adults.

Dave Roberts

Publisher of Youthwork, the leading Christian youthwork magazine. He is Chairman of Brainstormers, the youth leader training event. Dave is Editor of Alpha, a major monthly Christian magazine, and has written on youth culture.

Brian Spurling

Leadership Training Manager for Crusaders. Before that Brian was a secondary school teacher, and further back still, an aircraft pilot.

Phil Wall

National Youth Evangelist with the Salvation Army since 1990. Phil is involved in training and equipping young leaders, conducting celebrations and youth weekends, and with Feet First, Frontline and On Fire 1995.

Pete Ward

Archbishop of Canterbury's Officer for Youth Ministry. Pete founded Oxford Youth Works, to practise relational youthwork, and to train others to do the same. He co-authored a training book, *Youthwork, and How To Do It*, and has written other books on youth culture and youth worship.

Lyn Watson

Currently Regional Director (South), Lyn has worked for the YMCA, Y Training Services for the past twelve years. Y Training Services focuses on training unemployed young people and adults.

Richard Wilkins

General Secretary of the Association of Christian Teachers, involved with support and representation services for Christians in and concerned about schools. Richard was formerly a primary school teacher and head of Religious Education at a comprehensive school.

Elaine Williams

Coordinates teaching materials for Crusaders. Before that, Elaine taught modern languages in a secondary school, where she also had a pastoral role.

Foreword

When General Eisenhower was asked to illustrate the essential ingredient of leadership, it is said that he placed a piece of string on the table in front of him and then attempted to push it across the surface. Having failed to shift it that way, he then showed his audience just how easy it was to move if you pulled instead of pushed. 'That's what a leader's job is all about,' he said, 'the leader must always lead the way'.

All of us who are responsible for youth leadership have a task which is to do exactly that—to lead the way into the future. But what sets a youth leader apart is his or her ability not to dream about the future, but to understand and shape it. We call this vision. It is vision that enables a leader to identify the opportunities and possibilities ahead, as well as the problems and threats that the future poses, and to deal with them constructively.

The ongoing health of any local church group will always be dependent on its leaders' ability to lead with a strong and developed sense of vision into the future. Proverbs 29:18 states: 'Where there is no revelation, the people cast off restraint'. This means that to aspire to leadership is to carry a huge responsibility. As Charles Sorenson puts it, 'It isn't the incompetents who destroy an organization. The incompetent never gets into a position to destroy it—it is those who have achieved something and want to rest upon their achievement who are forever clogging things up.'

The only thing that is here to stay is change. Change is a fundamental principle of the universe. 'When people shake their heads because we are living in a restless age,' said George Bernard Shaw, 'ask them how they would like to live in a stationary one and do without change'. But though change itself is nothing new, what is new is the rate at which it is now taking place and at which it is constantly accelerating. This speed of change has had a profound effect on all institutions, including the local church, because any organization which is unable to keep responding to and changing with its cultural environment is bound to suffer badly. So instead of struggling against change or ignoring it, leaving it to impact our churches and youth work in an uncontrolled way, it is our task to shape and manage it constructively. We have a straight choice—either we accept change and adapt ourselves accordingly or we will find ourselves swept away by it, like King Canute trying to turn back the inevitable tide.

It is our task to grapple with the issues of how Christian faith relates and applies to the fast-moving, visually orientated, post-literate, pluralistic society of today's teenagers. It is too easy to assume that if we pray a bit harder and sing a bit louder, everything will somehow turn out all right. Prayer and dependence on God are vital. But we worship a God who expects us to use our brains. If we are going to make any real impact on our culture, we must do some serious thinking. There are no short cuts. No quick fixes. It is time to do the hard work of listening to the world around us, reflecting our findings in the light of God's Word and then, as a result, engaging our culture.

We live in a society where knowledge and experience are often presented as alternatives, even as enemies, each with its own army of defenders. The truth is, of course, that we need *both*, and that each validates the other. The interaction between knowledge and experience always provides the best way forward. That is why I think this book is such an important tool for all those seeking to understand and respond to the fast-moving currents of youth culture. Firstly, it is earthed in excellent research by an eminent statistician providing an accurate understanding of young people's needs and attitudes in the 1990s. Secondly, this is matched by the incisive comment and sharp insight of more than twenty of the most experienced Christian youth workers in Britain today.

My prayer is that the contents of this book will stimulate, encourage and challenge you as you develop and implement a vision for effective Christian youth work for today.

Steve Chalke Oasis Trust September 1994

Introduction

This book is constructed around the idea of a river flowing from its source to the sea. The journey passes through a stretch of upstream water into the rapids of adolescence. Here, when the water becomes troubled, Christians are challenged to throw a life-belt to swimmers in trouble and to help them to continue their journey in a boat which itself passes through a storm. In other words, most of us travel from the reasonable security of childhood into the turbulence of the teenage years, and some find companionship and meaning within the congregations and youth groups that make up the church. The church itself is the boat, a place of comparative safety and progress amid troubled waters. The different chapters, then, are grouped into sections corresponding with the journey down the river and the final chapter, by Michael Eastman, provides an excellent summary of the whole voyage.

Each of the nearly thirty contributors to this book is a practical Christian youth worker, someone who knows how young people think and what they feel. Each contribution makes use of statistics drawn from the Teenage Religion and Values Survey. This survey is fully described by the book of the same title (published by Gracewing, 1995) to which readers interested in the characteristics of the sample and the sampling procedure are referred.

Through the statistics quoted in most chapters, you will hear up to 13,000 young people speak. From that sample, which was drawn from sixty-five schools in England and Wales, a sub-sample is occasionally heard: this is the voice of church-going young people. Weekly church attenders comprise 11 per cent of the total sample, a figure which is consistent with other surveys. Of the total sample, 49 per cent are male and 51 per cent are female. The schools which provided the young people answering the questionnaire were asked to take pupils from the whole ability range in years 9 and 10 (thirteen to fifteen years of age). All the questionnaires were completed anonymously and the balance of participating schools matches, in terms of school types, that of state-maintained schools in England and Wales as a whole, including Church of England aided schools and Roman Catholic aided schools, as well as county schools.

Even by the standards of today's surveys, this sample is a large one. The particular advantage of a large sample, apart from the fact that it presents authoritative figures free of local bias, is that, when it is broken down into sub-sections—to year 9 and year 10 pupils, or to males and females—the sub-sections are still large enough to allow significant comparisons and generalizations to be made from them. Most of the chapters make use of these comparisons. Age trends and sex differences, therefore, are normally commented on by the contributors.

The idea of the publisher and the editors has been to blend the day-to-day expertise of youth workers with research findings based on a sample of more than 13,000 young people. The statistics give each contributor a wider horizon and a national perspective against which to measure his or her own experience; at the same time, the contributors are able to imbue the bare statistics with the experience of teenage life. Each contributor was asked to reflect on the statistics, to comment on them and to bring in other relevant information which he or she felt important. Afterwards, they were to make a theological assessment of the information presented and to draw a conclusion or to produce a practical application. As you read on, you will see how successful they have been. As a result, the book as a whole presents a set of hard statistics which have been put into their social context, and then reflected upon theologically and applied by experts in the dynamics of youth work.

The contributors are not drawn from any one particular brand of youth organization, but are deliberately taken from a spectrum of groups. They all have a concern for young people, and sometimes the frustration of young people with the apathy or distance of the adult world comes through. This is all to the good. We want to catch both the excitement and the pace of young people's lives, and to see problems from their angle. At the same time, we want to show that the church offers answers to these problems, and that sometimes young people are justified in their impatience and sometimes they are not. The contributors, naturally, call on the Bible, but the use of the Bible does not result in one monolithic approach to youth problems. It leads to creative and varied solutions.

When we consider life 'in the boat', in the church, there are occasions when disagreements come to the fore. Should there be 'youth churches', boats cut adrift from the main galleon, or should young people as a matter of policy be integrated into the main congregation to which they are attached? Some think one thing, and some think another. The issues are discussed and the editors have not attempted to stifle the debate. We think that what matters is that young people live Christian lives of integrity and grace. The exact context of their lives cannot be determined from tradition or scripture.

In the same way, when we consider the way ahead, we have not attempted to harmonize evangelism and social action, as if the two were mutually exclusive. Both have their place in the life of the Christian community and each is important in its own way. Ideally, they go together, but sometimes they are separated. And if social action has a political tinge, that should come as no surprise. There will be some young people who feel a vocation to serve God in the political arena just as others will wish to serve more or less obtrusively in education or other forms of secular employment. And, if young people are going to vary in their political opinions, it is no surprise that the contributors diverge in their political judgements. Some are critical of the present government's policies, while others see them as the result of common sense. Yet many of the contributors are agreed in their presentation of a historical analysis of modern youth culture. The children of the 1960s are the parents of today's youth. Misunderstandings between parents and youth arise because of the cultural changes which have taken place in the interim. Moreover, certain ideas have been tried and have failed. Complex programmes do not seem to work, and government provision, partly because money has been switched to pensioners, spends less on young people's leisure centres. Instead, the money for the young has gone into the expansion of higher education, which is well and good, but leaves a big hole in the provision for those who do not choose to take the higher education route. The breakdown of family life and the altered patterns within the traditional family caused by the prevalence of television, video, computer games and long-term unemployment have significantly contributed to the fragmentation of the world in which young people live. In this respect, they are the easy prey of the manipulators of fashion and teenage consumerism, to sexual relationships under the legal age and to the false hopes offered by drug-taking. The peer group is bound to become influential in the absence of a strong and stable family against which to offset external pressures.

This book is designed to help all those who care about young people. There is something here for youth workers, of course, but teachers, parents, social workers and clergy will all find stimulation within these pages. Our text deals with ideas and possibilities. It does not directly give you 101 things to do in a youth meeting or a classroom, but it does point to ways you might improve your contact with, and relationship to, young people. Christians will find here words to spur them to better relationships with the young and point them towards productivity in the service of Christ.

References

As a deliberate policy we left out of the analysis reported here pupils who belonged to non-Christian faith communities, for example those who identified themselves as being Buddhist, Islamic, Jewish, Hindu, Mormon, Hare Krishna or Jehovah's Witness. We hope to turn attention to some of these groups in subsequent publications.

William K Kay
Leslie J Francis Carmarthen January 1995

Section One: Source

Dave Roberts

Youth Culture

It is tempting to think that the phenomenon of a high-profile teenage culture, with its parading of sexual desire (Take That), alienation (Kurt Cobain and Nirvana) and satanic anger (Slayer), is a relatively recent development. However, although the impact of teenagers on the media and society is a relatively new development, the emotions on parade have been universal throughout history. We do not need to read the Bible for long before we discover the headstrong David, confident in his God and ready to fight the Philistines; or the idealistic and rebellious Absalom, convinced that he knew better than his father the king. Elisha the prophet was mobbed by a gang of young men, who despised his age and insulted his hairstyle. Josiah the king, raised in the ways of God, drove idolatry from the land at the tender age of sixteen. The Bible is by no means blind to teenagers, perhaps reflecting the Jewish understanding that you were an adult from the age of twelve, even if you were not considered mature until you were in your forties! The energy and idealism of the biblical teenager is seen to have had both good and bad effects, sparking faith in David and prophetic action in Josiah, but rebellion among Elisha's youthful enemies and in Absalom. Underlying the emotional intensity of the teenager are the intellectual and sexual developments that come with puberty, and the emotional developments associated with finding work and perhaps leaving home in the late teens. Intellectually, the brain moves beyond concrete, black-and-white thinking and can begin to think abstractly. There is often a strong desire to know how the world works and how it can be improved, sparking both a search for meaning and an uncynical idealism. Sexually, the teenager faces desire which he or she often despised or mocked as a pre-teen (parents will no doubt understand; the average eight-year-old male feigns vomiting if he sees a couple kissing!). The teenager may be unclear about the appropriateness of his or her desires, frustrated at the lack of opportunity to express them and worried that he or she does not fit the cultural pattern in terms of respect or desirability. Emotionally, this all collides with the new demands of the workplace or of tertiary education, and with the frequent need to cope alone after years of parental protection. The teenager faces an intense period of character formation in respect of his or her attitudes towards power, sex and meaning. These issues always emerge in youth culture, whether that culture is at the fringes of society or is a dominant force.

Youth culture and the need to address its concerns have been on the Western churches' agenda in recent centuries. The nineteenth-century growth of the YMCA, the Boys Brigade and other youth ministries are cases in point. Given the universal nature of teenage struggle, it is not inappropriate for the church to address teenagers' questions and problems. Most churches would seek to do this by integrating teenagers into mainstream church meetings, and also by holding additional meetings where the teenagers' concerns can be tackled. This brings together two principles. First, the unity of the church and the desire for a body of people to represent a wisdom and a community that transcend divisions of class, race, age and gender. Second, the desirability of speaking to sections of society in their 'mother tongue', much as the disciples did in the Book of Acts, chapter 2, which set the precedent of cross-cultural mission. The real issue for the church in the past thirty years, however, has been the emergence of successive waves of youth culture that are more universal, via electronic media; that change faster, because jaded consumers want something that is unique to their generation; and that are less and less intelligible to previous generations. Conveying the gospel in the language forms, parables and metaphors of a previous generation can lead to a failure of communication. The young person thinks, 'I don't know what they mean and, as a result, I'm not sure they would understand.' To understand how all this has evolved, we need to go back a little further than thirty years. The biblical picture of the family as the primary source of nurture was not difficult to maintain in agrarian and family- orientated societies. The birth of the Industrial Revolution and the consequently increasing urbanization began to undermine the rural family. The family no longer necessarily worked together. Social interaction outside family and neighbourhood gatherings meant that a regular social life, independent of parents, could develop. This separation increased with the growth of mass education. Although this was no bad thing, it meant that the state school system would eventually become both a passive and an active tool of social engineering. The passive aspect arose out of the five-day-a-week peer-group influence, and the potential tension of loyalties between the family, the young person and the peer group. Nonetheless, the young person still belonged firmly to the family until his or her own marriage. This was rooted in financial realities, and it meant that wide-scale, overt, sexual exploration was not easy. Three factors eventually conspired to place youth culture on the centre stage of society, and to spark the youth culture phenomenon and its impact on church life: growing affluence, which slowly gave teenagers greater financial independence; the university education system, which institutionalized a late-teen peer group; and the invention of the phonograph and the radio, which allowed the stirrings of the teenage potential for cultural expression to have a wide impact. At a time when teenage wealth had never been greater, namely the 1950s, the television began to make its mark. Elvis Presley, a gospel/country/ rhythm-and-blues singer, who might only have captured a cult audience in a few states, was able to short-cut the route to fame via regional radio stations, and to rocket into teenage consciousness through television. His implicit questioning (through his dance routines) of the sexual morals of the Christian United States was but a hint of the wider questioning of materialism, sexual morality and religion that would take place in the 1960s.

Youth Culture

The combination of the new mass media and the coming into adolescence of the huge number of children born in the post-Second World War baby boom brought down the average age of the population in Western society. Business writer Peter Drucker notes that in the United States it fell to seventeen. The media shifted to reflect the interests of these consumers, who were eagerly targeted by the advertisers. As the years passed, and abortion and the use of the pill rose, the average age increased again, to the late-thirties. The feasibility of a vibrant youth culture with its own dress codes and musical styles has remained. However, the idea that young people could change society or rebel against their parents has largely disappeared. Unless someone is a child of religious parents, what is there to rebel against? Non-Christian parents themselves probably experimented with drugs and had premarital sex. The ability of teenagers to consume, and the means to do so with some degree of financial independence, will mean that 'youth culture' will always be with us. Because young people want to be different from the youth of the previous decade—but not from the youth of two decades ago—they will often evolve new styles. Dance is one example of this. In the 1990s, house music (essentially dance-orientated) is slowly evolving into pure dance and indie dance (similar to that which gave birth to The Who), and into an ambient or psychedelic music similar to the progressive rock genre of the early 1970s. Grunge music is the punk music of the 1990s; although the look is different, the underlying philosophy of nihilistic hopelessness is the same. For the Christian youth worker, an appropriate response to youth culture has two aspects. First, the influence of youth culture must be acknowledged. It expresses itself through television, film, music, books, computing and radical socio-political movements such as New Age travellers. It impacts the life of the churched and the unchurched alike. How it does so is discussed elsewhere in this book. The way in which you respond should be based on the key principles of

Christian life and witness, which might be summarized as follows:

◆ The truth remains the truth. The ethical and moral basis of Christian life and discipleship does not change. Our belief in a historical, human and divine Jesus, who made it possible for us to be reconciled with God through his atoning death, does not change.

◆ Old truth, new clothes. The Bible suggests that Jesus, Peter and Paul made their message particularly relevant to the hearer, addressing his or her explicit needs and thoughts. Jesus spoke to the heart about the issues that lay behind the different questions posed by the rich young ruler, the Pharisees and his own imperfect disciples. Peter and the other disciples, under the influence of the Holy Spirit, spoke in the mother tongue, the day-to-day language, of their hearers (Acts 2). Paul tuned into the concerns, culture and thought patterns of his Greek audience at Mars' Hill.

◆ New generation, same needs. Although you need to be aware of the thoughts, symbols and heroes of contemporary youth culture to help you to cross the bridges of communication, the issues you address will remain the same. Thoughtful, integrated youth ministry will want to take account of the abiding undercurrents in the lives of adolescents. Are you addressing issues of identity, fashion, sexuality, power, materialism, intellectual doubt and racio-political concern?

◆ Does your youth ministry vision have a deliberateness about it? Youth ministry from the 1960s to the 1980s often seemed to be characterized by pragmatism: 'music is the only way to reach this generation'. Or it was a desperate and superficial attempt to entertain young people in order to stop them slipping away. Many of the writers in this book will explore a better way, one that embraces good music and entertaining presentation, but one which says that a young person who 'learns by doing' at school and in the workplace should be encouraged out of passivity and into local, church-based Christian service. Outreach must also have a strong relational element, rather than a 'hit-and-run' evangelistic emphasis.

◆ The positive fruits of adolescence are zeal and energy, idealism and adventurousness. If we can alert our young people to the richness of life in a multi-generational church and also respond positively to their special needs—with Christian apologetics, a positive view of sexuality, opportunities for mission and outlets for concern about social justice—we will be responding to the siren calls of youth culture without being lured into the minefield of generational conflict.

Colin Bennett

2 Politics, the Church and Young People

> The government of the people, by the people and for the people, shall not perish from the earth.
> *Abraham Lincoln*

> Here comes the new boss, same as the old boss.
> *The Who, We Won't Get Fooled Again*

> I am puzzled about which Bible people are reading when they suggest religion and politics don't mix.
> *Archbishop Desmond Tutu*

In the early 1980s, a young student teacher on placement in a local comprehensive school held a mock general election in a Social Studies class. The class went well, with the students setting up a hustings where the candidates could answer questions about their political choices and the policies which each party held. It was obvious that none of the candidates had a clue about any of the policies of any of the political parties, despite having had a number of lessons about what each party believed.

That student teacher was me and I have always been puzzled since about young people and politics. Why did this situation arise? What was the difficulty in making an impact? What could or should I have done differently? This section explores some of the issues surrounding the whole area of young people and politics.

When we reflect on the statistics resulting from the Teenage Religion and Values Survey, we can see clearly that, in response to the statement 'It makes no difference which political party is in power', there is little difference between the responses given by the total sample, and by individual boys and girls, and whether or not they attend church. There are few significant differences and, thus, we can draw some general conclusions:

about 50 per cent disagree with the statement that it makes no difference which political party is in power;

about 30 per cent are uncertain about the political party in power;
20 per cent agree that it makes no difference which political party is in power.

To put it another way, about 50 per cent have an interest in the political party in power, 30 per cent are 'floaters' and 20 per cent appear in some way to be disenchanted with or cynical about the political system.

We can see in the book *Young People's Understanding of Society*[1] by Furnham and Stacey, in their chapter on politics and government, that many surveys have been carried out on young people's attitudes, as well as many studies on political attitudes and about how young people feature in the political framework. Interestingly, Cochrane and Billings' study in 1982 stated that 50 per cent of young people felt that politics was a dirty business and that politicians did not care about what ordinary people thought; it also stated that about one-third believed that real decisions are not made by government, but by the powerful forces which control it. Certainly, the Teenage Religion and Values Survey highlights a political attitude concerning young people. A very interesting idea would have been to look at what political knowledge this group of young people had when making their decisions. Indeed, Milson, in his book, *Political Education*,[2] suggested that one of the main stumbling-blocks to political education in schools and churches was the fear that young people would become indoctrinated and forced to think in certain ways.

However, the general lack of political awareness revealed in Stradling's report (Stradling, 1977) must make depressing reading for anyone who is concerned about the future of our representative democracy and the prospects for greater participation by the public. There is something essentially paradoxical about a democracy in which some 80–90 per cent of citizens are insufficiently well-informed about local, national and international politics to know not only what is happening, but also how they are affected and what they can do about it.

Most of the political knowledge which young people do have is clearly of a rather inert and voyeuristic kind, and of little use to them, either as political consumers or as political actors. Later work by Fernham and Gunther (1983, 1987, 1989) confirmed this, finding that the level of adolescent knowledge about politics was much the same as before in the United Kingdom. The best predictor of political knowledge was not media usage, but expressed interest in political affairs. There was, however, some indication that those who watched more television news tended to have a greater political knowledge. We can see, therefore, from recent statistics, that a high percentage of young people's attitudes to politics is either negative or ambivalent, and that this is a reflection of the population in the United Kingdom at large (verified in a number of adult surveys).

Theological considerations

So, we ask ourselves, what impact does this have theologically? It is concerning this precise point that Stott, in his book, *Issues Facing Christians Today*,[3] says:

> *As Christians, we have two choices when it comes to political considerations: either 'escape' or 'engagement'. 'Escape' means turning our back on the world in rejection, washing our hands of it and steeling our hearts against its agonized cries for help. Too many of us Evangelicals either have been or maybe still are irresponsible escapists. The only thing that matters is to rescue the perishing. Thus we have tried to salve our conscience with a bogus theology. In contrast, however, 'engagement' means turning our faces towards the world in compassion, getting our hands dirty, sore and worn in its service and feeling deep within us the stirring of the love of God which cannot be contained.*

I would argue that only by adopting the latter do we really proclaim the gospel in people's lives. It is not enough simply to blurt out the gospel message that 'Jesus loves you' and then retreat; we need to be engaged and agonizing with those people who are going through agony, as well as with those people who are enjoying life. Theologically, the concept of politics means concern or engagement with the whole of our life in human society; politics is the art of living together in a community. When we are talking about politics, therefore, we are not looking merely at the science of government.

Once we are clear about this, we can ask whether Jesus was involved in politics. In the latter, narrow sense, the answer is a negative one. However, in the broader sense of the word, he revealed himself as one who had come into the world in order to share in the life of the human community, and he sent his followers into the world to do the same. It may not have been Jesus' mission to be involved in party politics (that does not mean that we should not be involved in this way!) but he was clearly political because he offered an alternative to the *status quo*. Our world not only needs caring for, but it also needs transforming, which, for the youth worker, may be a difficult and dangerous task, and one from which we could all too readily run away.

Implications for youth workers

Our task is, therefore, clear: we should be encouraging our groups of young people to engage at every level of active decision-making, not only in the political decision-making processes of political elections, but also in meeting the wider mandate of encouraging a 'salt and light community'; a community that will mean life, not survival; a community that will mean the church 'making a difference'. 'But how?' you may ask.

From a survey taken in 1983, it was concluded that those young people who, for whatever reason, are interested in politics expose themselves to more of the media's political output and help us learn more about it. What we now need to know is what makes children or adolescents interested in politics in the first place; and whether their political interest leads to increased political knowledge and behaviour, as demonstrated in voting preferences, standing for election or involvement in canvassing. Clearly, Furnham and Gunther would say that the more you encourage somebody to become a political person, the more they pay attention to it; and the more they see the need for engaging in decision-making, the more interested they will be in that kind of area. Thus, we need to realize that this is part of our mandate: to encourage and assist young people to take an interest in all decision-making processes (not just party political, but in all aspects of life!).

Unfortunately, there are no easy 'tips' to help to achieve this. The main way is by your role model as a youth worker—being someone who is enthusiastic, particularly in the area of socio-politics, and encouraging your church to get its hands dirty in the social and political arena. In a training sense, the use of games and simulations with a biblical approach to decision-making will help you to begin the process of making disciples who are decision-makers. For instance, use tools such as 'Star Power' found in Milson's book, *Political Education*;[4] also, 'The Trading Game' and 'Rights and Wrongs' in *It's Not Fair* by Christian Aid are both good 'starters'.

In a wider setting, some interesting work by the British Youth Council (BYC) could help your young people to gain hands-on experience of party politics. Their work has shown that only one in five eighteen- to twenty-four-year-olds voted at the last general election—a staggering non-registration rate four times higher than the rest of the population. The Projects Officer at BYC, which acts as an advocate for increasing participation in society, examined why so many young people were not voting. Her findings, published in the journal *Youth Clubs*[5] pointed to young people being disenfranchised (meaning 'cut off from society') because of homelessness, poor housing, youth unemployment, low pay and poll-tax avoidance. In response to this, BYC organize and publish information aimed at encouraging young people to play their full role in the democratic process. As part of this initiative, they have for the past three years organized 'Youth and Parliament Days' when young people have the chance to find out what Parliament does, questioning Members of Parliament and parliamentary representatives directly on issues of interest to young people. For further information, write to them about your young people being involved in one of their events.[6]

If our mandate from Matthew 28 as workers for the church is to make disciples, then we need to be aware that disciples should be decision makers. We are called to be both disciples and decision-makers, disciplining our young people to follow our example. However, the results of the Teenage Religion and Values Survey support the view that we still have a long way to go in making disciples of young people in this nation today.

In summary, when looking at young people's attitudes on party politics, we see an alarming lack of interest, indicating that many young people may well be unconcerned with affairs of decision-making in general, irrespective of their values and beliefs. We have seen this confirmed by other surveys which demonstrate that this is no new phenomenon, but rather a general reflection of the society in which we live. The advice to the Christian youth worker, however, is to seize every opportunity to encourage young people actively to make the decisions that affect them on a day-to-day basis; young people need to get used to negotiating, following through and reflecting on their experiences. Helping young people to take decision-making seriously and thoughtfully, and helping them to realize that decision-making is a first step along the road to effective Christian discipleship, is to enable them to be 'bringers' of the kingdom of life in a world short of good news.

It makes no difference which political party is in power

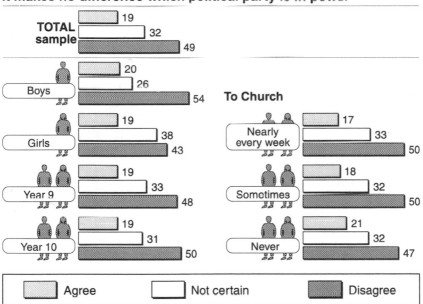

Source: Teenage Religion and Values Survey of 13,000 pupils in England and Wales. All figures refer to responses to the statement immediately above this diagram. The left hand column shows, at the top, the responses of the total sample which is divided, in the middle, into responses of year 9 and year 10 pupils. The right hand column deals only with the 11% of the total sample who attend church.

References

1. Milson, *Political Education: A Practical Guide for Christian Youth Workers*, Paternoster Press, 1980.
2. A. Furnham and B. Stacey, *Young People's Understanding of Society*, Routledge, 1991.
3. J. Stott, *Issues Facing Christians Today*, Marshall Pickering, 1990.
4. *It's Not Fair*, Christian Aid, 1993.
5. 'A Vote for Young People', *Youth Clubs*, Youth Clubs (UK) Journal, April 1994.
6. The address for the British Youth Council is: Projects Officer British Youth Council 57 Charlton Street London NW1 1HU

Russ Oliver

3

An Irrelevant Church?

As part of the Teenage Religion and Values Survey, the statement 'Church seems irrelevant to life today' was posed to a large number of young people for their response. I feel that the results were a fairly true representation of youth culture as we see it today. The bulk of those approached fell into the 'not certain' category. This comes as no surprise, because it is a typical response of young people going through adolescence, not wishing to make any commitments and avoiding life-changing decisions. This is obviously contrary to the fact they are, out of ignorance, continuously making these choices through their actions or inaction.

More girls than boys disagreed with the statement, again reflecting the current imbalance of male and female representation within our churches. I believe that a number of factors explain this situation:

◆ During adolescence girls mature faster than boys, not just physically, but emotionally and spiritually also. As a consequence, they are often in a position to make these difficult decisions earlier in life.

◆ This emotional development generally means that girls respond to the friendship offered by churches and identify with a relationship with God. Boys may often have a greater independence and do not want to be seen acquiring assistance or friendship. Such terms, and talk of love, often alienate many boys.

◆ Social activities offered may often appeal more to girls.

◆ Churches are generally dominated by females and this attracts young women.

Obviously, the response to the statement changes for those who attend church regularly, with more than 50 per cent disagreeing that church is irrelevant to life today. Conversely, those who never attend church agree with the statement. Within both categories, nearly 50 per cent of those questioned were undecided.

This indicates to me that, unfortunately, the church has not impacted, interested nor responded to a vast number within this large undecided category.

Sadly, many churches are highly irrelevant. The gospel and scripture contain guidelines for living which will never date. These give us a framework for life, enabling us to present, impart, teach and experience a relationship with God within any culture or group of people. Unfortunately, we have at times lost sight of this, and have become legalistic and religious, alienating all but a small percentage of our vast and varied society.

These characteristics are totally opposed to scripture and are part of the underlying reasons for which some of our churches are irrelevant today. Our buildings, songs and language leave young people confused, bored and disillusioned. Many Christians focus on and hold more dearly the pews, buildings, songs and traditions of the church than a relationship with God and our commission in Matthew's Gospel to be salt and light to all people. The problem we face is that the infrastructure and the traditions of the church were all tools to facilitate our relationship with God, and they were, in their time, both culturally relevant and accessible. However, things change; and yet this has not been the case with many church denominations.

We now have to turn the tide in order to address the many groups of people within our communities. This means laying down some of the things that are dear to us for the sake of the gospel. It includes ditching Christian language; introducing wider styles of music within our worship which reflect the cultures surrounding us; using accessible buildings for our public meetings; taking the good news out through our actions, and not just through words; updating our publicity; and using audio-visual equipment to enhance our means of creative communication.

In addition to the irrelevance of our church culture, we are frequently intolerant of many groups of people. Often being naive of culture, we are quick to marginalize people because of our mind-sets and tradition. Many of the issues faced by young people today are similar to those once faced by ourselves. The issues have changed only in their increased intensity: the rise of marriage breakdown; the accessibility of drugs and alcohol; acceptance of diverse sexual activity outside marriage; and massive media persuasion and influence.

Still quoted is the phrase: 'When I was young'. This mentality frequently condemns the actions we see, often justifiably, but it ignores the reasons why these actions take place. Such statements show the ignorance of many of us to exactly what life is like outside our white middle-class Christian lifestyles. Let us remember, too, that we need to address other problems. Ephesians 6:12 says: 'For our struggle is not against flesh and blood, but against the rulers, against the authorities, against the powers of this dark world and against the spiritual forces of evil in the heavenly realms'. Too often, society—correctly—looks for practical solutions, but ignores the spiritual.

A clear moral value system needs to be identified in order to enable young people to live their lives. The questions to be asked within our churches about young people's behaviour and attitudes are:

◆ What is a moral issue?

◆ What is personal preference?

◆ Why are the young people displaying this behaviour?

◆ How can we help?

◆ What were we doing at their age?

◆ What is God saying?

◆ How can we encourage and include young people?

We have an apology to make to many generations for our exclusive church life. Now is the time to change, in order to allow young people who are searching for answers to have a value system, security and family, and to experience the all-inclusive love of our God. Young people should know that, whatever the venue, language or style of music, our belief is focused on a personal relationship with our caring, loving dad, God. Through this, and through the power in the name of Jesus, everyone will see the relevance of God in the physical and supernatural. The ball is in our court to make a difference and to respond to the new generation, and to see our nation taken for God.

The Church seems irrelevant to life today

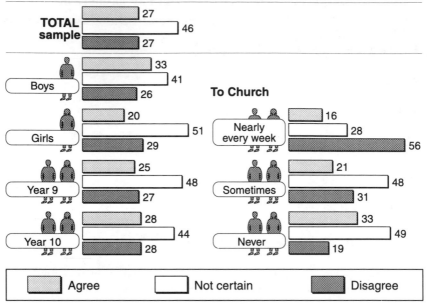

Source: Teenage Religion and Values Survey of 13,000 pupils in England and Wales. All figures refer to responses to the statement immediately above this diagram. The left hand column shows, at the top, the responses of the total sample which is divided, in the middle, into responses of year 9 and year 10 pupils. The right hand column deals only with the 11% of the total sample who attend church.

Pete Ward

4 Education

There is a difference between youth ministry and Sunday school work. This is not simply in the age range covered; it is also in the means by which youth ministers work with young people. The work of the church in Sunday schools is, however, extremely important for youth ministry. This importance can be considered in two different ways.

First, Sunday school forms the basis of Christian education and the socialization into full church membership of children born to Christian parents. Within the church, young people may graduate from Sunday school into the youth group or Pathfinders, and then into CYFA (Church Youth Fellowships Association) or the senior Crusader group. In this sense, youth ministers inherit the results of Sunday school. Sunday school is also important, however, as a means of reaching out to the children of families who may not regularly attend church. It is in this context that we should examine the results of the Teenage Religion and Values Survey in response to the question 'Did you regularly attend Sunday school?'

In the first instance, this survey gives us some reason to take heart. It would appear that more than one-third of the sample reported that they did regularly attend Sunday school between the ages of five and six. Again, almost one-quarter of those aged between nine and ten years also attended. It is no mean feat for the church to be in meaningful contact with such a sizeable proportion of the population.

The picture, however, is not entirely wonderful, because there is an alarming drop-off rate in the numbers attending Sunday school as we move up the age range. The survey shows that by the age of thirteen to fourteen years, only 7 per cent are regularly attending Sunday school. This picture roughly accords with the findings of Peter Brierley reported in *Reaching and Keeping Teenagers*.[1]

Clearly, we need to say that Sunday school, as a means of instructing children in faith and introducing them into ongoing Christian commitment, has some room for improvement. Those with specific expertise in the education of children in the faith will no doubt have a great deal to contribute towards a review of this aspect of the life of the church. Much needs to be done in curriculum development, training of Sunday school teachers and in the involvement of parents in the education of children in the faith. My concern at this point is to bring some observations to bear on this issue from my own area of youth ministry.

◆ There seems to have been a remarkable change in the culture of evangelical churches in the past twenty years. I would characterize this change as being a move away from a generalized ministry to the local community, towards an increased concentration on church-related matters. In the area of work among children, this has meant that we have tended to focus upon ministry to whole families. The family service has become part of this, as has the tendency for Sunday school to interconnect with the main morning service in church. The net effect of this trend has been that nominal churchgoers and those who do not attend church are less able to send their young people to Sunday school without attending church themselves. It also has to be said that, at the same time, changes in patterns of leisure, such as car ownership and a general rise in prosperity, have meant that many families are engaged in activities which have kept non-Christian young people from church-based activities such as Sunday school.

◆ One result of concentrating upon children of churchgoing families has been that the culture of the Sunday school has reflected a more intense and committed Christian family life. Family, church and Sunday school have become connected in our minds to a large extent. The effect of this has been to create a problem for Christian young people as they pass through adolescence. To move from being a child to being recognized as a young person is a difficult and, in our culture, an extended transition. It is this transition that we identify as adolescence. Transition to adulthood involves gaining some distance from the family. When faith, church and family become as closely identified as they appear to have become in many churches, young people often feel the need to press the pause button on their faith to get some space to do their growing up. This, in part, explains the decline in Sunday school attendance around the ages of thirteen and fourteen, the average time of the start of puberty.

◆ *Reaching and Keeping Teenagers*, the title of Peter Brierley's book, is somewhat telling. There is some pressure from Christian parents and from church leaders for youth ministry to be the means by which the church stops the flow of young people away from the church. For some people, youth ministry is essentially concerned with 'keeping teenagers'. I would argue that much of the current trend towards the employment of full-time youth ministers is, in part, driven by the anxieties of Christian parents, who see their young people moving away from the family as they go through adolescence. It is a tricky question, then, for the youth minister to decide how much he or she should encourage the growth of a right measure of independence among young people, in the recognition that this leads to maturity and adulthood, and how much they should follow the agenda implicitly laid down by the parents within the church. Given this perspective, youth ministry should be challenging those charged with the development of Sunday schools to come up with a means of helping young people to grow towards full maturity, rather than creating a culture from which they apparently feel compelled to escape in such large numbers.

◆ There is a further issue raised in my mind concerning the role of the Sunday school. At one time, work among children was seen as a means of outreach and of spreading a generalized knowledge of the faith. The trend towards ministry to families has increased the price of gaining a knowledge of the faith. One could argue that one meaning of the term 'unchurched' is the way that, by our policies on Sunday schools, family worship and baptism, we have 'unchurched' large numbers of the population as we have sought to create more identifiably 'Christian communities' in our churches. As a youth minister deeply involved in outreach, it is noticeable how much easier it is to bring young people to the faith in their teenage years if they have had some previous experience of the church. It is quite remarkable in my experience how often this has been through Sunday school or a church choir. As Sunday school reflects more and more an exclusively committed Christian culture, these contacts will continue to decrease. This will inevitably make evangelism among teenagers even more difficult than it already appears to be.

References

1. Peter Brierley, *Reaching and Keeping Teenagers*, MARC, 1993.

Did you regularly attend Sunday school (i.e. at least once a month) at these ages?

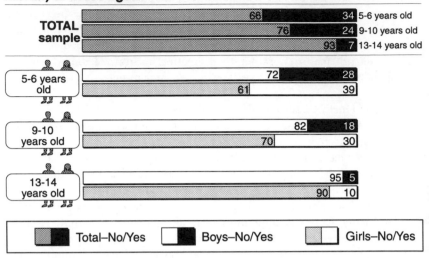

Source: Teenage Religion and Values Survey of 13,000 pupils in England and Wales. All figures refer to responses to the statement immediately above this diagram. The left hand column shows, at the top, the responses of the total sample which is divided, in the middle, into responses of year 9 and year 10 pupils. The right hand column deals only with the 11% of the total sample who attend church.

Section Two: Upstream

Richard Wilkins

5

School-days

As part of the Teenage Religion and Values Survey, teenagers were asked to respond to the statement: 'My school is helping me to prepare for life'. There was very little difference between the answers given by boys and those given by girls. It might be claiming too much, therefore, to say that either boys or girls are more far-sighted and purposeful than the other, or that the curriculum is sexist, on the strength of a 2 per cent difference in agreeing or disagreeing with the statement. There are, however, significant differences in the responses given by church attenders. We will look at these later.

A comparison of affirmative responses between years 9 and 10 shows a fall of 5 per cent in the older age group. We can be fairly sure that this trend continues and steepens in year 11. A report in 1994 for the Department for Education, *Truancy in English Secondary Schools*,[1] showed that truancy of all kinds increases by 11 per cent between years 10 and 11. The figures from the Teenage Religion and Values Survey are for two different year groups surveyed at the same time. If the current year 9s follow the trend of the current year 10s, in 12 months' time 5 per cent will no longer agree that school is helping them to prepare for life. They will be divided almost equally between being uncertain and being convinced that the answer is 'no'. Because they will be nearer to the beginning of the 'life' for which school may or may not be preparing them, this is, on the face of it, worrying. We need to explore this difference between 'school' and 'life' which is built into the question. It may tell us something about how young people's attitudes work.

School-days are meant to be left behind. Those who truly feel that their days at school were the happiest of their lives have not had their experiences in the expected order. Schools are built to be passed through. At least, that is the way matters are seen by the adults who plan education. Schooling is a means to an end—to a healthy, useful, secure, reasonably prosperous, successful and, with all that, happy life. Understandably, education is designed for future use. As young people advance into adolescence, their teachers and parents increasingly justify the inconveniences of education in terms of what it will do for them in the future. You would think that as life beyond school drew nearer, school itself would make more sense, as a winding track up a mountainside seems worthwhile as the summit comes in sight. Quite the reverse seems to happen. Where there is movement in the figures, it shows the travellers along the educational trail rather less convinced than before that this is the way to their destination.

There are several reasons why the adult guides seem less persuasive as time goes on, and some reasons are more obvious than others. One strong possibility is that the adults seem unable to agree about which parts of education matter. Furthermore, each of the separate secondary school subjects seems to demand total commitment. Subject-specialist teachers are not always as aware as they need to be that whereas their subject commands at least two-thirds of their own working attention, it may represent only one-eighth or one-tenth of the year-10 student's curriculum.

To cope with such issues, schools today increasingly have staff who take an overview of each student's work pattern and general direction; such teachers are called 'managers of learning' or a similar term. This is necessary, although more traditional schools might view such appointments as a betrayal of belief in knowledge for its own sake. But even with a managerial overseer the problem remains: 'life', for which the school is supposed to be preparing students, reveals no adult with a full timetable of ten activities which look anything like school subjects. School, therefore, is a community in which the adult exemplars are one- or two-subject specialists, while the pupils for whom the school exists relate to them as ten-fold specialists rather than as integrated people.

Another factor interrupting the sense of progress from school to adult life is that as the latter draws closer, young people find the prospect more and more threatening. It is also, of course, fascinating, and that fascination dawns in ways that distinguish it from the childhood curiosity they experienced at school. But the adult world's looming menace, especially perhaps the uncertainties of relationships and careers, seems vast and heavily armed compared with the childlike securities represented by school. The school may seem inept in preparing them for 'real life'.

There could be a loop effect here. Those young people most determined to leave school are most acutely aware, they think, of the inadequacies of school in preparing them for the plunge into the adult world. On the other hand, part of the quest for further education may conceal a desire to remain for longer within a sheltering institution. Who can blame those who feel that way? College, like school, exists for its students, whereas the workplace exists for its customers. To stay in the educational womb is to be 'better prepared for life' and to be counted as 'successful' at an early stage. O'Keefe found that 58 per cent of truants still wanted to continue their education beyond the school-leaving age.[2]

One of the main reasons, however, for jaded attitudes to school relates to my reason for persistently putting 'life' in quotation marks. It may be a peculiarly adult viewpoint that sees school as a preparation for 'life'. This is understandable and justifiable if schools are thought to be places that exist for afterwards, places to leave. Young people themselves echo this, and they are quite sincere when they voice this kind of view of school. Many a school lesson is interrupted with, 'What use will this be to me in getting a job?'

Yet at the same time, young people at this age are becoming aware, with mingled fascination and fear, that they are very much alive *now*. It is not natural, or at least it is not emotionally comfortable, to view such a time-consuming section of their lives as being all about the future, when the sap is rising and the peer group is fizzing with possibilities. This is a time of life when part of them is straining at the leash to become adult, while adults seem to be holding them back and keeping them in childhood, or else pushing them on at a pace that is not their own. The future is under adult control, or under no control at all.

There is some security in 'now'. During their school years, young people are in what the Canadian educationist Kieran Egan calls the 'romantic' phase, in which wild passions, soaring ambitions, all-consuming friendships, absorption in nature and obsessions with power all accompany strange dreads and a mortal horror of being bored.[3] It is the 'Dead Poets Society' phase, with its unspeakable secrets to which only the rarest of adults can be admitted. As Stevie Smith observed:

Fourteen-year-old, why must you giggle and gloat, Fourteen-year-old, why are you such a goat? I'm fourteen years old, that is the reason, I giggle and gloat in season.

It is at this age, when young people often feel sealed off from the past and not yet admitted to the future, that they were asked in the Teenage Religion and Values Survey (by adults) whether school was helping them to prepare for life. But life is now! While they themselves are realizing how little they knew of life before, everyday adults with their indifference to boredom or even their liking for it do not seem very much alive. What is 'life' if it lies in the future? So much is new; life is now. These times may never come again.

If all this is true, the fact that two-thirds of the people questioned agreed that their schools were helping them to prepare for life amounts almost to a ringing endorsement of schools' good intentions, if not their effectiveness. At an age when personal chemistry, biology and private sociology shriek that school is a bind, a two-thirds majority saying that school is doing a reasonable job is a vote of confidence. To refer again to O'Keefe's research,[2] 54 per cent of all truants said that *most* or all their lessons were useful, while avoidance of *particular* lessons or their teachers was by far the most common reason for truancy.

Of course, convinced sceptics will say that the affirmers are shouting in the teeth of their experience merely to make sense of life. No one likes saying that much of their life is spent on futile drudgery, so they do not say to the researchers what they may not dare to say even to themselves. Evidence against this view arises in the very alienation that some students do disclose. Years 9 and 10 are the years when the very brightest students 'go off', often displaying the most obnoxious arrogance that their teachers ever have to face. Much of this is the testing of boundaries and trying out their teachers' convictions. Underneath is a determination to make the most of life. They recover and excel, but if final judgement were made on them at the end of year 9 many who later graduate would be expelled. Their apparent schizophrenia is a part of growing up, but the part of them that wants to conform may well come out in answer to questionnaires.

The other part of them carries its distrust of adults' good intentions all the way. There is a widespread, morale-enhancing view amongst voluntary youth workers that they are the real confidants of the younger generation. Well, that depends on whom you ask, and on who does the asking. Paul Corrigan's study of urban education, *Schooling the Smash Street Kids*,[3] revealed that young people regarded youth workers as middle-class do-gooders, 'teachers in disguise'; and that they saw youth clubs as 'good places to meet outside'. The symbolism may have changed (more detached youth workers) but the truth remains that young people want to conduct most of their lives out of adult earshot. It is adults in general, not teachers in particular, from whom young people feel distant, not wanting to be driven by alien ideals.

What are the answers? Some lie in the provision of more precisely nuanced education. Adult communications with young people that relate to their needs and feelings stand a good chance of promoting knowledge, skills and understanding that will be useful in the future. Keiran Egan has explained a possible way of doing that in *Romantic Understanding*[4], relying heavily on young people's emotional development at that age. However, the mix of emotion and rationality varies with individuals and time, so the precise matching of the needs of adolescents is difficult in class-sized groups.

Another solution is to persuade young people that, although education is very important for them all, their use of schooling to supply their individual needs will vary from person to person. Preferred learning styles need more careful identification. My older daughter is convinced that her 16-plus exam results were better than they might have been because she revised for them during a teachers' strike. Other students might have been ruined by the same accident of history.

Finally, a belief that the world and the future make sense is likely to be educationally positive. The higher correlation of church attendance with confidence about the school's effectiveness might be merely two symptoms of conformity. It is equally likely that confidence in schooling springs from a mental atmosphere of confidence in the God who has the world and the future in his hands. Christian faith and optimism do not always go together and, in any case, the optimism may be unrealistic; but if there is a God who revealed himself in Jesus Christ there is hope, and hope inspires the learner's will.

References

1. D. O'Keefe, *Truancy in English Secondary Schools*, Department for Education, 1994.
2. O'Keefe, *Truancy*.
3. Paul Corrigan, *Schooling the Smash Street Kids*, Macmillan, 1979, pages 121–122.
4. Keiran Egan, *Romantic Understanding*, Routledge, 1990.

My school is helping to prepare me for life

Source: Teenage Religion and Values Survey of 13,000 pupils in England and Wales. All figures refer to responses to the statement immediately above this diagram. The left hand column shows, at the top, the responses of the total sample which is divided, in the middle, into responses of year 9 and year 10 pupils. The right hand column deals only with the 11% of the total sample who attend church.

Michael Eastman

6

Working With Disadvantaged Young People

Increasing numbers of young people are the casualties of the upheavals and changes in a society undergoing rapid transition. The varied turbulence described in other chapters affects most deeply those with least going for them. By some estimates, as many as one-third of the young experience disproportionate disadvantages. They are pushed out, forced under and held down. Most are trapped within an underclass of the urban poor concentrated in our inner cities, outer estates and run-down industrial areas. Some in rural areas experience similar lack of choice and bleak futures. The conclusions of the Archbishop of Canterbury's Commission on Urban Priority Areas ten years ago still hold good.

> *Yet the overall impression is clear. It is that there are sizeable groups of young people who are trapped in UPAs (Urban Priority Areas) who only gain attention when they become a threat, who are denied equality of opportunity and life chances, and with whom the churches have little or no contact.*
>
> *It is difficult to exaggerate how alienated these young people are: from adults' ideas of how young people should behave; from their peers of different social classes; from agencies they think of as acting on adults' behalf and not usually in the interests of young people, e.g. from the police; from schools; and from the church.*[1]

These young people are labelled failures by an education system increasingly dominated by tests and league tables. The piecemeal dismantling of the Youth Service, with an emphasis on performance indicators, inputs, outcomes and contracts, has subjected youth work to the categories of 'the market'. Grants have been cut, youth clubs closed, youth workers made redundant in the very areas where they are most needed. In this much-vaunted privatized world, voluntary agencies are overstretched and tend to cater for those making fewer demands.

Endemic long-term unemployment and homelessness compound the mixture, along with family breakdown and serial marriages. Too many of the young people feel betrayed and let down by all the adults in their lives. They are sinned against more than sinning, experiencing firsthand the effects of poverty and powerlessness and lack of choice. They are effectively disenfranchised, denied the possibilities and potential inherent in their creation in God's image.

This is a global phenomenon. Across the world, there is an orphaned generation experiencing exclusion not integration. It is most acutely seen in the exploding cities of the two-thirds world, particularly in the plight of street children exterminated like rats in sewers.

'Faith in the City' reported:

Alienation—the making of people, not least young people, to feel themselves to be 'outsiders'—is from a particular order that is felt to be unresponsive and uncaring.[2]

We have heard firsthand of the fear of the destructive potential of young people. We have sensed the latent violence as we have walked along the streets; we have seen groups of young people with nothing to do, nowhere to go and with nothing to lose.

I wouldn't go out without a pair of scissors to defend me.

If someone steps on your toe every day, and if they keep on doing it, you might do something drastic.[3]

Such young people develop remarkable survival skills. They beg or steal, or squat or sleep rough. They work in the black economy, deal in drugs, work the benefit system, living day to day. They seek ways to escape, keeping on the move, migrating to city centres, playing the slot machines, sniffing glue, drinking, taking drugs, viewing video nasties, chasing their dreams and fantasies. They create their own tight subcultures for mutual support and security, where each belongs and is given a sense of identity in street gangs, territorially or ethnically defined. When driven to it, such young men and women exploit their own youthfulness and, in turn, are exploited by those able to politicize their discontent and by those with money to buy their bodies, drugs and their illegal skills. So young victims become menaces, the carriers of AIDS, bearers of unwanted children, threats to persons and properties, finally to be put away in 'secure institutions'. These are doubly sinned against as well as sinning, scapegoated for the failures of others as well as their own.

Jesus set out his messianic mission at the outset of his ministry:

The Spirit of the Lord is upon me, because he has chosen me to bring good news to the poor; he has sent me to proclaim liberty to the

*captives and recovery of sight to the blind; to set free the oppressed
and announce that the time has come when the Lord will save his
people.*[4]

He was at home among the outcasts on the edges of the society of his day, who
were ostracized by the religiously pure and excluded by the politically powerful.
Jesus is the friend of alienated people. Sadly, thousands of young people cannot
experience his friendship because the Messiah's people exclude them from most
of our churches and many of our Christian agencies. Frontier youth workers in a
variety of projects and units know what it takes to go beyond the comfort zones of
the conventional Christian world. Lasting relationships cannot be forged at a
distance. Effective Christian frontier youth work combines three broad
approaches in many different forms.

Without street presence there is no contact. Incarnation is at the heart of
mission. Those who bring the friendship of Jesus must become at home among
the outcast young, whoever they are and wherever they are located.

*Young people often gravitate to the city centres for a variety of
reasons. Those who can afford the pubs and clubs go there. For those
who cannot, the city centre may be a meeting place, where they can
congregate, perhaps in a particular arcade or cafacutee.*

*'Going down town', 'hanging around', 'doing nothing' is a
common experience as are reports of 'contacts' with police and
security guards.*

*Contact with young people in these locations across the country is
usually the work of detached youth workers. We affirm their
importance in this situation: the ideal is for such workers to be part of
a team (including centre-based workers) and with a proper support
system.*[5]

These young people need safe places, where they are valued unconditionally by
those who seek their true well-being. Coupled with this, they require crisis
provision which addresses their immediate needs: whether for a job or a roof over
their heads; someone to talk to; refuge from abuse and exploitation; a square
meal; second-chance education; or access to specialist help. In such contexts,
sustained long-term relationships are possible through which they sense the
friendship of Jesus for themselves. Their own stories and the story of Jesus
become personally linked.

This is demanding work with no quick fixes. It requires 'an infinite capacity
for being let down'. Those who make up the teams given to such ministries need
together to embody and exemplify the new wine of God's kingdom through the

gift and power of God's Spirit. Primary mission of this kind requires primary church planting. Appropriate forms of worship, celebration, prayer, Bible study and mutual caring are needed, which create and sustain new, indigenous communities of Messiah people where those who serve and are served experience and explore together Christ's life and purposes for each other.

Those so engaged through ministering with and among the casualties of our fragmented society inevitably come to challenge the causes. This advocacy gives voice to the voiceless. It is prophetic to those who hold power and make decisions which affect the lives of young people. Such communities learn what it is to confront the 'principalities and powers' which destroy, demean, degrade and exploit the young. In so doing, they at times find themselves at odds with the dominant values of many churches and fellow Christians. As Jesus himself knew, those who seek the forsaken become outcasts, too. It can be a lonely and misunderstood calling.

The demands of God's mission among and with those who are geographically close but culturally distant is as challenging and urgent as that in other lands. Those engaged in such frontier mission have pioneered the way. Where are the others to join them to form a growing missionary movement, able and willing to bring good news to the poor of this frontier generation of young people?

While some of the answers are to be found elsewhere in this book, it will take a major attitude change in the Christian community to mobilize for such frontier mission. Most churches and many Christian youth agencies operate strategies for institutional maintenance and extension. By some estimates, about 90 per cent of Christian youth work resources are concentrated on the 9 per cent of young people in touch with the churches. Specific programmes are directed to retaining the young once they have embarked upon their teenage years. Despite all the energy and dedicated effort put into such work, overall decline has continued throughout the past fifty years. This has bred a defensive attitude. New initiatives have to break the mould. If every congregation and Christian youth agency set aside 10 per cent of its resources for mission initiatives among dispossessed young people, mould-breaking would begin.

Recent developments, such as YFC Urban Emphases, Crusaders' thrust into Urban Priority Areas and Oasis' homelessness project, are signs of hope. Joint ventures, such as non-alcoholic bars, the Earls Court Project, converted pubs such as the Brown Bear in South London and the Kings Arms at Bishop's Stortford, point the way. YWAM, Time for God, Careforce, Frontline, Voluntary Evangelism, place some young volunteers in frontier situations, many of whom catch a vision for frontier mission. Among new ways of worship and of being church are Shal Church in Grimsby, JOY in Oxford, and NOS in Sheffield. They point ways for the future. Long-standing projects, such as Kaleidoscope, Cambridge University Mission, Shrewsbury House, Oxford Kilburn Club, All Souls Club House, Knights Association of Christian Youth

Clubs and Oxford Youth Works, are places where others can come and learn, by doing, and then go and develop new ventures elsewhere.

Almost 1,000 frontier initiatives are linked through Frontier Youth Trust. It takes courage, tenacity and commitment to long-term, consistent unspectacular ministry in order to sustain such ventures. There is often little to show in terms of new Christians added to those congregations which support them. In different ways, they seek to care for the whole person and the whole community. God's mission includes being God's good news by working for the total well-being of each person and their families, and the neighbourhood. It means telling the story of the life, teaching, ministry, death and rising again of Jesus Messiah. It involves discipling others and working for social justice.

Such a missionary movement requires a new strategy for church planting and church growth. Current congregational extension and congregational cloning perpetuates the cultural and class captivity of the Christian community. If frontier churches are to arise from frontier youth work on-the-job training is needed, which combines learning by doing; missiology with urban ministry; sociology and professional youth work skills; cross-cultural communication with interpreting the Bible; practical theology with creative worship; spiritual warfare with community organizing; spiritual formation with practical discipleship. It should tap the rich resources of Catholic, Pentecostal, Charismatic and Evangelical traditions, as well as the experience of the Majority Black churches, the newer churches and theologies of the two-thirds world where the cutting edges of frontier mission are found.

Alongside denominational and Christian youth work agencies, the support networks such as Frontier Youth Trust, which links together upwards of 3,000 frontier youth workers, have developed. A focus in the United Kingdom for practitioner networks and any Christian agencies, including those in youth work, education and child care, and the criminal justice field, is provided by the recently established Frontier Forum, through which new collaborative strategies are being forged.

The Spirit is renewing the churches for such a time as this. God's call to reach the least of the lost generation remains insistent and urgent. Will his people reorder their priorities and rise to the challenge or will God's good news continue to be denied to the dispossessed young people because we chicken out?

References

1. 'Faith in the City', Church House Publishing, 1985, page 315.
2. 'Faith in the City'.
3. 'Faith in the City', page 316.
4. Luke 4:13–19.
5. 'Faith in the City', page 317.

7 Peter Gilbert

All Change

Have you ever experienced the disruption of an interrupted train journey, when the guard calls out 'All change'? The inconvenience and hassle of trying to gather together all your gear, carrying it all with you, hoping not to lose anything, anxious lest you leave anything behind, and a little insecure about making the connection and resuming your journey? Will you have as good a seat? And with whom? Will you get there on time? Will you get there at all?!

All change brings with it the potential for a crisis of security. Change can challenge identity, relationships and function. When, as in the lives of adolescents, it is literally 'all change'— socially, mentally, spiritually, emotionally and physically—all the ground shifts simultaneously. There is, therefore, little wonder, that, insecurity, fear, worry and anxiety are key words to understanding the angst that lies behind the transition from child to adult. Adults can all too often forget or minimize the fears generated by adolescence. The statistics from the Teenage Religion and Values Survey presented in this section may serve to remind us, as youth leaders, teachers and parents, just how keenly change is felt.

For many young people, adolescence is most clearly marked by the onslaught of puberty. Other interrelated life areas are changing, but it is often physical growth and sexual development that provide the most clearly identifiable evidence of these changes. Both the individual and the onlooker mark, and remark upon, such changes in the physical realm, and it is here, too, that many worries are generated. Whereas it is true that teenagers reach their peak in their potential for sexual reproduction (and energy!) at around eighteen years of age, it has also been estimated that the average adolescent *thinks* about sex about once every fourteen minutes! So physical and sexual developments naturally affect the mental and emotional processes as well as merely bodily symptoms, and they will also have a 'domino effect' on relationships. Statistics indicate that anxieties are not solely about the 'sexual act' or sexual activity, but also about perceptions of self and of others. The adolescent is seeking to relate his or her feelings to a wider social context: 'Where do I fit in—sexually, physically and emotionally—to society?' To go back to our original paragraph, 'Will I have as good a seat? And with whom?'

For many girls, puberty starts as early as ten years of age; for many boys, it begins some time after the age of eleven. The sample of 13,000 boys and girls aged thirteen to fifteen questioned for the Teenage Religion and Values Survey is therefore likely to reflect the views of people in a kind of crisis of change. For the girls, menstruation will probably have started, with its potential for fear, embarrassment and the hormonally produced mood swings that often accompany it. Fatty tissue—at the hips, thighs, buttocks, and breasts—is also likely to increase, as is the growth of body hair on legs, underarms, and around genitalia.

For boys there will be the probable settling of the voice to a lower register, possibly accompanied by uncontrollable vocal inflections ranging from embarrassing high-pitched squeaks to lower, deep-down growls! Fatty tissue (puppy fat) may be replaced by muscle, and hair will develop on legs, arms, underarms, genitalia, face and perhaps chest. External genital development will be marked by a lengthening and filling out of the penis and testicles, with an increased capacity for penile erection, sperm production and ejaculation—often, initially, through nocturnal emission ('wet dreams') and through masturbation.

Anxiety

If we can be aware of this type and level of physical change when we look at some statistics on anxieties faced by young people about their sexuality, we shall have a better context for understanding and for drawing out later any practical implications. The teenagers were asked to respond to the statement: 'I am worried about my sex life'. The resulting statistics do indicate that the level of anxiety decreases as the individuals get older, particularly where those worries relate to teenagers' views of themselves and to how others see them. Thus, 17 per cent of year 9 pupils express worries about their sex lives, but that figure reduces to 16 per cent by year 10. Attractiveness to the opposite sex is *not* a worry to 45 per cent of year 10s. Only 43 per cent of year 9s, however, are unworried by this. This shift in the statistics lends weight to the idea that, as the first (and perhaps the most startling) wave of puberty recedes, so individuals gain in security and anxiety declines. Experience must also be a factor in this statistical shift. A teenager questioning his or her attractiveness to members of the opposite sex will become less worried once successful dating relationships begin! I would suggest that one of the factors behind the decline of worry about sexuality is that more year 10s are sexually active than year 9s. Surveys vary, but about 30 per cent of young people have experienced sexual intercourse by the age of sixteen (years 11 to 12).

This surmise is backed up when we examine the statistics on worry about AIDS. Unlike the other statistics mentioned above, the fear of AIDS *does not* decline with age. Rather, there is an increase in worry from 61 per cent in year 9 to 62 per cent in year 10. AIDS-related worries are the predominant anxieties expressed in the Teenage Religion and Values Survey: 62 per cent admit to them, compared with 50 per cent worried about getting on with other people, 32 per cent worried about attractiveness to the opposite sex and 17 per cent worried about their sexuality. The increase in worry about AIDS may well indicate that sexual activity, and therefore an increase in one possible source of AIDS, is more prevalent with increased age. It is encouraging that the percentage of weekly churchgoers who express concern is lower (58 per cent) than that of non-churchgoers (62 per cent). A further cause of the increase may be attributable to an increase in AIDS awareness through media exposure.

It is interesting to see that there appears to be a gender bias to some of the anxieties recorded. More girls than boys worry about their attractiveness to the opposite sex (35 per cent compared with 28 per cent). Perhaps this statistic reflects society's sexist weighting to the male as initiator/hunter in relationships and to the female as hopeful recipient of male attention. It also underlines the effectiveness of the massive media market aimed at young people, which feeds on the insecurity of personal self-worth and self-image, and targets females in particular through magazines, diets, make-up and so on. Teenagers in the United Kingdom spend £18 million per week on magazines, music, clothes and make-up.

Churchgoers and anxiety

Apart from the lower level of worry about AIDS among churchgoers, every other category scores higher levels of anxiety for regular church attenders! Some 56 per cent of churchgoers worry about getting on with others, whereas only 46 per cent of non-churchgoers express concern. Getting on with the opposite sex is a concern for 37 per cent of churchgoers, compared with 29 per cent of non-churchgoers. While 18 per cent of churchgoers worry about their sex lives, the figure for non-churchgoers is 15 per cent. This gap is also perceptible amongst those non-churchgoers who classify themselves as believers in God, uncertain or atheists. In general, believers are more worried than agnostics who, in turn, are more worried than atheists. Perhaps not surprisingly, agnostics tend to score highly as being uncertain/undecided about to how to interpret their feelings.

For the churchgoer, denomination seems to produce no clear overall pattern of response to these anxieties. The clearest trend seems to be a kind of self-assurance in Anglican churchgoers, only 54 per cent of whom are concerned about how they get on with others, compared with 60 per cent of Roman Catholics and Free Church attenders. Looked at from the other perspective, the same trend emerges: 22 per cent of Anglicans are unconcerned about their ability to get on with others, compared to 18 per cent of Roman Catholics and 17 per cent of Free Church attenders. Because churchgoing is *not* the norm for the age range sampled, could it be that the figures for Anglican churchgoers represent the children of more 'established', more 'socially confident' families? These young people might be expected to be more confident and assertive, more aware of social influence, than their non-churchgoing peers.

What can we infer from this analysis of the statistics? Our first lesson must be that there still is a considerable amount of fear and anxiety prevalent among young people, and that we should not underestimate the insecurity that such fear engenders. There is still room for the exploration of subjects such as self-image, self-worth, assertiveness and sex in the programmes of any youth worker, leader or teacher. The figures suggest that there are boys and girls who believe that they are sexually attractive, but lack the social confidence to express it; the mixed youth-work group can still provide a safe and monitored environment for social interplay. Such a forum may also avoid the concept of 'unequal yoking' as described in 2 Corinthians 6:14. Our second lesson must take into account the fact that anxieties abound among believers, more so than agnostics who are, in turn, more anxious than atheists. What are we to make of this?

One message is clear across the statistics: if you want an unstressed, anxiety-free, low-pressure life, do not expect that becoming a Christian will immediately solve all your problems and remove all your worries. But if you are up to a challenge, will take a risk and live with tensions, but know ultimately who you are, what you are worth and where you are going, then follow Jesus Christ. And every youth worker, leader and teacher worth their salt should charge themselves up to that challenge, working *through* anxieties and not avoiding them.

I am worried about my sex life

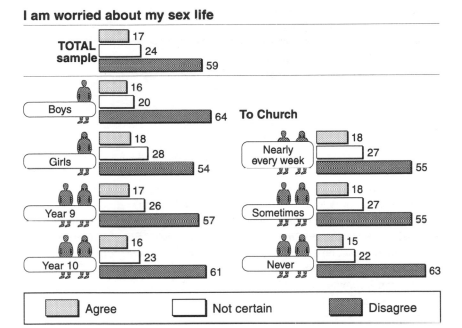

To Church

	Agree	Not certain	Disagree

Source: Teenage Religion and Values Survey of 13,000 pupils in England and Wales. All figures refer to responses to the statement immediately above this diagram. The left hand column shows, at the top, the responses of the total sample which is divided, in the middle, into responses of year 9 and year 10 pupils. The right hand column deals only with the 11% of the total sample who attend church.

47

8 David Bruce

Self-esteem

Sharon saw her boyfriend, Michael, talking to one of the youth workers who came to her West Belfast housing estate each Saturday. She moved to where they were standing and, without waiting, interrupted their conversation. 'You want me to sandbag for you tonight, Mick?' 'Yeah, sure, whatever you like,' replied Michael, barely registering that she was there. The youth worker looked puzzled. 'I'm sorry, Mick,' he said, 'but I don't understand what Sharon just asked you. What did she mean by sandbag? I haven't heard that one before!' 'Oh, that's simple enough,' said Michael with a shrug of his shoulders. 'I'll nick a car later on and Sharon'll come with me. She'll get in the back and park herself on the parcel shelf so that if I crash through an army checkpoint, the soldiers won't shoot because she'll be in the way. Get it? Sandbag. Simple.'

As the youth worker reflected on this later, he came to see that central to Sharon's many problems was a lack of self-worth. She saw in her bedroom mirror each morning not an attractive, gifted young woman setting out to win over the world, but an inanimate object filled with sand. A bullet-stopper. What has made her feel this way about herself? Unemployment? Discrimination? Religion?

Out of a similar crucible a black teenager, fed up with his lifetime of discrimination and racial put-downs, scrawled on a banner hung in his room for all to see, 'I'm me and I'm fine, 'cause God don't make junk.' Amidst the brash bravado and enthusiasm this was good theology.

In some parts of the United Kingdom, teenage suicide has been increasing for years. Take Karl, for example. He was sixteen, keen on (and good at) sport, with a circle of friends who admired and liked him. He had some difficulties at school, but nothing out of the ordinary when compared with hundreds of others his age. One Monday afternoon, his father found him slumped across the front seat of the family car in the garage with the engine running. He had deliberately sealed up the cracks around the door with an old blanket, had turned on the car radio and sat eating a bag of sweets until the fumes made him pass out. Next day his girlfriend received his suicide note in the mail saying, among other things, 'At least now, I won't have to pretend'. Karl didn't feel he was worth much as a person.

Teenagers don't know what to make of themselves. On the one hand, they can often appear desperately overconfident: they dress, dance and rave to make a statement and to stand up to (and to face down) authority—no meek acceptance of the *status quo* here. On the other hand, they can also spend hours agonizing about sexual emotions, stumbling and stuttering with the self-assurance of Bambi when faced with someone to whom they are attracted.

The Teenage Religion and Values Survey shows that most teenagers today say that they feel fine about themselves; about two-thirds of the group questioned disagreed with the statement, 'I feel I am not worth much as a person'. Of course, that leaves a colossal one-third who were either not too sure or who thought, 'Yes, this describes me.' It seems that boys are slightly more sure of themselves than girls, but the difference is not great. Looking at the question again through the filter of church attendance, however, reveals something very important. Here we see that the regular church-attenders have a much higher self-esteem than those who attend irregularly or never. Why might this be?

Critics of Christianity have long asserted that religious faith bears down on the natural worthiness of the human spirit, sapping people of their potential and rendering them guilt-ridden subjects of a manipulative system of domination. There has been some justification for this view, given our history. The Irish writer, James Joyce, expresses something of his anger against Christianity in *Portrait of the Artist as a Young Man*. His youth was dominated by a Catholicism which seemed to him heavy on guilt and depravity, but light on grace and forgiveness. It is hard to imagine a teenager subjected weekly to a diet of sermons in which the horrors of hell are described in these terms: 'The blood seethes and boils in the brains, the brains are boiling in the skull, the heart in the breast glowing and bursting, the bowels, a red-hot mass of burning pulp, the tender eyes flaming like molten balls.'[1]

Protestant orthodoxy does not escape criticism either. Many Christians have sung the hymn 'Beneath the Cross of Jesus' and have been helped by it. Some time ago, John Stott told an assembly of ministers and Christian leaders gathered for a conference that he had actually 'repented' of singing one verse of the hymn as it was originally written by Elizabeth Cecilia Clephane:

And from my smitten heart with tears Two wonders I confess:
The wonder of his glorious love, And my own worthlessness.

In many modern hymn books the last two words have been replaced by the word 'unworthiness' which is possibly a more biblical assessment of the human condition. This is not to soft-peddle the seriousness of sin, but it is to oppose with vigour those who would shamelessly manipulate the tender human spirit to feel worthless when exposed before God, or to make someone grovel perpetually in a way far beyond the intention of the Lord who reaches out to save them. Anthony Hoekema in his little book, *The Christian Looks at Himself*,[2] quotes a piece of research by William Counts, in which he found a clergyman saying, 'I feel I've preached an effective sermon when I've left my congregation feeling guilty.' Quite so. If that is what the preacher sets out to accomplish then it is far more likely to be he who has done it than the Lord. Many adults today have a warped view of faith and, more tragically, of God, because they were frightened into a decision 'for' Jesus at an early age by unscrupulous preachers who stressed the penalties of failing to 'decide'. Failure is built into the entire presentation: you need to decide because you have failed to measure up; you will fail yet again if you do not decide today.

Nevertheless, the Teenage Religion and Values Survey points up an encouraging trend, which is that churchgoing young people today are not emerging from their encounter with Christian teaching bowed down under a burden of self-loathing—rather the reverse. Of young churchgoers, 56 per cent said they disagreed with the statement, 'I feel I am not worth much as a person', compared with 31 per cent of those who sometimes attend church and 18 per cent who never attend. One hopes that this is because churchgoing young people have discovered something seminal about themselves in relation to their Creator. Sinful we all undoubtedly are, and must rightly come to appreciate the full force of our judicial guilt before a holy and righteous judge; but forgiven we may all be, because there is grace! Jesus Christ, the Son of the Father's love, subjected himself to the Father's wrath that we, who are the objects of the Father's wrath, may become the sons and daughters of the Father's love.

The love of God compels us forcibly away from a negative view of ourselves to the most positive view—indeed, to a view which is beyond us to comprehend in this present age. God has invested everything in us, including the ultimate domestic harmony of his household, because we are to be the collective bride for his Son. Knowing this, it is difficult to have an entirely negative view of oneself.

In reaching young people who are outside of church structures, we have at our disposal the best news imaginable for them. Maybe the 'scene' will tell them that they are nothing more than sandbags or objects. Maybe the prospect of unemployment will lead them to the view that they merely represent depressing statistics rather than vibrant opportunities for optimism. Maybe the suspicion of older generations, too busy to listen and too cynical to care, will convince them that no one is interested anyway. But the people who follow Jesus can say to them, 'He loves you and will not stop loving you. He has plans for you that you would not believe. He alone can help you make sense of the horrors grabbing at you, and give you peace.'

References

1. James Joyce, *Portrait of the Artist as a Young Man*, Panther, 1977, page 112.
2. Anthony Hoekema, *The Christian Looks at Himself*, Eerdmans, 1975, page 16. *Quoting William M. Counts, 'The Nature of Man and the Christian's Self-esteem'*, *Journal of Psychology and Theology*, January 1973.

I feel I am not worth much as a person

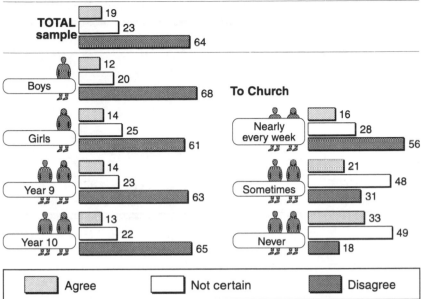

Source: Teenage Religion and Values Survey of 13,000 pupils in England and Wales. All figures refer to responses to the statement immediately above this diagram. The left hand column shows, at the top, the responses of the total sample which is divided, in the middle, into responses of year 9 and year 10 pupils. The right hand column deals only with the 11% of the total sample who attend church.

9 Rana Johal

Race

This section investigates the attitudes of young people to the number of black people living in Great Britain. The underlying issue is the incidence of racism among young people. Those surveyed were presented with the statement 'There are too many black people living in this country', and were asked whether they agreed, disagreed or were uncertain about the assertion. For the purpose of this exercise, the term 'black' included all people who are not white.

A report by the Commission for Racial Equality, *Race Through the 90s*[1] defines racism as follows:

> *Racism is the belief that some races are superior to others, based on the false idea that different physical characteristics—such as skin colour—make some people better than others. Scientists have now thrown out the old idea that people can be divided into four basic 'races'.*

The good news is that, overall, almost two-thirds (65 per cent) of the sample group disagree with the statement, a further 16 per cent are uncertain and only 19 per cent agree that there are too many black people living in the United Kingdom (see tabulation). If we look at the results from a gender perspective, a more interesting picture develops. Of the boys, 54 per cent disagree, 18 per cent are uncertain and more than one-quarter (28 per cent) agree. Of the girls, 76 per cent disagree, 13 per cent are uncertain and only 11 per cent agree.

Looking at the statistics from an age perspective, we see that 67 per cent of year 9 pupils (age thirteen to fourteen years) disagree with the statement, 15 per cent are uncertain and 18 per cent agree. There is a slightly more disappointing picture with year 10 pupils (age fourteen to fifteen years); 63 per cent disagree with the statement, 16 per cent are uncertain and 21 per cent agree.

If agreement with the statement is an indicator of racist attitudes, one in five young people between thirteen to fifteen years of age exhibits some degree of racism; it also appears to be more than twice as prevalent among boys than girls. The 3 per cent difference between year 9 and year 10 pupils who agree with the statement may indicate that racism increases as children get older.

The young people questioned in this survey fell into three different subgroups: those who attend church nearly every week; those who sometimes attend church; and those who never attend church. These three groupings provide some interesting responses. More than three-quarters (77 per cent) of those who attend church nearly every week disagreed with the statement, whereas 12 per cent were uncertain and only 11 per cent agreed. Of those only attending church sometimes, 69 per cent disagreed, 15 per cent were uncertain and 16 per cent agreed. Those who never attend church show the most startling results: 60 per cent disagreed with the statement, 16 per cent were uncertain, and almost one in four (24 per cent) agreed.

There seems to be a direct correlation between the incidence of racist attitudes among young people and the frequency of church attendance. Those who never attend church are *more than twice as likely* to be racist as those who attend nearly every week. It would seem that church attendance somehow affects young people's attitudes towards race. Nevertheless, 19 per cent of the whole sample group and 11 per cent of those who attend church regularly agreed that there are too many black people in the United Kingdom.

To put the issue into perspective, the 1991 census figures for the population of Great Britain[2] indicate that the total non-white population is a mere 5.5 per cent. However, more than 50 per cent of the ethnic minority population lived in the south-east in 1991. The greatest concentration was in Greater London, where 20 per cent of the population are from an ethic minority. Rural areas generally comprise less than 1 per cent ethnic minorities, whereas metropolitan districts and London boroughs have more than 5 per cent. Furthermore, the population of ethnic minority groups tend to be in the younger age ranges, about 60 per cent compared with about 40 per cent of the white population.

With a black population of only 5.5 per cent, why is it that such large percentages of the young people surveyed believe there to be too many black people in the country? More importantly, why is it that 11 per cent of regular churchgoers and 16 per cent of occasional churchgoers agree with the statement? It may be that the uneven distribution of the non-white population leads people to think that there are far more black people in the United Kingdom than there actually are. Or it may be that a well-informed white majority does indeed consider a black population of 5.5 per cent to be too much. A further reason may be Britain's white cultural heritage which, in regard to non-whites, is at best prejudiced and at worst racist. Three main factors may have created this situation:

Anti-Semitism

Early on in the history of the church there arose the accusation that Jews were 'Christ-killers'. As the church's understanding of Christology developed, the accusation became that of 'deicide'. Jews were seen as rejecters of God, and worthy of persecution and misery until, just before the Second Coming of

Christ, they accepted Jesus as Messiah. When the church became the official religion of the Roman Empire, this anti-Jewish 'theology' resulted in laws which, in turn, underpinned the succeeding Germanic traditions. As Europe developed, so did the concept of 'Christendom'. The persecution and vilification of Jews became an accepted part of the legal and theological framework of the Christian states, culminating eventually in the Holocaust. Ironically, it was the Holocaust that brought an end to the overt anti-Semitism of the European (supposedly Christian) nations.

European expansionism

European expansionism, which began with the expeditions of Christopher Columbus and Vasco da Gama, led to a new understanding of colonialism. The Christian nations of Europe saw the new lands opening up to them as gifts of God's grace, provided for their possession and to be used in any way they saw fit. To provide further justification for the subjugation of large numbers of people, white biologists and scientists also developed new theories and classifications of race (for instance, describing black people as subhuman). Not surprisingly, the 'white race' was seen to be the most advanced and highly evolved of the races. It therefore had a natural right to subdue and rule over those races 'lower down' the evolutionary scale. Furthermore, superiority of the white race was seen not merely as biological, but also intellectual and cultural. These concepts were most clearly demonstrated in the British Empire, which Lord Macauley described as the 'triumph of reason over Barbarism'.

Myths

There have arisen a number of myths in Britain about the presence of black people. In his book, *Understanding Race Relations*,[3] Keith Trobe considers several myths which have become a part of the white British understanding about immigration. These are as follows:

immigration is a recent development;
all immigrants are black;
all black people are immigrants;
Britain is being swamped by immigrants;
many more people enter Britain than leave;
anyone can come and live in Britain.

As with all myths, repetition has led many to believe that these are facts. The truth, however, is to the contrary: the three factors outlined above have produced false myths, excuses for expansionism and bad theology. Instead, Christians must base their understanding and teaching about race on the Bible.

The biblical position on race is quite clear:

◆ All human beings are made by God in his image. He considers all people worthy of dignity, respect and justice. The notion that there are several 'races' or subspecies of *Homo sapiens* is both biblically and biologically insupportable. God is, in one sense, the Father of all humans. As such, he sustains, loves and makes available his grace for all humans, irrespective of skin colour, language or physiognomy. (Genesis 1:27, 11:1–9; John 3:16–17; Acts 17:24–28)

◆ All humans are sinful and need God's forgiveness. There is no individual, tribe, nation or culture that is free from sin, and it is, moreover, foolish to suppose that any one 'race', nation or culture is in some way superior to another. We all pay the price for this universal human trait. (Genesis 3; Romans 1:18—2:4; 3:23)

◆ Faith in Christ makes people one. All Christians, whatever their colour, culture, nationality or sex, are conjoined in Jesus into a new body, the church. This unity is more than spiritual and is to be demonstrated in tangible ways. (Acts 2:1–41, 10:34–36; Romans 1:16; Galations 3:26–29; Ephesians 2:11–22; James 2:14–26; Revelation 5:9–10, 7:9)

◆ God works with people of all 'races'. Abraham was the Iraqi-born father of Israel, Zipporah the Nubian wife of Moses. The Queen of Sheba, Rahab the Canaanite and Ruth the Moabitess were forebears of King David and Jesus, and the Egyptians, Persians, Romans, Greeks, Libyans and Arabs all had a share in God's plan for the redemption of humankind. Clearly, God does not view humans in terms of 'race'. Neither does he favour one 'race' above another. (Genesis 12:1–5; Exodus 2:15–22; Numbers 12:1–16; Joshua 2:1–14; Ruth 1:1–7; 2 Chronicles 9:1–12; Song of Songs 1:5–6; Mark 15:21; Acts 2:5)

◆ God cares for foreigners. The Israelites were given strict instructions about foreigners in their land. Foreigners were to be treated 'as fellow Israelites' and loved 'as you love yourselves'. The parable of the good Samaritan was used by Jesus to demonstrate how ethnic background is irrelevant in terms of obedience to God. Peter's vision, and the Jerusalem Council that followed, demonstrated how God himself does not restrict his grace to any race or ethnic group. (Exodus 22:21; Leviticus 19:33–34; Psalm 146:9; Malachi 3:5, Luke 10:25–36; Acts 11:1–18)

To summarize, racism is of direct concern to the church. The results of the Teenage Religion and Values Survey, if we take together those who agree with the statement and those who are uncertain, indicate that possibly more than one-third of white youngsters between the ages of thirteen and fifteen have racist attitudes. These attitudes are formed by factors which are in direct opposition to biblical teaching and demographic evidence. The church has an obligation to teach biblical truth regarding race. However, 23 per cent of regular churchgoing thirteen- to fifteen-year-olds have racist attitudes or tendencies, and there is much to be done.

The survey indicates that negative attitudes towards blacks may increase with age—a swing of up to 4 per cent between years 9 and 10. Clearly, we need to reach children with the truth as early as possible. In *The Early Years*,[4] Iram Siraj-Blatchford cites evidence that racial awareness begins as early as three years of age, and with it begins racial prejudice and discrimination. Home life and parental influence play an overwhelming part in the early development of racial attitudes. What does this have to say about church work with very young children in the context of the family?

When it comes to racist attitudes and gender, we are faced with yet another problem. Thirteen-to fifteen-year-old boys revealed twice the levels of racist attitudes as the girls. Indeed, agreement with the statement and uncertainty together show that 46 per cent of all the boys were in some way influenced by racist attitudes. It seems that there is something that tends them towards racism. What does this mean for the church when we are so bad at reaching males? The MARC Europe English Church census of 1979 showed English church attendance, by sex, to be 45 per cent male and 55 per cent female. A follow-up census in 1989 showed the figures to be 42 per cent male, 58 per cent female (these are the latest figures).

A church that is poor at reaching males is also going to be a church that fails to have significant influence in the male subculture. The matter would seem to be of particular urgency, because there is an apparent difficulty in reaching and keeping young people in the church past the age of fifteen years.

Assuming that we can get young people into the church, what kind of example do we then set them? It seems that there is still an antipathy to colour. Power structures are still in the hands of whites. Even missionary organizations and evangelicals hoping to reach out to non-white peoples appear to keep power in the hands of whites. Not only do potential converts have to respond to a gospel adjusted for white sensibilities but, having responded, they have to worship, pray and socialize with white-directed structures designed for white cultural sensibilities.

Perhaps I am being a little too hard, but with such a church in Britain, it is not entirely surprising that as many as 23 per cent of regular churchgoers and 31 per cent of occasional churchgoing thirteen- to fifteen-year-olds have some racist attitudes. There is, however, much that can be done to redress the situation:

◆ Educating the church about non-white British cultures, and helping the church to deal with the truth that some people are both non-white and British.

◆ Educating the church about the role of black people in its history.

◆ Ensuring that non-white spirituality and theology are seen and taught as equally valid beside white, Western and Greek philosophical traditions.

◆ Opening up church power structures to black Christians; positive discrimination may be helpful in achieving this end (a biblical precedent can be found in Acts 6:1–7).

◆ Sharing partnership and resources with black Christians to facilitate integration, perhaps through the auspices of bodies such as South Asian Concern, the Alliance of Asian Christians and the Afro-Caribbean Evangelical Alliance. This may also help the church to deal with a demographic opportunity: young people constitute 60 per cent of the whole black population in Britain.

Once we can act together, British Christians, black and white, can deal with the tragedy of racism in Britain. Racism affects the white child as much as the black child. The black child develops a confused sense of self-identity and self-esteem; the white child develops an equally damaging sense of superiority based on erroneous stereotypes. Before long, young people are prepared to insult, abuse and assault one another simply because of skin colour and culture.

The church has a responsibility to share God's perspective on race with everyone. Today's thirteen- to fifteen-year-olds are tomorrow's leaders, and we must exercise our responsibility with ever-increasing diligence and commitment.

The following quotation is a fitting end to this chapter. It comes from Ronald Sider's book *Evangelism and Social Action*,[5] and it offers both hope and a warning:

If God has reconciled us to himself, but cannot reconcile us to each other, then the whole thing is a fraud.

References

1. Commission for Racial Equality, *Race Through the 90s*, 1992 (revised 1993).
2. Social Trends 24, Crown copyright, 1994.
3. Keith Trobe, *Understanding Race Relations*, Stanley Thornes, 1991.
4. Iram Siraj-Blatchford, *The Early Years: Laying the Foundations for Racial Equality*, Trentham Books, 1994.
5. Ronald J. Sider, *Evangelism and Social Action in a Lost and Broken World*, Hodder and Stoughton, 1993, page 81.

There are too many black people living in this country

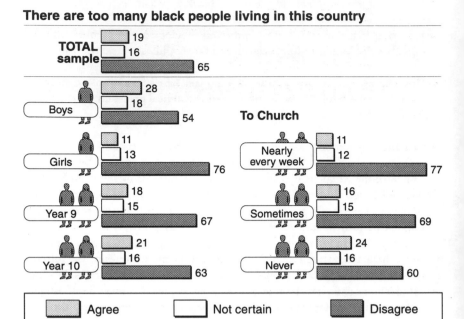

Source: Teenage Religion and Values Survey of 13,000 pupils in England and Wales. All figures refer to responses to the statement immediately above this diagram. The left hand column shows, at the top, the responses of the total sample which is divided, in the middle, into responses of year 9 and year 10 pupils. The right hand column deals only with the 11% of the total sample who attend church.

10

Sue Rinaldi

Society's Expectations

No one can escape effectively from the particular customs, principles, flavours and modes of life that identify and fashion each society. Whatever age the individual, everyone is subject to certain limitations and opportunities. Forces—or pressures—are exerted morally, ethically, socially and spiritually, and it is vital to examine them, especially in young people. Of course, not all pressures have a negative effect. Some produce positive values in the lives of individuals, however challenging and disturbing such pressures may be in the short term. The aim is not to eradicate all pressure from young people's lives. Rather, it is to help young people to interpret and handle pressure in order to mature, and to enable them to appreciate their own contribution to life and its rewards.

'Change is here to stay.' How true this is of the characteristics of each new generation! Each generation sees definite shifts in priorities, values and identifiable trends. Some change is due to an intrinsic need to find a fresh identity, and independence from former ways and thoughts. The characteristic of tradition—'this is the way it has always been and must continue to stay'— usually provokes reaction and rebellion in young people. The search for alternatives becomes high on the agenda.

The process of learning

There is an expectation that each new generation will learn from the one before. However, although this is spectacularly true in science and medicine, for example, it is debatable whether this is the case in morality, ethics and spirituality. With the loss of moral consensus, what one person sees as progress or the benefits of freedom, another perceives as the consequences of a disintegrating moral framework. Without doubt, we are living in a society that frequently challenges all the foundational standards of life and thought created by a Christianized society. Many see a moral framework as old-fashioned, irrelevant and an unjust restraint on personal freedom.

Young people of the 1990s are, whether they know it or not, surrounded by the philosophies of 'relativism' and 'existentialism'—the belief that there is no absolute or ultimate truth, no set standards of right or wrong. Instead, the belief is that truth and morality depend on the individual and vary from one individual to another. The spiritual and moral experimentation of the last few decades seems to have produced a generation of young people with no agreed moral code to consult. What is more, many bear the scars of family breakdown and have lost any real sense of respect for authority. This moral void, and the irrelevance, for many, of Christianity and the church, provide a lethal cocktail for a spiritually searching, often-confused and hurting group, however full of potential that group may be.

A closer look at the 1990s

Teenagers, with their varied experiences, thoughts and emotions, have to find within themselves a basis on which to build their adult lives. Circumstances ranging from tragedy to success, and emotions ranging from loneliness to joy, become a melting pot from which the values and direction of the adult emerge. Can we describe these teenage years more closely?

Whose identity?

The search for identity is a huge pressure in a culture that asks us to define ourselves by what we look like and what we do. Hunger for identity, together with a longing to belong, often channel into intense peer pressure. Subcultures within subcultures develop according to varied tastes in music or clothes, social-class groupings, living conditions or educational opportunities. Experimentation and 'finding oneself' is the norm as individuals reject the established boundaries and align themselves with new groups in their search to find identity and belonging. At times, even personal values are trodden underfoot and discarded. When damage is self-inflicted unintentionally and unknowingly, it is very sad. This search for identity within peer groups can influence many things: dress code, for example—one can easily spot the 'fashion victim' or the 'goth'! The recent exploration into the art of body piercing could be interpreted as a cry for uniqueness or, alternatively, as a submission to peer pressure. Let us not forget that these variables of youth culture fuel a huge industry coldly manipulated for profit. How happy is the company that convinced young people they must have 70 training shoes! The rebellions of the 1990s' teenager are often cynically stirred up by a marketing conference!

One major pressure felt by young people and reinforced by the media is to search for the perfect model image. Advertisements and magazine features constantly promote the 'ultimate' denim jeans, the 'choice' hairspray, the 'perfect' figure, the aftershave that guarantees success with the opposite sex. As such, they impose a standard which consumers must strive to reach. Personal success, at least on the surface, is sold at the price of a product. Beauty tips, healthy eating plans and exercise routines abound as our minds are teased by the media. In moderation, these can be a positive contribution to lifestyle, but an obsession to 'fit in' and 'look right' may mean that the real person is never discovered. Instead, he or she remains hidden under a weight of worthlessness and rejection. In some cases, this poor self-image can result in depressive tendencies, eating disorders, illness and suicide.

Pressures from outside

Insecurity and instability within the home create unwelcome and often destructive pressures on young people. The breakup and decline of family life appears on the increase, corrupting the most valuable qualities of love and security. Dissension, violence or the fear of losing a parent can produce all kinds of disturbing behaviour and anti-social attitudes; they can affect whole value systems and patterns of life.

There is also an intense pressure on the sexual ethics and behaviour of young people. Teenagers themselves often highlight this area as the most difficult. Their sense of inadequacy, inferiority and rejection is strong because they fear that they are not living up to the sexual standards (real or fabricated) of their friends. The pressure, therefore, is to live in a society where a moral framework does not matter, resulting in the advice, 'if it feels good, do it!' The moral erosion which results then encourages teenagers to ignore the positive physical and emotional benefits of virginity until marriage; and virginity is discarded by trading with a stranger.

High incidences of teenage pregnancies have resulted in an increasing rate of abortion and single-parent families. Commitment within marriage is considered unrealistic, resulting in an increasing divorce rate and extra-marital affairs. The increasing awareness and fear of AIDS and other sexually transmitted diseases has given birth to a 'condom culture', where we encourage safer sex rather than give moral education.

The Office of Population Censuses and Surveys published statistics in June 1994 which showed that 'one of the most striking trends in recent years has been the dramatic increase in the number of births occurring outside marriage'. In fact, births outside marriage now make up 31 per cent of all live births compared to 14.4 per cent in 1982. These are only a few of the effects of the erosion of biblical moral values. Teenage magazines, lyrics to chart songs, readily available pornography, television 'soaps' and declining standards of censorship only serve to reinforce this erosion. Within an environment of 'anything goes' and a lack of clear guidance, it is no wonder that young people are struggling for breath as the pressure for sexual adventure overwhelms them.

Similar to the reaction against 'the bomb' in the 1960s, there is a pressure facing the 1990s' young person regarding the quality of the future. This time, it is more generally related to the environment. There is increasing awareness of ecological issues, increasing understanding of the scientific facts and increasing thirst to fund projects and alter lifestyles—all to secure a healthy and valuable future for coming generations. These ecological facts appear so worrying that some people might feel like disappearing under a cloud of despair. It seems, however, that young people are responding the opposite way. There is a genuine concern among the new generation to make financial and economic decisions which benefit the environment. As an article in a national newspaper commented, 'young people are far more sensitive to cruelty, both to animals and to people. They are less racist, more environmental, more philanthropic. They are more aware of what goes on in the world and more generous.'

A casual glance at society is sufficient to see that there is a spiritual search among young people. The quest for long-term fulfillment through materialism and hedonistic pleasure seems to have lost its impetus. Unfortunately, we also seem to be living in an age where many young people never see Christianity or the church as a valid alternative worthy of consideration. They see them as old-fashioned and totally irrelevant to today's culture and needs. The pressure to fall in line with this thinking is immense, and those voicing the opinion that Christianity is dynamic, relevant and positively life-changing are risking their reputation for normality and are likely to find themselves operating within a minority. It could be, however, that young people are not rejecting Jesus, but rejecting the cultural package he is wrapped in.

11 Pete Ward

God in Our Lives

There is currently much talk about 'the unchurched' in Christian circles. Youth ministers have often been heard to say, to a startled and amazed church audience, 'Of course, most of these young people were totally unchurched.' Despite the growing popularity of the term, however, the definition of 'unchurched' is unclear.

In popular youth ministry, 'the unchurched' sometimes means those young people who have no connection with the church. Often linked with this is the idea that they have no biblical knowledge or concept of what the gospel message might be. In using the term, youth ministers may well be concerned to say something about the effectiveness of their evangelism in reaching young people who previously had never been contacted by the church. This is encouraging, but at the same time the use of this term requires a degree of caution.

One question about the word 'unchurched' is this: why are we starting to use it instead of more traditional phrases such as 'non-Christians' or 'unbelievers'? Could it be that the term implies that the gap between those who attend church and those who do not is growing ever wider? Could it be that those of us within the church are starting to feel that large sections of the population no longer have any concept of what the Christian faith is about? In previous generations, we may have assumed that a 'non-Christian' would be someone who has considered the Christian faith and who has concluded that it was not for them. In the 1990s, our tendency is to assume a total ignorance of the Christian faith in the case of the vast majority of young people.

It is in this context that a particular response from the Teenage Religion and Values Survey should make us think again. In reply to the question 'Do you believe that your life is being guided by God?', 45 per cent were clear that this was not the case. Looking at the other extreme, only 7 per cent responded 'Yes, definitely' to the same question. The percentage of those who have a live 'spiritual' encounter with God is clearly and predictably low. Between these extremes, however, there exists a vast number of young people who are either 'not really sure' (34 per cent) or 'not certain' (14 per cent) that their lives are being guided by God. In other words, although a large number of young people did not perceive a link between God and their daily lives, an equally large number (48 per cent) were sitting on the fence.

In the light of these findings, the question of what we mean by 'the unchurched' becomes even more problematic. The Teenage Religion and Values Survey does not necessarily support the view that outside the church there is a vast wasteland of unbelief. The survey is supported by other research, too. In 'Young People, Religion and Values Today',[1] Leslie Francis finds that 66 per cent of young people who believe in God but do not attend church say that they pray; he also finds that 9 per cent of those who do not believe in God do the same. In all, we are presented with a strongly contrasting picture of young people's religious behaviour.

If we are to believe these findings, and they do accord with my own personal experience, then certain ideas which lie behind the popular use of the term 'unchurched' need to be considerably revised. While it is true that the vast majority of young people do not have any church connections and, perhaps as a consequence, have little working knowledge of the Christian faith, we need to recognize the fact that many young people are open to an experience of God through prayer or guidance.

To set this observation within a theological framework, the use of the term 'unchurched' to refer to young people has some serious problems in that it implies that God is limited in his activities to those who attend church! To the contrary, God is all-powerful and all-loving.

There is one further consequence of the findings from this report. In our outreach and evangelism, we should take account of the fact that many young people will have already had some religious experience. It is true that church may not yet be a factor in their lives; and the way the young people will talk about guidance or prayer may be limited or even confused in its doctrinal content. However, we must try to understand and to value what God may already have done in a young person's life. At the very least, this survey should encourage us to reach out to young people who may be nearer to God than we think!

References

1. Leslie Francis, 'Young People, Religion and Values Today', *Believing Without Belonging*, The Essex Hall Lecture, Unitarian Information Department, 1994, page 9.

Bill Hogg

Pleasure in Leisure

One nation under God has turned into one nation under the influence of one drug: television, the drug of the nation, breeding ignorance and feeding radiation.

This generation of young people is the MTV generation, child-minded by the electronic babysitter. Our researchers have indicated that the most significant slice of young people's leisure time is spent parked in front of the television.

Of course, young people are not perpetual couch potatoes. They do engage in physical and social activity. The sample questioned for the Teenage Religion and Values Survey, for instance, preferred swimming to soccer and enjoyed angling as a leisure pursuit. Soccer proved less popular among regular church-going young people than their non-attending or infrequently attending peers. This could reflect a clash of interest between Sunday League games and church activities. Not surprisingly, soccer is far more popular among boys than girls (89 per cent of boys surveyed are footballers compared to only 28 per cent of girls). Unlike the United States, where there are girls' high school soccer leagues, girls in Britain are not encouraged to play soccer. Angling is even more of a male preserve (only 4 per cent of female respondents are anglers). There is no significant difference between the churchgoers and non-churchgoers when it comes to swimming.

Despite its popularity, the youth worker might want to think through whether or not football, or any competitive sport, should be a part of youth activities. By its very nature, competitive activity, while involving some, excludes others. Tony Campolo observes: 'The world functions in a way that often excludes certain people and makes them feel like rejects, but the church should never do this.'[1] I am not trashing sports—I am simply raising the question of what is to be done with those you exclude and those who do not perform well. It is no fun being the last kid picked for 'sides'!

Television watching is a daily pursuit, however, for all but a tiny group (4.4 per cent) of those surveyed. Some 27 per cent had a daily television fix of more than four hours. The media moguls are not ignorant of the power of television to mould the young. Ben Johnson, a director of MTV, was asked if MTV influenced young people. He responded 'We don't influence eleven- to fourteen-year-olds.

We own them.' Jerry Mander, for fifteen years an advertising executive, said of television, 'I learned that it is possible to speak . . . directly into people's heads and then, like some other-worldly magician, leave images inside that can cause people to do what they might otherwise never have thought to do.'

There are big bucks to be pulled from the pockets of the teen consumers. In 1993, 'America's 28 million teenagers spent $57 billion of their own money. In Europe, Latin America and the Pacific Rim, a swath of more than 200 million teenagers are converging with their American soul mates in a vast, free-spending market that circles the globe.'[2]. Our young people are aggressively targeted by well-researched advertising campaigns. Coca Cola has spent two years studying 'the global teenager'. Rivals Pepsi have pushed Pepsi Max in television advertisements featuring teenage adrenaline junkies who live on the edge and enjoy dangerous sports. We need to be aware that the advertisers are out to ambush the emotions of the consumer generation.

'Major's Children '93', a survey conducted by the Trustee Savings Bank, found that young people's favourite television programmes were 'Neighbours', 'Home and Away' and 'Gladiators'. Chess and news programmes were deemed 'turn-offs'. What are we to make of the popular soaps? Noel Edmonds recently panned 'Neighbours' as 'lightweight rubbish'. The medium is not concerned with truth or substance, but image: 'Straight teeth in your mouth are more important than the words that come out.'

Professor Tony Campolo comments, '. . . television is one of the 'principalities and powers' and no one would question the fact that television moves us. Films are 'principalities and powers' and they mould us, too. As a matter of fact . . . most of you . . . are moulded by the media far more than you are moulded by the Holy Spirit. That's something we have to change. We must stop being controlled by the media. We must struggle to allow ourselves more and more to come under the control of the Holy Spirit. It is easy to see that we are media creations by the way we dress, the way we talk, the way we act, that almost everything we do is influenced by the media'.[3]

We are also seeing the emergence of a visually sophisticated Sega/Nintendo generation, which is becoming increasingly passive and private in its leisure. Television is not a social activity. An *Independent on Sunday* national opinion poll discovered that 55 per cent of eleven- to sixteen- year-olds own their own television, and 10 per cent of boys have their own video cassette recorder. Many young people spend their leisure time in isolation. A Channel 4 documentary revealed that only 3 per cent of young people play computer games under parental supervision. Many young people are withdrawing into a fantasy world.

Psychologists Robert Kubey of Rutgers University and Mihaly Csikszent Mihalyi of the University of Chicago conducted a thirteen-year study to explore the impact of television watching. The researchers discovered that watching television, particularly for long periods of time, creates low moods. The longer you watch, the less able you are to concentrate. You become increasingly drowsy and bored. As time goes on, you become sadder, lonelier, more irritable and more hostile. The plug-in drug has created a generation who will slouch on a couch and let the world pass by. Rather than 'seizing the day', they grab the remote control and engage in 'channel surfing'. Scottish Television featured a film, 'Around Seventeen', about young Scots on their way to becoming elite Kosbies. A drill sergeant boasted: 'They come off the street as couch potatoes and we turn them into soldiers.'

The MTV generation poses an evangelistic challenge to the church. How can the bookish church communicate to the visually sophisticated teenager with a short attention span? How can the youth evangelist compete with the way in which television grabs the viewer? Television has short transmit times: most well-produced advertisements have an image every two or three seconds. A bad advertisement features the store's proprietor talking to the camera ('This is my shop. I'm paying for the advertisement, so I'm going on the television'). The most boring advertisement has a still picture with a voice-over. If you look at the leading soft drinks commercials there is an explosion of activity with constantly changing visual images. Tricky angles and special effects combine with the unusual to maintain visual capture; for example, you view the action through the eyes of the hero or—you are not just a fly on the wall, you are involved! The preacher, therefore, stands in front of an impatient audience!

We need to recognize that the church often uses outmoded methods in cross-cultural communication. We need to work hard at involving our audience in our communication. We need to be visual; to use drama and dance and interactive methods. The youth evangelist must be a good storyteller. Sermons need to be full of word pictures.

In fact, we need to follow in the footsteps of Jesus. His communication was unpredictable and full of visual imagery. His parables and the Sermon on the Mount contain 2,320 words, 348 visual images and nineteen questions. Jesus also uses the word 'you' 221 times, making his preaching direct, personal and immediate.

Jesus would have been an excellent MTV preacher! According to Gregg and Ralph Lewis, MTV has 42 per cent fluency; in the Sermon on the Mount, Jesus has 65 per cent! I believe in preaching. I also believe it is a sin to switch off young people by sharing the message of the gospel in a dull and predictable way. We must communicate with style!

References

1. Tony Campolo, *The Success Fantasy*, Kingsway, page 69.
2. Shawn Tully, 'Teens: The Most Global Market of All', *Fortune*, 16 May 1994.
3. Tony Campolo, 'You Can Make a Difference', *Word*, 1985, page 57.

Angling

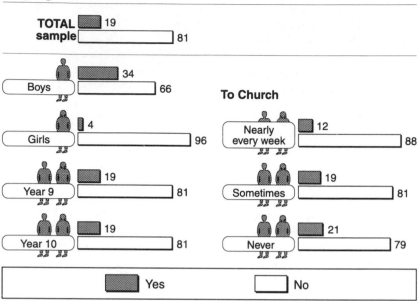

Swimming

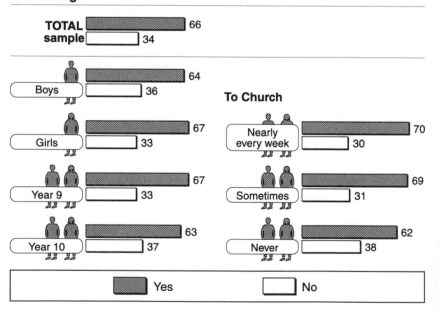

Soccer

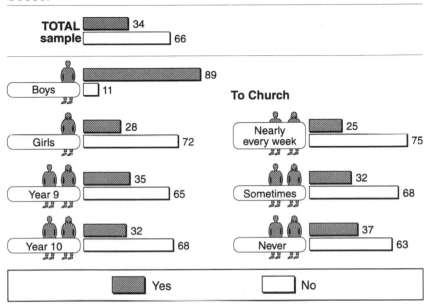

Source: Teenage Religion and Values Survey of 13,000 pupils in England and Wales. All figures refer to responses to the statement immediately above this diagram. The left hand column shows, at the top, the responses of the total sample which is divided, in the middle, into responses of year 9 and year 10 pupils. The right hand column deals only with the 11% of the total sample who attend church.

13 John Allan

Young People and the Law

Who commits most crime in British society? The young. More than half of all offenders are under the age of twenty-one; one teenager in four claims to be willing to carry out a credit card fraud should it become possible; and by the age of thirty-five, seven males in twenty will have a conviction for a recordable offence.

How interesting, then, that 62 per cent of teenagers say, in response to a statement in the Teenage Religion and Values Survey, that: 'The police do a good job'. There would not have been the same level of agreement back in the 1960s—when youthful sit-ins, demonstrations and student protests were the order of the day, and 'mods and rockers' rioted on the sea front at Clacton. The 'pigs' were the natural enemies of young people, even though society was then much more law-abiding than now. What explains the change in attitude?

This confidence in the police is reflected by every group surveyed. Girls (64 per cent) were slightly more pro-police than boys (59 per cent), and younger pupils more so than older ones; churchgoers were much happier with the police than non-churchgoers. But the differences are not huge. Today's young people are more conservative about law and order than the last generation.

Why? Perhaps there are two main reasons. The first is *apathy*. The young people of the 1960s and early 1970s who raged against the system wanted to see things change. They believed that a better society could be built by their generation, and the media encouraged them to believe so, not least because young people were accorded an importance and a respect which they do not receive today.

By contrast, at the last general election in Britain, 2.5 million young people failed to vote. Graham Hitchen of the British Youth Council says: 'Many young people believe that taking part in the electoral process will have no impact on their lives. They seem to share the view of one well-known British politician that "if voting changed anything they would make it illegal . . .".' Young people feel sidelined in society, and matters of government, policing and authority seem remote from them.

The second reason for the survey result may be *fear*. Young people are the perpetrators of most crime, but adolescents are also most likely to be the victims of crime, especially where violence is involved. Among many teenagers there is a perception that life is less safe than it used to be, and there is a greater desire for law and order then a decade ago. Today's teenagers grew up under Thatcherism.

The one thing which the Teenage Religion and Values Survey result *does not* demonstrate is the existence of a strong morality among young people. In fact, the reverse seems to be true: there is a moral opportunism among most young people today which stems from a decline in generally accepted standards, the refusal of parents to give a firm lead to their families and the 'born to shop' approach to life which encourages individuals to relate to society primarily as consumers with rights, rather than as citizens with responsibilities. Not many recognize absolute values.

Those that do often do not apply them: 43 per cent of unmarried teenage Christians surveyed in 1991 were sexually active by the age of nineteen. Recently, I had a lively debate with seventy intelligent seventeen-year-old girls who were firmly convinced that abortion was absolutely wrong. But in the van on the way home, several of them admitted, 'If I got pregnant, I wouldn't think twice . . . you can't let your life be wrecked . . .'.

Young people are uninterested in political and legal issues because they realize that they do not count for much. Many feel that they have no future. In 1988, only 22 per cent of those who left school at sixteen went into a job, compared with 60 per cent a decade earlier. In 1985, Peter Everett had already commented:

> *Perhaps it should not have surprised anyone that whereas the optimism of youth in the 1960s had found expression in a variety of causes, from CND to Save the Whale, the pessimism of the 1980s has led to an outbreak of patriotic sentiment and cries of 'I'm all right, Jack'.*
>
> *A MORI poll during the Falklands conflict found that young people were more in favour of military action against Argentina than were their elders. In the NOP poll of 1983, a majority supported the reintroduction of National Service.*

If young people support the *status quo*, it is not because politicians have been good to them. As the number of older people in Britain increases, there are few votes in youth issues; at the last general election, none of the major parties highlighted young people in their manifesto. The Youth Service has been quietly squeezed almost out of existence (and although cuts in the National Health System and in education have attracted outraged cries of public protest, few voices have spoken up for youth workers). Fifty years ago, the McNair Report recommended that there should be one qualified youth worker for every 300 young people aged thirteen to nineteen years. At the time of writing, however, authorities in England and Wales are falling far short of even that basic target.

The campaign group Youthaid has calculated that 68,000 under-eighteens in Britain are currently without jobs, training or benefit. Since the government abolished general entitlement to income support for sixteen- and seventeen-year-olds, most unemployed young people in this group have not been officially recognized or counted. Legally, they have no rights. They are no one's responsibility until they are older.

This marginalization of young people means that they can easily be exploited. The abolition of the minimum wage has led to a dramatic fall in the amount that young people can earn. The Low Pay Unit estimates that 40 per cent of school-age children are working part-time, and that nearly three-quarters of them work illegally. This is either because they are too young to work at all, or because they are working the wrong hours or because they are too young for the job they are doing.

There is not even the safe haven of a youth culture which repels adults and gives teenagers some sort of badge of identity. Everybody seems to be listening to rock music; parents refuse to grow up and be their age; young adults, rather than teenagers, are the arbiters of taste and fashion.

The effect of this media-sponsored psychological homogenization of different life stages falls under the heading of 'youthification'. The natural instability of youth, once viewed as simply a stage in life, is now projected on much of adult society and presented as a normal attitude towards life. Few purely 'adult' norms or expectations distinguish generations.

If this is the position young people are in, how should Christians respond? There seem to be four important points to make.

First, we must remember that *young people matter to God as much as anyone else*. The Bible is full of very young people—David, Jeremiah, Samuel, Mary—who God picked up and used when others would have sidelined them. 'Don't let anyone look down on you because you are young,' Paul warned Timothy. And so our churches must consciously aim to provide the encouragement, empowerment and recognition that young people need, rather than unthinkingly to adopt the general attitude of society.

Second, *youth must not be idolized.* We do teenagers no favours by treating them as a special breed; that was the mistake of the 1960s. Tony Tyler of the *New Musical Express* reflects:

I think one of the things to lament, perhaps, about the teen boom of the 1950s through the 1970s is that it force-fed a couple of generations with false expectations. It made them seem to themselves more important than they really are . . . But they were a market and it was essentially a market force. And I'm afraid when you take away the market, you take away the interest. That's why it's finding its own level again.

A great deal of the cynicism and suspicion of young people today derives from the fact that they know how the last generation were fêted. And they realize how quickly that flurry of importance passed into history. Once bitten, twice shy.

Third, *we need to help teenagers to focus on responsibilities as well as rights.* We need to help young people see that they can make a significant contribution; that life is not just about individual survival, about keeping an eye on the main chance and serving one's own interests; that absolute values are important. Even among Christian teenagers, the idea of giving one's life away in order to find it is often an unfamiliar concept. Yet the more we encourage young people to grow into service and self-sacrifice, the more their sense of self-worth develops.

Many political strategies for dealing with youth problems today are penal ones. (If you do not join a training scheme, you will get no benefit. In the United States, if you play truant from school, your family's benefit will be cut.) There is more and more evidence that these strategies are failing. Young people do not respond to increasingly severe penalties; they respond to challenges that offer them some hope.

Fourth and finally, *we need to respond to society's lack of youth resources by being willing to step into the gap.* Christians were active in youth work many years before there was any statutory provision! And we need to recognize that in today's pressurized, distorted, bewildered society, young people need youth workers more than ever before. Perhaps it was to meet such needs that God put us in Britain today.

The police do a good job

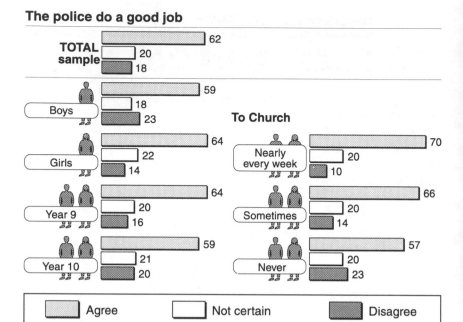

Source: Teenage Religion and Values Survey of 13,000 pupils in England and Wales. All figures refer to responses to the statement immediately above this diagram. The left hand column shows, at the top, the responses of the total sample which is divided, in the middle, into responses of year 9 and year 10 pupils. The right hand column deals only with the 11% of the total sample who attend church.

14 Michael Eastman

Enough to Do?

**For many young people, how to spend their leisure time is the question ...
thinking about this in itself is one way in which time will be passed.**[1]
The 'spare time' available to young people depends on the age and life-stage
reached. It is that time which is not spoken for, when school, college or work
obligations have been taken care of. It is usually available during the evening, at
weekends and during holidays. Institutions may provide a rich environment
with 'lots of things to do', but these things go with being a pupil, student or
employee.

The question of 'what to do?' relates more to chosen contexts and activities
than to everyday life. 'Thus development of the individual as well as factors such
as social class, ethnicity, location may affect what the individual perceives to be
accessible or appropriate in terms of spare time activity.'[2]

Perception is governed less by what is available than by what the young
person wants to do now. If present aspirations are not fulfilled the young are
inclined to say they are bored! The major exception to these generalizations
comes when young people are unemployed (see Chapter 22). 'Spare time'
becomes 'time to kill'. Lack of money restricts the options. Poverty reduces
choice. For some young people, survival, food, shelter and warmth are of
primary concern. Necessity rules.

The 10 per cent of the population whose living standards have not increased
over the past thirty years have experienced deep alienation, as opportunity and
choice have increased for the majority. Perceptions about provision are closely
related to how to fund it. The moves towards contracting out and privatization
have significantly shifted the balance towards the better off, and away from the
impoverished. Youth clubs have closed in those very areas of our decaying inner
cities, run-down outer estates and isolated rural communities where they are
most needed. The ideology driving provision of public services has, since 1979,
made for more uneven distribution of resources and more inequality of choice.
Commercial activities are concentrated where there are those who can pay. As
these trends continue, those with the least disposable income suffer most.

The overall picture indicates other long-term trends. 'The crucial thing to
note here is the shift from activities specifically organized and directed at young
people, through casual activities; into commercial (mainstream) provision. In

terms of leisure usage this is not a pattern that will be significantly disrupted over the next few years, as it springs from deep-seated, socio-cultural, as well as physical and psychological factors'.[3]

This shift is to be put alongside the determination of the government to double the number of young people in higher education within a decade. Already there has been a dramatic increase in the numbers and range of young people aged sixteen to nineteen in further education. 'Because a growing proportion of young people spend their days in institutions of education rather than diverse work places, fewer need youth centres in order to meet their peers. Neither do so many depend on Centres to supply them with a space that is their own—education and other institutions perform that function.'[4]

'The adolescents of all ages and stages of development spend a great deal of their time at home, especially the girls, as they begin to withdraw from some of the more "teenage" orientated activities'.[5] This is confirmed by later studies: 'the majority of young people spent more and more time in the home . . . We are seeing a paralleling of adult interests in young people's leisure usage'.[6] At times, young people seem to take over the shopping malls, pubs, discos, arcades, fast food outlets and some restaurants! This reflects the insistent pressures in our society for us all to be consumers.

Contract is expressed through payment rather than personal commitment. The growth in leisure and fitness centres marks the same trend. Ten-pin bowling exists alongside aerobic classes in the same building. The recent re-emphasis on team games in the school curriculum conflicts with this trend. It is too early to judge the effect. The ways young people regard and use their leisure time are identified,[7] and it appears that these ways have largely continued into the 1990s. The age range of those attracted to and participating in uniformed organizations and youth units providing for young people has come down.

Youth clubs attract a younger clientele. The figures in the Teenage Religion and Values Survey tend to reflect this. Young teenagers still opt into provision. Older teenagers have moved much more to adult patterns of leisure use. The mid-teens are ambivalent. They are less inclined to join on the terms set by the providers and want increasingly to take part on their own terms, but as yet have neither the mobility nor financial means to do so.

A further significant factor in this mix is the shift of resources in the United Kingdom. We are an ageing population. By the year 2021, more than 18 per cent of the population will be over sixty-five. In 1991 the figure was 16 per cent, which compares with 11 per cent in 1951. In 1991, 11.5 million people were under the age of sixteen. Twenty years previously we had 14.5 million under-sixteens. This has shifted the national psyche. The schools closure programme is one highly visible consequence. We are less inclined to invest in the young and more inclined to provide for the old who are living longer and more healthily with greater disposable income.

'Faith in the City' noted a local shift in responsibility for youth services, from those running the education services to those providing leisure services. The Commission argued for the retention of an understanding of youth work as 'a means of social education of young people, with its emphasis on their developmental needs'.[8]

The slogan 'Creators not Consumers' echoes this. It is a call to engage young people as participants. The shift, from training adults to be youth and community workers to training them in informal education skills, is significant here. Youth workers are employed in many places, including colleges of further education. Not only do the provision and opportunity depend on who you are, they also depend on where you are. 'The migration of people and the movement of capital, employment opportunities, private enterprise and voluntary effort is increasingly away from the Urban Priority Area districts to the more sylvan and salubrious areas of the South and East'.[9] This results in a lack of amenities.

'Faith in the Countryside' concluded, '. . . for those young people who lack parental resources or who live away from accessible countryside where urban facilities are but a short journey away, rural living can be narrow and confusing. In particular, the growing teenager can find even the largest and most suburban of villages a backwater of experience where facilities for leisure time are confined to those for younger children only and where access to jobs and job training can present a special problem'.[10]

What are the implications of this broadly drawn picture for the youth work of churches and Christian youth organizations? We must take seriously the impetus of young people towards adopting adult styles of using their leisure time at an earlier age. Our mind-set needs to change. Churches and organizations which concentrate on young children tend to view teaching older teenagers as the culmination of their work. The young, however, wish to leave childhood behind.

Our youth work should therefore be about enabling transition and integration into adulthood rather than extending childhood. 'Providing for' should give place to 'doing with'. Where there is multiple choice available, the collective resources of a young group can give access to a wide range of opportunities—to go places and experience new possibilities within the security of people who know each other. The youth group should be a means of unlocking new possibilities.

This needs a flexible, come-and-go approach, with the emphasis on relationship, not provision. Some non-alcoholic bars and drop-in ventures achieve this well. Twelve- and thirteen-year-olds are becoming eager for this switch. We should anticipate it, not deny it. The emphasis should be on liberation into a world of choice and opportunity, not retention for the sake of the institution. This has significant implications for how the young are disciplined and how they are regarded and treated by older Christians.

Our young people need mentoring at an earlier age, so they are able to participate as creators in their own faith journeys. The over-sixties, who growingly dominate congregations, were schooled in the previous provision models which reinforce dependence. In those areas where facilities and opportunities are lacking for young people, the Christian community should use its collective strength through its youth agencies to extend choice.

This requires the transfer of wealth and resources from the more favoured to the less. Christian youth work in inner cities and outer estates, decaying urban areas and impoverished rural situations should not be Cinderellas left to fend for themselves. *Careforce*, *Time for God*, *Frontline* and similar schemes enable some transfer of resources. But these schemes and others like them ought to be sustained beyond the one year they usually last. Expectations are raised, experiences extended and horizons widened.

Unfortunately, however, hopes are dashed and disillusion grows if the benefits are not maintained. All too easily, the young people who should be benefiting actually suffer—at the expense of the extended horizons of those who give their time. Christian youth work needs to be undertaken where the young congregate in their leisure time. Schools and particularly college campuses are the places where young people feel at home; so are the streets, pubs, discos, shopping centres, arcades, leisure and sports centres, where the young go.

Releasing, training and supporting these teams effectively is a major challenge ahead of us. As leisure and styles change much more, Christian youth work will need to take place outside the safety zones of our congregations and youth organizations.

References

1. *Young People in the 1980s—A Survey*, HMSO, 1983.
2. *Young People in the 1980s.*
3. *Young People and Youth Work—Some Comment on Trends.*
4. *Young People and Youth Work.*
5. *Young People in the 1980s*, page 31.
6. *Young People and Youth Work.*
7. *Young People in the 1980s*, chapter 2.
8. 'Faith in the City', Church House Publishing, 1985 page 320.
9. 'Faith in the City', page 23.
10. 'Faith in the Countryside', Churchman Publishing Ltd, 1990, page 90.

In my area there lots of things for young people to do in their leisure time

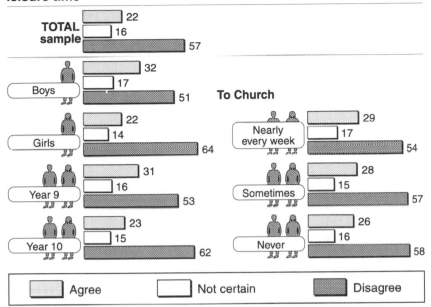

TOTAL sample
- 22
- 16
- 57

Boys
- 32
- 17
- 51

To Church

Girls
- 22
- 14
- 64

Nearly every week
- 29
- 17
- 54

Year 9
- 31
- 16
- 53

Sometimes
- 28
- 15
- 57

Year 10
- 23
- 15
- 62

Never
- 26
- 16
- 58

Agree   Not certain   Disagree

Source: Teenage Religion and Values Survey of 13,000 pupils in England and Wales. All figures refer to responses to the statement immediately above this diagram. The left hand column shows, at the top, the responses of the total sample which is divided, in the middle, into responses of year 9 and year 10 pupils. The right hand column deals only with the 11% of the total sample who attend church.

Section Three: Rapids

15 Grahame Knox

Substance Use

The average home contains about thirty products that give off a vapour at room temperature and which can be sniffed. They range from glues, paints and petrol to lighter fuels, nail varnish removers and a variety of products in aerosol sprays. Originally glues were the substances most used, hence the term 'glue sniffing', but because a number of other volatile substances can also be used, there has been a general acceptance of the term 'solvent abuse'.

Research among young people has shown that the most vulnerable age for sniffing is between twelve and sixteen and that most sniffers, who are predominantly male, are introduced to the practice by friends. For the majority it is a case of 'one try only'. Only a minority of solvent abusers indulge in the habit long-term. However, everyone who experiments with solvents is at risk. Recent figures (1991) showed that 122 young people died from solvent abuse, forty of them experimenting for the first time. Solvent sniffing tends to be a group activity and the age cut-off point for sniffing tends to be when young people are able to purchase alcohol in pubs and off-licences.

The misuse of glues and solvents is not illegal. In fact, the only legal action which can be taken relates to suppliers. Shopkeepers can be prosecuted for selling products to young people if it can be proved—a difficult task—that they knew that the products were going to be misused.

In 1985, a survey by the National Campaign Against Solvent Abuse revealed that about 17 per cent of teenagers at school admitted to inhaling glue or solvents at least once. In recent years, programmes of education and the continuing publicity about the dangers of sniffing have provided more information to young people. However, the Teenage Religion and Values Survey revealed that 19 per cent of young people disagreed or were not sure with the statement that it is wrong to sniff glue. The degree of disagreement and uncertainty is higher in

81

boys than girls, 22 per cent compared with 17 per cent. As we know, teenage boys are more likely to experiment with solvents. Although young people who indicated regular church attendance polled a higher anti-glue sniffing response than their peers, nearly one in seven disagreed with or were not certain about the statement.

Trends do change, however, and recent research has shown that glues are now sniffed by perhaps only 30 per cent of users, although aerosols, butane gas and other volatile substances are increasingly used. The sniffing of lighter fuel now accounts for more solvent-related deaths. In the survey, young people responded to the statement, 'It is wrong to sniff butane gas', with just over one in four disagreeing or being uncertain. This higher response may well reflect a changing trend in perception—that is, of sniffing glue compared with other solvents. Again the amount of disagreement with the statement was higher in the boys polled. Young people who were regular churchgoers were again more resistant to the prospect of sniffing solvents but, having said that, one in five young people in that group still either disagreed with the statement or were unsure of where they stood on the issue.

The physical effects of sniffing solvents are well known. When inhaled, solvents produce feelings of intoxication similar to alcohol which can last from a few minutes to half an hour. Solvents act like other depressant drugs, slowing down the nervous system, breathing, heart rate, thinking, judgment and balance. Shortly after sniffing, a young person can experience a 'hangover' and headaches, which may also lead on to feelings of irritability, depression, nausea and fatigue. Unpredictable effects may include hallucinations, blurred vision and loss of memory. Recent evidence has shown that prolonged abuse can cause damage to the lungs, liver, kidneys and bone marrow. Solvents also irritate the lining of the stomach and can lead to loss of appetite and weight. When the solvent vapours come into contact with lips, mouth or nose they can burn the skin. It is quite common to see skin burns and sores around the noses and lips of sniffers.

A few deaths have been caused by sniffing glue from small bags held to the nose and mouth. Many more deaths, however, have resulted from inhaling aerosols or butane gas, and from suffocation when plastic bags have been placed over the head. Young people have also died in accidents, through drowning or burns when influenced by the intoxicating effects of solvents. Sniffers looking for other substances to provide the solvent-induced intoxication may become an easy target for people selling illegal drugs. Some people believe that sniffing solvents can easily become a training ground for other drug abuse.

There is no single reason which explains why young people experiment with solvents or other drugs. Actually, reasons and explanations are usually thin on the ground, taking second place to such phrases as 'everybody was doing it', or 'it makes me feel good'. Behind the scenes, though, experimentation may result from the need for acceptance and to be part of a group; and the fear that to refuse a substance will lead to rejection by friends. Curiosity or boredom may lead some young people to seek for the experience that drugs can provide, as they search for thrills and excitement. Some young people may feel trapped by circumstances. Drug misuse provides a means of escape, a chance to forget their family problems or difficulties at school. For others, it is a way to rebel, to shock, to be different from everyone else. Real drug dependence may still only effect a minority, but it is known that many more young people experiment with illegal drugs. Drug misuse may start in an apparently harmless or casual way, but even though it may stop well short of dependence and addiction, all drug misuse involves taking risks.

The term 'drug' covers a wide range of substances. Some are controlled substances, illegal to possess, such as cocaine (which is becoming increasingly popular with young people today). Others are drugs more readily accepted and encouraged by our society, such as alcohol. Drugs are also viewed by some as 'hard' or 'soft'. This is misleading because the so-called 'soft' drugs, such as cannabis (the most widely used illegal drug in Britain), are not without danger. These unhelpful descriptions only mislead people into thinking that certain drugs are safer than others. A more accurate way of understanding drugs is to study the effect they have on the human body.

Stimulants

These drugs stimulate the nervous system, increase physical and mental activity, and enhance alertness and confidence. On the one hand, they include caffeine in coffee and nicotine in cigarettes; on the other, they include amphetamines, cocaine and the modern, rave-culture 'designer' drugs—for example Ecstasy, a stimulant with hallucinogenic effects. Once the drug effects wear off, the user usually has a feeling of severe fatigue. The increased stimulation may result in the user becoming confused, frightened and anxious, sometimes to the extent of anti-social and aggressive behaviour.

Depressants

These work by reducing the activity of the central nervous system. They have a calming effect and make the user feel relaxed. They also interfere with the making of reasoned judgements and decisions and slow down the accuracy of responses. Examples of depressant drugs include alcohol, opiates (heroin) and tranquillizers.

Hallucinogens

Hallucinogens alter the user's perception of reality. The main drugs in this group are the controlled drugs LSD and cannabis. They can produce hallucinations which are unpredictable and generally uncontrolled. According to a recent survey in 1992 it was estimated that about 5 per cent of fifteen- to sixteen-year-olds (about 250,000 people) have tried LSD or Ecstasy, usually in the context of a rave. Liberty Cap mushrooms (magic mushrooms) produce a similar effect. The mushroom grows throughout the United Kingdom, fruiting between September and November. Large doses can result in very unpleasant side-effects.

Those who begin to misuse drugs regularly can quickly become dependent. Most common is *psychological* addiction, when a person needs to repeat the sensations of euphoria or sedation that the drug brings. All drugs are psychologically addictive; this can be every bit as destructive as physical addiction and often far more difficult to break. Taking drugs can also cause changes in the body so that it cannot function normally without the continued presence of the drug. Without regular doses the individual will experience a physical reaction or withdrawal symptoms. This is *physical* addiction.

It has been said that we live in a drug-orientated society. The use of alcohol and cigarettes is socially and widely accepted. Drugs are commonly and frequently prescribed as an answer to an emotional or physical problem. The modern drugs of the rave culture influence thousands of young people. So how should we live as Christians in this kind of society? What does the Bible say about drugs?

The only drug mentioned by name in the Bible is alcohol. The Old Testament writers referred to wine as a gift from God (Psalm 104:13–15; Proverbs 3:9–10); and Jesus' first recorded miracle involved the changing of water into wine at the wedding at Cana. However, the Bible also clearly warns that real drunkenness is wrong and is not an option for the Christian (Galatians 5:21; Ephesians 5:18). Instead we are encouraged to exercise responsibility and wisdom in our own lives, and to be an example to those around us.

> *Be very careful, then, how you live—not as unwise, but as wise,*
> *making the most of every opportunity, because the days are evil.*
> *Therefore do not be foolish, but understand what the Lord's will is.*
> *Do not get drunk on wine, which leads to debauchery. Instead, be*
> *filled with the Spirit.*[1]

Clearly, in forming a Christian view, our response to the more socially accepted drugs is just as important as our response to illegal substances. Both the view that the human body can be the temple of the Spirit (1 Corinthians 3:16–17), and the idea that, as Ephesians 5:18 suggests, being filled with the Spirit is a replacement for alcoholism, may be used as pointers towards the construction of a Christian approach.

Most young people will already be learning at school about drugs, their effects and their dangers. This does not mean, however, that the use of alcohol, solvents, Ecstasy and other drugs cannot be discussed positively in a Christian context. Young people in the church are not immune to the pressure of friends and peers, and it is important that the youth ministry of the church provides opportunities for young people to explore 'pressure points' and discuss situations which affect them daily.

In order for a youth leader to help to educate young people about drugs, and to prevent possible drug abuse among the young people they have contact with, three elements are necessary. First, they need to be informed about the nature of the substances; second, they must be aware of the general situation regarding drugs in the local area; and third, they should know where to get advice and assistance. A local drug advice centre should be able to provide all the information and help needed.

If you discover that a young person in your group has had a minor involvement with illegal drugs—perhaps a 'one-off' experiment at a rave—or if someone admits to sniffing solvents with friends, do not panic! The degree to which you can help depends on the quality of your relationship with them, and often it can be handled quietly and sensitively between you and the parents of the young person involved. Your attitude needs to be one of care and genuine concern for the person. Look beneath the surface of the drug use and offer counsel on any deeper issues involved. For example, what feelings led them astray in the first place? Were they scared, or sad, or bored? Why? They may need to talk seriously about these issues. They may also need encouragement to form new friends and new interests, to help them to move away from those who have influenced their drug use.

However, if a young person's drug misuse is more serious, recognize your limitations and proceed with great care. Take advice. Your friendship, support and prayers are important, but other professional sources need to be mobilized to help a young person to a full and lasting recovery.

Finally, at some time in youth ministry you may find yourself with a drugged person who requires emergency help. Remember:

if the person is drowsy but awake, find out what they have taken, walk them round and keep them talking, and ask someone to phone for an ambulance;

if the person is unconscious, loosen his or her clothes, place him or her in the recovery position, make sure nothing is blocking the nose or throat, and ask someone to call an ambulance;

if the person is tense and panicky, keep him or her in a quiet darkened room, talk in a calm reassuring voice, find out what he or she has taken, stay with the person, and ask someone to call for an ambulance.

References

1. Ephesians 5:15–18.

It is wrong to sniff glue

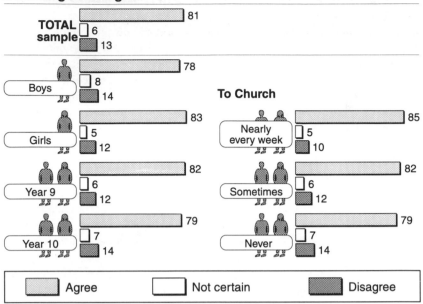

TOTAL sample
- Agree: 81
- Not certain: 6
- Disagree: 13

Boys
- Agree: 78
- Not certain: 8
- Disagree: 14

Girls
- Agree: 83
- Not certain: 5
- Disagree: 12

Year 9
- Agree: 82
- Not certain: 6
- Disagree: 12

Year 10
- Agree: 79
- Not certain: 7
- Disagree: 14

To Church

Nearly every week
- Agree: 85
- Not certain: 5
- Disagree: 10

Sometimes
- Agree: 82
- Not certain: 6
- Disagree: 12

Never
- Agree: 79
- Not certain: 7
- Disagree: 14

Agree / Not certain / Disagree

It is wrong to sniff butane gas

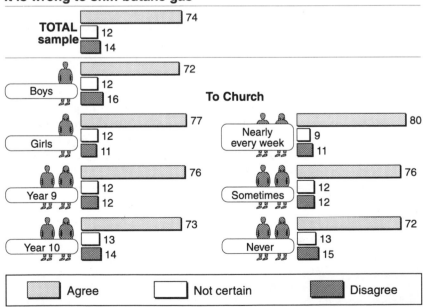

TOTAL sample
- Agree: 74
- Not certain: 12
- Disagree: 14

Boys
- Agree: 72
- Not certain: 12
- Disagree: 16

Girls
- Agree: 77
- Not certain: 12
- Disagree: 11

Year 9
- Agree: 76
- Not certain: 12
- Disagree: 12

Year 10
- Agree: 73
- Not certain: 13
- Disagree: 14

To Church

Nearly every week
- Agree: 80
- Not certain: 9
- Disagree: 11

Sometimes
- Agree: 76
- Not certain: 12
- Disagree: 12

Never
- Agree: 72
- Not certain: 13
- Disagree: 15

Agree / Not certain / Disagree

16 Richard Wilkins

Under-age Sex

As part of the Teenage Religion and Values Survey, young people were asked to respond to the statement 'It is wrong to have sexual intercourse under the legal age (16 years)'. The figures show that 46 per cent of young people either agree or are 'not certain' that under-age sex is wrong, while 54 per cent are convinced that it is not. Differences between boys and girls vary sharply on both definite answers. This confirms a traditional difference. Even so, nearly half the girls (48 per cent) say that sex under sixteen is not wrong, and less than a third (29 per cent) think it is wrong. Permissive attitudes increase significantly in the older part of the sample, with 6 per cent fewer favouring abstinence in year 10 compared with year 9, and 8 per cent more giving the permissive answer.

This is a question about attitudes and beliefs. It does not provide evidence of practice, nor tell us if opinions have varied over a period of years. There are surveys from earlier periods and with older age groups that give us an idea of changing attitudes, but the answers to this question must be hedged with some caution. In other words, they shed little direct light on the oft-stated axiom in the sex education industry that 'more than 50 per cent of young people are sexually active by the time they are sixteen'. This uncertain linkage between surveyed opinion and personal practice needs exploring. We may reasonably conclude that opinion and practice will tend to follow each other, though in what order we cannot generalize with certainty. But in trying to outline communication, support and pastoral strategies, we need some informed speculation on what needs, attitudes and beliefs are implied in these answers.

For example, there may be various reasons for saying that sexual intercourse below the age of sixteen is not wrong. Two obvious reasons are: 'I do it already and it hasn't done me any harm', and 'I would do it if I had the chance and don't see why I shouldn't'. Additional reasons, however, include, 'It's not for me because I personally think it's wrong, but I don't see what the law has got to do with it' or, more probably, 'I don't want sex until I feel ready for it, but many of my friends have had sex, I like them and take my ideas from the group, so I suppose it can't be wrong'.

On the other hand, we have no idea whether sexual practice is inhibited in all cases by a belief that it is wrong. Indeed, for some that may be part of its attraction. We could, therefore, be faced by large numbers of cross-over practitioners, with abstainers saying that sex under sixteen is not wrong, and strenuous practitioners saying that it is wrong.

Finally, before settling into what the answers might really reveal, we should note the 'Augustine factor'. Augustine of Hippo, who now carries much of the blame for a long Christian tradition of sexual repression, says in his *Confessions* that he was so anxious to parade his sexual prowess that he boasted of conquests he had never made. It is true that Augustine is not denying the real randiness of his youth; he is only saying that he was not quite as randy as he made out when he was a hot-blooded youngster. Forty or so years ago, it used to be taken as a general rule that those who had most to say about sex were the least likely to have experienced it. Something of that scepticism might still be in place when evaluating survey answers. Furthermore, in a culture where overt sexuality is constant and obtrusive, it might take considerable courage to say, even to someone with a clipboard, that it is wrong to resist the urge which seems to drive everything.

With all due reservation and scepticism, however, we must concentrate on the possibility that the young people questioned meant what they said. Assuming that, what do they want sex for? This unfashionable question is increasingly being pushed today. Traditional cultures, with all their taboos and restrictions, did at least have some social and historic uses for sex. Our present culture no longer offers sensible reasons for the clamorous urge. In an overpopulated world, the sheer quantity of sexuality is surplus to the requirement of prolonging the race. Even for that purpose, reproduction without two-person intercourse seems every day more of a scientific possibility. Conservation of property by inheritance has largely ceased, since the Second World War, to be a matter of commanding social importance. Moreover, sex as an expression of love and loyalty can hardly convince the children of strife-filled homes and separated parents. And then there are AIDS and herpes, and other sexually transmitted diseases. Sex in our developed world seems to lead to nothing but trouble. It may be that in modern minds sex does not immediately connect with concepts of right and wrong, so the survey question did not make obvious sense. Never mind the law, the Bible, the Pope or the Christian Union; sex is actually a senseless disease of the human race.

Actor and journalist Stephen Fry wrote in 1985, 'We have inherited this instinct to rut as we have inherited other instincts once necessary for survival. But these vestigial urges have no place in a rational, intelligent community that can determine its own destiny.' And he concludes: 'Besides, I'm scared I may not be very good at it.'

If you are young at heart and in touch with the youth culture you will cry out that this inhuman rationalism is quite unrealistic. You are probably right. Sex for the adolescent is attractive because it is there. Pointless it may be, but it offers at least a moment of world-eclipsing ecstasy which blots out the rational hells of life. Sexual intercourse is only one expression of a complex maturation process which makes us alive to other human beings as desirable persons. This 'sexualization' of life and the world is actually what makes us want to serve, give and sacrifice for other people. Our sex-saturated culture might well channel all that is noble, just and right about growing up into a desire for coitus, but that is truly only a part of the life that young people grow into.

Could it be that a falling average age for first intercourse (sixteen according to the 1991 Wellcome Survey into Sexual Behaviour in Britain—a girl in the United States recently became the world's youngest-known mother at eight) is telling us something? Sexual intercourse is a form of play—and nothing else. Play is appropriate to lower age groups. Not only are films, magazines, books and advertisements giving young people sexual role models to emulate, the adult world can tell them nothing about sex except that it is play, and play is what children do. Sexual activity may be given more serious names in later life, as when some promiscuous celebrities are described as 'sexual athletes', but the principle is the same. For all its passion and ardour, sex is at best recreational and at its most basic a form of nervous and hydraulic relief. To call it play, of course, does not mean it will be confined to the young. Psychologist John Huizinga maintained that play is not an emulation of adult behaviour; rather, adult civilization is a prolongation of play.[1] Sex may have a future after all.

Even so, Christians are required to explore the connection between sexuality and spirituality. It is both obvious and mysterious. Ardent liberators of the young urge the necessity of early sexual intercourse like charismatic evangelists. There is little doubt that devotion to Christ and devotion to a sexual partner employ some of the same emotional faculties. High levels of devotional enthusiasm, and genuine access to the Holy Spirit's blessings, are found among both convinced virgins and the recently jilted. Spiritual commitment may tail off during a courtship. The old spiritual counsellors knew what they were about when they strove against 'mismating with unbelievers'. The discharge of emotions upon another human being leaves less passion for the Lord, even if the object of love is a fellow believer. Styles of devotion, as found, for example, in the words of worship songs, which appeal to middle-aged congregations whose sexuality is, shall we say, seasoned, look open to charges of displaced eroticism. They are not necessarily wrong; there are worse things to do with surplus eroticism than to sing worship songs.

More than one-third (37 per cent) of 'nearly weekly' churchgoers did not think that sex under the age of sixteen was wrong. The breakdown by denomination is remarkable, showing greater tolerance of under-age sex among Roman Catholics than among Anglicans or members of Free Churches. In both of the latter, adult role models are more likely to be married, although disapproval of sex outside marriage is as high among Catholics as among Anglicans. Cause and effect here are difficult to locate. The age of consent tends to be lower in some Roman Catholic countries (for example, it is twelve in

Spain). Protestants may think that the confessional's easier forgiveness (but is it easier?) is relevant, and they may smile as they remember Cardinal Newman's words, 'I have long thought, even before I was a Catholic, that the Protestant system, as such, leads to lax observance of the rule of purity'.[2]

All such thoughts must be balanced by a query about whether the minimum age of sixteen is biblical—of course it is not. Jesus may well have been born to a fifteen-year-old mother; nevertheless, whatever the legal age limit, sex before it is, in biblical terms, 'fornication'. This, and considerations of health, emotional and physical abuse, along with the obvious concerns about sexually transmitted diseases and pregnancy, make early sexual experience a crucial issue for Christian youth workers.

Help seems to lie in presenting alternative lifestyles. First, it seems clear from young people's responses to the CARE video, *Make Love Last*,[3] that many do not like being railroaded into sex, and welcome an affirmation of virginity as, at least temporarily, a valid option. Many a conversion, especially among boys, is welcomed as an escape from the tyranny of sex. Second, the complex package that comes with sexual development has, in the past, been expressed in other than sexual ways. Apart from sex, there is very little romance in life today. Heroes have feet of clay, war is wrong, art is ghastly, the future is bleak, the environment is doomed and people do not live happily ever after.

Harry Blamires' book, *The Christian Mind*,[4] was famous for its intellectual challenge; but its last chapter was about romanticism. Blamires saw the appeal to the lawless emotions as the way to communicate with young people. 'Nothing,' he said in 1963, 'is now more tragically out of date than the public school conception of the young man making his sterilized, clean-limbed way through life, shoulder to shoulder with all the other good types who wear short pants and play the game.' We know that. The trouble is that we are not good at projecting the Christian life in genuinely romantic ways because we depend too heavily on a culture where romance apart from sex and violence is dead. Other generations knew how to do it. That is why God's call to the mission field had such a heroic ring, and why so many women (yes, women, the romantic gender), answered the call and went. It may have led to all sorts of unrealistic expectations but it fulfilled God-given desires in positive ways. Young people are equally attracted today to opportunities of service; preparation for such service should not douse the emotions in secular realism.

Similarly, Christian discussions about sex can recover the best forms of romanticism, by dwelling on the nature of love as a reflection of heaven. The lover's feeling for the beloved is derived from an anticipation of the beloved in glory; as such the feeling is subject to the life of heaven that we can have on earth now. The aim of love is not deflowering but adoration, both of the beloved and the God from whom all love derives.

If any of this is to communicate itself to young people, it must be seen in the lifestyles of Christian adults. Healthy, controlled sexuality in the young requires some heroic restraint and, sooner or later, it needs some inner light that eclipses sexual demand and puts it in its place. But there are changes that adults must make. Christians must get beyond their current presentation of sexual intercourse as something wonderful, rich, and God-given, which is, nevertheless, only right for people who can afford a mortgage.

References

1. J. Huizinga, Homo Ludens: *A Study of the Play Element in Culture*, Routledge and Kegan Paul, 1949. Quoted in Susanna Millar, *The Psychology of Play*, pages 189–190.
2. J. H. Newman, *Apologia Pro Vita Sua*, Fontana, 1959, pages 18–19.
3. Video: *Make Love Last*, 1A Productions, with Teacher's Pack and Student Worksheets, by State of Flux, all 1994, distributed by CARE.
4. H. Blamires, *The Christian Mind*, SPCK, 1966, pages 173ff.

It is wrong to have sexual intercourse under the legal age (16 years)

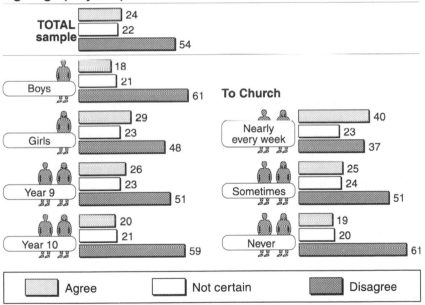

Source: Teenage Religion and Values Survey of 13,000 pupils in England and Wales. All figures refer to responses to the statement immediately above this diagram. The left hand column shows, at the top, the responses of the total sample which is divided, in the middle, into responses of year 9 and year 10 pupils. The right hand column deals only with the 11% of the total sample who attend church.

17 John Allan

Popular Religion

For the last two years, the churches in my city have carried out a survey designed to show who goes to church on a typical Sunday. The survey covers the broadest possible range of churchgoing and style of worship, and each year it has shown one fact very clearly: young people have less to do with the church than any other group in the community.

The change in the figures is quite striking. Up to the age of fifteen, children are over-represented in church: 30 per cent more city children go to church than one would estimate by using figures from the national census. In the fifteen- to nineteen-year-old group, however, there are three or four per cent *less*. For young people in their twenties, that figure shoots up to 60 per cent!

I do not think that my own home town (sleepy, predominantly white and markedly middle-class) is particularly unusual unless, perhaps, youthful churchgoing is higher there than it is elsewhere. But right across the country, it is clear to see, young people are bored and repelled by the church. Does this mean that they have no interest in the supernatural? Or—as many Christians have claimed —are young people simply diverting their interest elsewhere, into a fascination with the occult and all things mysterious?

Two items of the Teenage Religion and Values Survey provide us with some little evidence. First, when presented with the statement 'I believe in black magic', about one in five agreed, and another 30 per cent were not sure. There is certainly an openness to the possibility of unknown spiritual powers which was not as evident just a few years ago. Since the heyday of the psychic 'stars' of the 1970s—Uri Geller, Matthew Manning and Doris Stokes, for example—and the rise of New Age spirituality in the 1980s, many young people have become less dismissive of offbeat possibilities.

But it remains the case that 51 per cent of those surveyed dismissed the idea out of hand. Black magic does not work. And this reflects the fact that half the young people today have no place in their lives for spiritual answers of any kind; they are exclusively concerned with the here and now. It is a material world, and girls just want to have fun. Christianity's significant opponent is not magic and mysticism, but the bleak, amoral, hedonistic materialism which fills the horizon for most teenagers. It certainly is not the case that all non-Christian young people are turning to the occult for spiritual satisfaction; a large number see no need for any satisfaction beyond the material realm.

Paradoxically, it seems to me, this is why many teenagers of my acquaintance love horror films such as 'Nightmare on Elm Street': they do not believe any of it. Their response to such films is very different from the response of earlier generations of teenagers to 'The Exorcist' and 'The Omen', for instance. There, the worry that 'some of this might be true' was part of the *frisson*. But nowadays, although supernatural elements feature in most children's television teatime serials, heavy metal bands play with satanic concepts and horror fiction for young adults sells as never before, there is less real belief in the supernatural than before. I have a selection of teenage novels before me as I write: *Whispers from the Dead*, *The Possession* and *Haunted*. In each of them, the supernatural element is used simply as a mechanism to move the plot along, to focus the interest on what really matters in the story: the interplay of relationships between the characters. The reader need not believe in ghosts or curses any more than a film audience needs to believe that a Western provides a historically accurate description of the United States in the nineteenth century.

(It would be interesting to speculate on how this ties up with the 'unbelieving Christianity' currently promoted by figures such as John Hick and Don Cupitt, and for which the Rev. Anthony Freeman lost his job: the philosophy which recognizes the Christian framework as a powerful myth that can shape one's life, although in a 'realist' sense, it is simply not true.)

The young people in the Teenage Religion and Values Survey were also asked to comment on the statement 'I believe in my horoscope'. Here, opinion was fairly evenly divided: about one-third agreed, one-third disagreed and the remaining one-third were not sure. Older teenagers were slightly more likely to believe than younger ones, and girls much more likely to believe than boys. This probably reflects the fact that girls are more open to religious and metaphysical ideas than boys; almost any religious youth event will contain a much larger percentage of girls.

Why are horoscopes more likely to command belief than black magic? Perhaps part of the answer is that astrology is less of a systematic, organized practice. Young people recoil from established religion in any shape or form; and whereas black magic also has implications for your lifestyle, astrology is more neutral. The kind of supernatural realm with which today's materialistic teenagers feel safe is a mechanical, impersonal one—incorporating a neutral power which can, potentially, be harnessed and controlled. Perhaps some day we will understand the workings of the planets and be 'on top of' astrology; even scientists such as Hans Eysenck are saying so. But black magic? The very notion seems superstitious.

The most interesting feature of the 'horoscope' response is the large number of young people who regularly attend church and yet believe in the power of astrology. A majority of those who are in church every week would not be prepared to dismiss it. Those who attend 'sometimes' are more likely to believe in astrology than those who never go. This shows quite clearly that the church is not teaching young people very effectively, at least where this area of the 'pop supernatural' is concerned. Considering the amount of evangelical time which is often spent in issuing warnings against occult practices and the horror with which many Christians regard non-Christian forms of divination, such a failure is quite striking.

Today's non-churchgoing young people seem to be not so much 'post-Christian', or even non-Christian, as pre-Christian. It is not that they have rejected Christianity; rather, that they have simply not been confronted with anything much to reject. Because most have never encountered the real thing, a minority of teenagers are fascinated with other spiritual possibilities, from delving into New Age beliefs to experimenting with ouija boards. But this group is still a minority (New Age believers, for instance, tend to recruit from the next generation up), and the majority of British young people have few spiritual preoccupations of any kind. Again, it is a material world. What should Christians be doing in this situation? There are five options.

First, we must develop an apologetic which lets young people see just why Christianity is an important subject for them to consider. The large number of 'don't knows' in the survey results reflects the fact that this is a 'floating voter' culture, in which young people have often despaired of arriving at hard-and-fast conclusions about spiritual matters. Believers are tolerated, but not if they try to spread their ideas to others. ('If you want to be religious, fine, but don't tell me what I ought to think, all right?')

Second, we need to help young people see that a consistent world-view is possible. Most of them have only a bundle of assorted convictions, tied loosely together: don't be bad to your mum, tolerate gays, save the environment, be true to yourself, make as much money as you can. But they have no worked-out position, and one of their frequent objections to Christianity (or Marxism or Islam) is that it decides everything for you; it leaves you no 'freedom'. The result is that they are coasting along on a few sketchy moral guidelines of the most subjective kind, and when faced with a real problem—bereavement or family breakdown, for instance—they have no resources with which to cope.

Third, although we need to be aware of youthful interest in the occult we do not need to be obsessed by it. In a climate which will tolerate any view, however bizarre, dangerous ideas and practices can easily mushroom. However, it is possible to overestimate the depth of teenage fascination with occult matters and to fail to spot that the *real* enemy is anarchic materialism.

Fourth, we need to be aware that conversion is likely to be a long-term job. Teenage evangelism is carried out among people who have only a rudimentary understanding of the Christian claims and lifestyle (compounded by the fact that many of them think they understand it much better than they do). Leading a teenager to Christ is only the start of a battle; making every subsequent thought obedient to him is not, in a culture like theirs, going to happen overnight.

Fifth and finally, we need to be especially careful with young people who grow up within the Christian culture. We must be aware that from a fairly early age they will be conscious of a severe tension between the outlook of the world they inhabit at home and the atmosphere they breathe everywhere else they go. We need to ensure that we equip them to cope with this tension, to help them to recognize clearly the difference between true and spurious versions of the supernatural, and to bridge their two 'cultures' without being faithless to the one and overwhelmed by the other.

I believe that fortune-tellers can tell the future

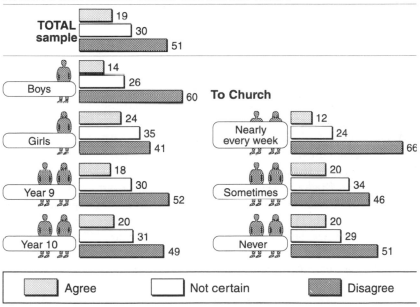

Source: Teenage Religion and Values Survey of 13,000 pupils in England and Wales. All figures refer to responses to the statement immediately above this diagram. The left hand column shows, at the top, the responses of the total sample which is divided, in the middle, into responses of year 9 and year 10 pupils. The right hand column deals only with the 11% of the total sample who attend church.

18 Bill Hogg
Crime

Archbishop George Carey told a conference in London: 'To see the devastatingly low self-esteem and hopelessness of youngsters on the fringes of crime in our inner cities is most dispiriting'.[1] Across the Atlantic, US Attorney General, Janet Reno, stated on 24 July 1994: 'If something isn't done about rapidly increasing juvenile crime, the nation faces losing a generation'.[2]

CBS News once reported that the seven top problems identified by teachers in US schools were:

talking out of turn;
chewing gum;
making noise;
running in the halls;
cutting in line (US English for 'jumping the queue'!);
dress code infractions; and
dropping litter.

Many teachers, parents and youth workers would gladly settle for tackling these 'top' problems! Tragically, by 1980 the top seven problems had been identified as suicide, assault, robbery, rape, drug abuse, alcohol abuse and pregnancy. Why the tragic shift?

A little more than one-third—36 per cent—of our young respondents saw crime as a growing problem in their area. Our researchers did not define 'crime'; nevertheless, what can we make of this? How can we evaluate this perception of a growing level of criminal activity? Does it mean that young people are afraid to go out at night? Are they aware of gang activity in their area? The term 'crime' could mean burglary, vandalism, drug crimes or sexual violence. *The Daily Telegraph* poll of 31 May 1993 found that, of the young people surveyed, many think it likely that they will be beaten up or mugged. When asked in the Teenage Religion and Values Survey about shoplifting, 85 per cent disagreed with the statement 'There is nothing wrong in shoplifting'. Churchgoing young people took a slightly dimmer view than their pagan peers.

In 1992, the number of crimes registered in Britain was 5.6 million. By 1994, the risk of burglary had become one of the highest in Europe. Moreover, 35 per cent of males under the age of thirty-five now have a criminal record; and more than half the offenders are under twenty-one.

We need to pause and reflect. We are called by God to touch broken young lives with the healing love of Jesus Christ. Statistics do not bleed, young people do! What do these trends mean? Why do young people get drawn into crime and caught up in gangs?

Rebels without a cause

Iain Grant, for thirty years the Director of New Zealand Youth for Christ, says this is the first generation to be bored with its own freedom. There is an aimlessness and purposelessness among young people. How does this create an impetus toward crime?

Luis Rodriguez is a former gang member, and author of *Always Running: La Vida Loca—Gang Days in L.A.* He writes, 'When I was in a gang, the only thing I felt I had control over was whether I lived or died. It was a powerfully empowering thing. I would deliberately put myself in the line of fire. It was a way of saying "I exist". Miraculously, I survived.'[3]

Sometimes, juvenile crime can offer excitement to otherwise bored young-sters—the adrenaline rush of attacking another bunch of kids in the park, or the prospect of escaping from the scene of damage without getting caught. Will the shopkeeper or security men catch us?

The drip feed of violence

Our culture has glamorized violence. Many of our celluloid heroes are 'shoot 'em up and shut 'em up' types. Some are wise-cracking, such as Mel Gibson's cute killer in *Lethal Weapon* and Bruce Willis' John McLane in *Diehard* ('Stay clear of the airport if McLane has booked a flight.'). Our video shops offer a grand procession of macho men who leave a trail of corpses in their wake: Clint Eastwood, Arnold Schwarzenegger, Steven Seagal, Jean Claude Van Damme, Chuck Norris and so on. Some films, such as *Clockwork Orange* and *Menace II Society*, have glorified youth violence in particular. Some of our music espouses violence, for example that of Gangsta Rap. Ice T's 'Cop Killer' got its performers into hot water in July, 1992; they excuse themselves by saying that the lyrics concerned express anger rather than instructions to kill:

> *I'm 'bout to bust some shots off, I'm 'bout to dust some cops off . . .*
> *Die, Die, Die, Pig, Die.*

The heavy-metal genre also has its exponents of violence. As Motley Crue say, in the charmingly-titled 'Bastard':

> *Out go the lights, in goes the knife, pull out his life, consider the bastard dead.*

On top of this, our young people can also participate vicariously in violence through video games such as 'Streets of Rage', 'Mortal Kombat' and 'Shenobi'. Of course, we cannot apportion the blame for society's ills solely at the video shop or cinema. However, there is truth in the old adage, 'garbage in, garbage out'. Jesus put it this way in Mark 7:21:

For from within, out of men's hearts, come evil thoughts.

The perpetual influx of violence and immorality, propagated in the name of entertainment by certain sections of the video industry, will have an inevitable effect on the actions of its consumer group—young people. We are facing a moral problem.

Society has jettisoned what Francis Schaeffer called 'true truth'. God has been handed his P45. Truth, and therefore morality, have become a consumer commodity: 'Discover and live by your own truth.' We live in the land of do-it-yourself religion and do-it-yourself ethics. Life is cheap, and abortions are commonplace. Christian morality has been abandoned. However, juvenile delinquents are not only the sinners who violate God's standards; they are sinned against, too. Youth crime is often associated with unemployment, drug abuse, depression and poverty. Burglaries and muggings are crimes mostly committed by males for money. Stolen property is sometimes resold for money to buy food and clothes, to pay the rent or to feed a habit. Hungry people are more likely to commit crime.

Crime can appear to offer a route out of the dehumanizing squalor of urban life. Crime, and drug-pushing in particular, can be easy money. Katie Buckland is a Los Angeles prosecutor who volunteers in the city's schools. Commenting on the rise of youth violence, she had this to say:

The only direction these kids receive is from their peers on the street, the local drug dealers, and other role models who engage in criminal conduct. The kids that are selling crack when they're in the fifth grade are not the dumb kids. They're the smart kids. They're the ambitious kids trying to climb up their own corporate ladder, and the only corporate ladder has to do with gangs and drugs.[4]

Major pieces in the tragic jigsaw of youth violence (and the upsurge of gangs in particular) are the breakdown of family and the breakdown of community. Indianapolis Prosecuting Attorney Jeff Modisett told *Newsweek*, 'It takes an entire village to raise a child, but the village isn't there for the children any more'.

John Perkins, veteran urban minister and activist for reconciliation, told *Christianity Today*:

It's no coincidence that as the church pulled from the problem areas, violence mushroomed. Our nation faces a crisis greater than the breakdown of the family—the breakdown of community. The burden lies with the church to change this.

Human beings were created in the image of a triune God to live in community. When God created Adam, he said, 'It's not good for man to be alone.' The isolationism and individualism of Western culture is not the way things are supposed to be! John Donne preached and wrote:

No man is an island, entire of itself. Every man is a piece of the continent, a part of the main; if a clod be washed away by the sea, Europe is the less . . . any man's death diminishes me because I am involved in mankind; and therefore never send to know for whom the bell tolls, it tolls for thee.

Gangs offer support, a place of belonging and a form of security. They produce a twisted sense of male identity where masculinity is affirmed and expressed through violence.

Sociologist and Baptist preacher Tony Campolo sees academic failure and the adolescent quest for peer acceptance as contributory factors to youth crime and youth gangs:

As a sociologist, I am convinced that feeling like a failure at school is a major cause of juvenile delinquency. Children retreat from classrooms and from teachers who make them feel unsuccessful, and look for some other group that will give them more positive feelings. The youngster who is willing to do something daringly antisocial can gain instantaneous praise from the gang that hangs out on the street corner. If being foul-mouthed, tough, and defiant are traits which the gang will praise, children craving for approval will quickly acquire them.[5]

We could view gangs as surrogate families or urban tribes. The gang leader is the father substitute. This is particularly the case in Los Angeles where the gang members have this in common: outside the gang they have no male role model— they are, almost without exception, from single parent families. 'Dad' is the gang leader.

Here we see an open sore in this emerging generation; they are the fatherless generation. Kevin Costner's portrayal of the fictitious criminal Butch Haynes in *A Perfect World* is a commentary on dysfunctionality. The escaped convict takes to the road with an eight-year-old called Philip. The film becomes a buddy movie with a twist: Haynes sees in the boy the childhood that he never had. They build a rapport as young Philip grows to love his captor like the father who has been absent from his life.

Butch Haynes, we discover in the film, had a prostitute for a mother and a father who, on the extremely rare occasion he was around, meted out violence. The last time Haynes saw him was when he was thirteen. At the end of the film, having been shot by an FBI marksman, the dying Haynes tells Philip where they were heading for. He shows the boy a postcard of Alaska and explains, 'That's where my daddy is.'

We have a hurting, aching generation, hungry for the love of a father. Some, like the celluloid criminal Butch Haynes, deprived of 'Dad' and schooled in crime, are walking time bombs. *We* know that the true and living God declares his love for widows and orphans. He longs to be Father to the fatherless and to pour into this generation's orphaned hearts his Holy Spirit of adoption. We must be agents of his healing love.

References

1. The Guardian, 22 February 1994.
2. *USA Today*, 26 July 1994.
3. *Christianity Today*, 18 July 1993.
4. *Newsweek*, 2 August 1993.
5. Tony Campolo, *The Success Fantasy*, Kingsway, 1994, page 39.

Right
Source: Teenage Religion and Values Survey of 13,000 pupils in England and Wales. All figures refer to responses to the statement immediately above the diagrams. The left hand column shows, at the top, the responses of the total sample which is divided, in the middle, into responses of year 9 and year 10 pupils. The right hand column deals only with the 11% of the total sample who attend church.

There is nothing wrong in shop-lifting

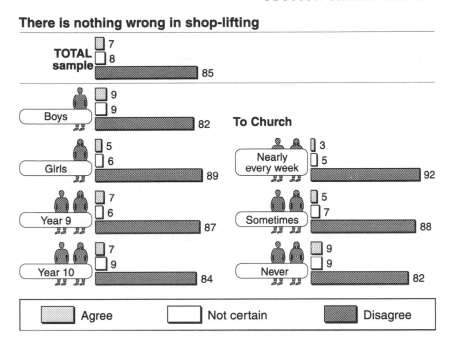

TOTAL sample
7
8
85

Boys
9
9
82

Girls
5
6
89

Year 9
7
6
87

Year 10
7
9
84

To Church

Nearly every week
3
5
92

Sometimes
5
7
88

Never
9
9
82

Agree | Not certain | Disagree

Crime is a growing problem in my area

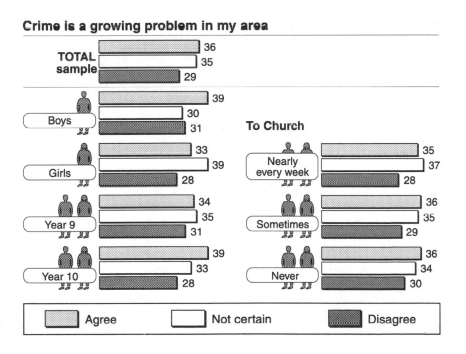

TOTAL sample
36
35
29

Boys
39
30
31

Girls
33
39
28

Year 9
34
35
31

Year 10
39
33
28

To Church

Nearly every week
35
37
28

Sometimes
36
35
29

Never
36
34
30

Agree | Not certain | Disagree

19 Grahame Knox
Bullying

The results in the Teenage Religion and Values Survey reinforce the view of many: that bullying is a real concern for thirteen- to fifteen-year-olds. A quarter of the young people polled agreed that they were worried about being bullied at school, with nearly as many again indicating uncertainty about their feelings on the issue. The survey also revealed that more than 28 per cent of girls said they were worried about being bullied at school. As young people enter the senior years of school their concern appears to lessen a little, although it is still significant. Interestingly, those young people who indicated a regular church attendance appear to be more worried about bullying than their peers. More than half of the young people who go to church nearly every week were worried or unsure about their feelings about being bullied at school.

With reference to other evidence, the concern expressed by young people seems to be justified. Another recent survey has shown bullying to be a major source of disruption and stress, with polls indicating that almost half of all teenagers are bullied in school at some time, and that one in five plays truant to avoid being bullied. A quarter of pupils in the same survey revealed that it made them ill. Many more suffered nightmares, and more than one-third did not know how to stop the bullying. A further survey of nearly 7,000 children discovered that 27 per cent of primary and 10 per cent of secondary pupils had been bullied that term. Ten per cent of primary pupils reported being bullied at least once a week. If this pattern is repeated across the country, it is estimated that 360,000 eight- to ten-year-olds are being bullied every week.

More people are realizing the very real long-term emotional damage that bulling does to young people. Bullying has serious repercussions. It would not be an exaggeration to say that for some it produces an emotional scar that will last for life. It has been linked to several suicides over the past two years. In a survey of young offenders, 92 per cent of those questioned said they bullied other children in school. This could imply that if bullying can be dealt with effectively in school, then this could have a significant influence on juvenile crime.

Bullying takes many different forms. It is not always physical, but often just a threat: 'We'll be waiting for you after school'; or 'My brother's a black belt and he'll get you.' Such threats work on the victims' fear, undermining their self-confidence. When pupils have been questioned, they have said that the type of bullying they feared most was having rumours spread about them, their family or their sexual relationships. This was followed by fear of physical violence, of being called names or of being deliberately left out of a group by their peers. Boys said they were most worried about verbal threats and rumours. Girls said direct bullying was the most stressful.

The degree of bullying that takes place in schools is often related to how seriously teachers, parents and children take the problem. Often, children and young people themselves have some of the most useful and creative ideas about what to do, because they know what is going on and where the bullying takes place. In some schools, creating pupil councils and building on the positive effects of peer pressure have lead to effective strategies to combat bullying.

We live in a violent world: watch the six o'clock news this evening! Violence surrounds us: an elderly person is mugged, a bank is violently robbed, there is a terrorist atrocity. Bullying, threatening behaviour and fighting in school unfortunately reflect the society in which we live. It is not just a 'phase' some young people go through, but a culture of violence and fear not only in school but in the adult world as well.

The church's role

What role can the church play to combat bullying? Certainly, representatives on school governing bodies and parents of schoolchildren can support and encourage the development of strategies to combat the problem. Increasingly, it is believed that crucial to combating the problem is a 'whole school policy', where everyone is involved—teachers, governors, parents, pupils and support staff. Firm policies involving counselling, and not just disciplinary measures, are important. Increased playground supervision and more extra-curricular activities may also be effective.

Closer to home, those with responsibility for children's and youth ministry in the church need to consider again the destructiveness of bullying, and to ensure that church activities are a haven from the influence of bullying. As youth leaders we may also wish to reflect on our own example to the young people in our care. We need to ensure that we discipline ourselves not to be violent in our behaviour, our language or our thoughts, and to be the example that God wants us to be in the world.

Within our church groups there may be young people who have been, or are continuing to be, the victims of bullying. At the very least, a number are worried about the possibilities of being bullied. More sobering still is the fact that some, perhaps unwittingly, are also bullies. According to the Teenage Religion and Values Survey, more than half said they were worried or uncertain about their feelings on this matter. Bullying is a 'live' issue for many young people which should be tackled at some point in the church youth programmes. As well as a spiritual perspective, we must also include practical suggestions on how to deal with particular situations. Small-group discussions and role-plays about bullying can be effective in allowing young people to give their views and share experiences, as well as to consider how they can support one another. We must also make available opportunities for individuals to talk alone with someone if they want to, and provide pastoral support and advice to help them to combat the effects and further influence of bullying.

I am worried about being bullied at school

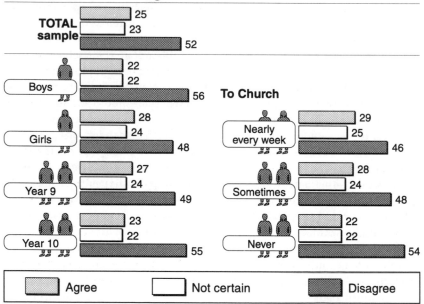

Source: Teenage Religion and Values Survey of 13,000 pupils in England and Wales. All figures refer to responses to the statement immediately above this diagram. The left hand column shows, at the top, the responses of the total sample which is divided, in the middle, into responses of year 9 and year 10 pupils. The right hand column deals only with the 11% of the total sample who attend church.

20 Sue Rinaldi
AIDS

'Everybody's doing it!' comments one teenage magazine; 'A smart girl's guide to sex' is included in another; sexually suggestive lyrics to chart songs are transmitted on the radio; an estimated 9,230 sexual acts are screened on television every year, and about 80 per cent of them are outside marriage. Young people are continually bombarded and stimulated by visual images and experiences of a sexual nature. To unscramble these messages and to formulate personal codes of sexual conduct and morality will probably be one of the most difficult challenges we face.

This task is further complicated by the decline and virtual disappearance of a consensus within society about our spiritual and moral natures. It has been considered 'out of fashion' to promote advisable standards of right and wrong, and 'in vogue' to consider all boundaries extinct, in the search for personal morality.

A headmaster was quoted as saying, 'You cannot give young people moral tuition about sex any more. They regard it as an intolerable intrusion on their privacy.' Every individual, regardless of class, age, status or circumstance, has a value system or a code of behaviour. This value system, with specific regard to sexual morality, is affected and shaped by a multiplicity of experiences and influences. These influences include family, friends, school, the media, individual conscience, and religious and societal trends. Throughout life, values are constantly challenged, strengthened or even destroyed.

It is interesting to look at the effects the 'swinging sixties' have had on the morals of today's generation. During that significant decade, creativity and experimentation were particularly enjoyed by people identified as 'hippies'— 'flower children' who talked of love, peace and communal living. A revolution of sexual abandon characterized their journey into self-expression and their investigation into behaviour without boundaries. Many people challenged all precepts of right and wrong, and their children, the 1990s' teenagers, have consequently reaped the fruit of their parents' departure from the *status quo*.

Pornography on tap

An ever-increasing amount of pornographic material containing explicit and degrading sexual activity has been published over the past few years. In addition, it has become more widely available and accessible. Teenagers today live in a world of lurid magazines, shrieking videos, telephone chat-lines and computer software offering a plethora of obscene and sexual pleasures on demand. The pornographic industry in the United Kingdom is reputed to be worth more than £100 million annually. It has been proved that sales of teenage magazines rise significantly when they include a pull-out sex supplement. The messages of magazines that are easily bought from high street shops are that sexual adventure is OK. As a by-product, those teenagers who fear that for some reason they are 'missing out' are put under pressure, and are made to feel they are in the minority—not living the lifestyles of the sexually experienced as portrayed in the articles.

Interestingly, only 31 per cent of thirteen-to fifteen-year-olds in the Teenage Religion and Values Survey agreed that pornography is too readily available. Indeed, 33 per cent disagreed. These figures may reflect teenagers' own definition of pornography: for, with every obscene act or image, the mind can become anaesthetized by degrees and more images will become acceptable. Or it may be the response generated by peer-pressure: to fall in line with the 'anything goes' philosophy. Boys tended to disagree more with the statement than girls.

The issue of censorship and availability of erotic material will continue to be hotly debated. There are those who wish to allow all kinds of material from hard-core to soft-core, giving the individual the freedom to accept or reject it. Then there are those who insist on the responsibility of people in authority to establish parameters; they wish to see a framework for protection and education, especially of the young, so that personal morality *can* exist in a hotbed of hormones. The overwhelming tragedy of pornography is that a person's value is measured by the degree of eroticism or sexual stamina they display—disguising and cheapening the full worth of the person. The degradation of women as 'objects of desire', slavishly pleasing men, the diversion into sado-masochism, the amoral sickness of paedophile rings and the savage increase of rape on our streets must sound the alarm: enough is enough. Speaking the truth about the real value of life and encouraging respect and dignity for the individual must be priorities.

The collective journey of sexual morality appears to have hit many crisis points within the last few years. Each crisis has caused individuals to question and ultimately reassess their own values and lifestyles. The present decade seems unique in that the sexual revolution appears to be waning. Current trends are towards sexual abstinence; celibacy is being seen as an equally valid lifestyle; and the advantages of monogamy are being promoted. Although these trends are only just beginning to emerge against a previous backdrop of sexual adventure and experimentation, what exactly is causing the change?

The AIDS crisis

A major crisis that has affected behaviour and attitudes has been the global onset of AIDS. Within the past ten years, significant steps have been made regarding the understanding of the HIV virus and the risks of infection. Aggressive prevention campaigns, educational strategies and statistical information have helped people to replace fear and ignorance with realism, practical help and advice. In the United Kingdom, the homosexual community was the first to be affected and, consequently, AIDS was labelled the 'gay disease'. This belief was soon challenged when evidence revealed that the HIV virus did not belong to this one community alone, but transcended all boundaries of colour, race and sexual orientation. HIV infection was now known to be passed on through heterosexual activity and drug abuse, as well as through homosexual activity. In the early 1980s, projected figures of HIV infection threatened an explosion of AIDS beyond belief, and created a climate of immense fear and paranoia—feelings which were only made more intense by ignorance.

Many organizations, in particular the World Health Organization (WHO), have brought new knowledge together with realistic statistical evidence and clear guidelines. They have supplied information on how to avoid HIV, and given practical help to those infected, and to their families and friends. Dr Michael Merson, director of WHO's global programme on AIDS, remarked, 'Aggressive prevention campaigns can make a real difference in the ultimate size of the pandemic. If we seize this opportunity, millions of people may be spared infection by the year 2000.' In June 1993, WHO revealed that 14 million people were infected with HIV worldwide—one in 250 of the world's population—with a conservative estimate that this figure may reach 40 million by the year 2000. In the United Kingdom the same source estimates that 7,500 people will have developed AIDS, with more than half dying from the disease. Nearly 30,000 people are officially reported as being 'HIV infected'; however, the true figure is likely to be 50,000.

There is no doubt that infection through heterosexual activity is steadily increasing. This has led to comprehensive educational programmes with particular focus on young people, prior to their becoming sexually active. Considering the fact that people today become sexually active at a considerably lower age, priority must be given to prevention campaigns at this level.

The Teenage Religion and Values Survey revealed that 62 per cent of teenagers between thirteen to fifteen years old are worried about getting AIDS. Whether male or female, the response was similar. Of the total sample, 21 per cent said they were not worried, leaving 17 per cent unsure. This survey must indicate that even more emphasis should be given to provide sufficient school-based education about AIDS, especially because this is not provided in most homes. Interestingly, those teenagers from the sample who attend church on a regular basis were only slightly less worried than those never attending church. Information and education about AIDS must, according to this survey, become higher on the agenda for churches and, in particular, in the youth work of churches. Unfortunately, statistics confirm that topics relating to sexual issues are embarrassingly avoided at church. Instead, the church should be leading the way in addressing real-life issues and voicing positive alternatives based on Christian ethics.

The AIDS crisis has caused young people to assess their own sexual behaviour and to re-examine their values. Motivation to adopt safer sex has resulted in a condom culture, as well as a growing trend towards fewer sexual partners, monogamy and even sexual abstinence. A greater awareness and dialogue about sexual behaviour and its often unrecognized consequences can only serve to benefit individuals and, ultimately, society. The hope is that such understanding will influence young people's choices in a practical way.

Positive alternatives

The present generation has emerged realizing that the consequences of the 1960s search for sexual utopia has been destructive as well as liberating. This realization is signalling some interesting new trends. Positive alternatives are being offered regarding sexual behaviour and moral values. A growing confidence and justifiable search for equality has opened the doors of opportunity for women in particular. A woman's worth is no longer locked up in the role of motherhood; she can choose a career before, or instead of, a family without attracting negative criticism. Celibacy or sexual abstinence is becoming a considered choice, free from the stigma of inferiority and oddness it has attracted over past decades. The positive alternative of monogamy or fewer sexual partners is also being chosen, helping to combat the sexually transmitted diseases as well as promoting the advantages of 'commitment for life'. The soaring incidence of divorce, the tragedy of family breakdown, the surge in teenage pregnancies, and the availability and trauma of abortion have all resulted in a reassessment of values. How much this reassessment will affect actual behaviour remains to be seen. The search for sexual morality is, indeed, an intricate and difficult one for every young person.

21 Heather Evans

Self-destruction

I haven't felt the excitement of listening to, as well as creating, music, along with really writing something, for many years now. I feel guilty beyond words about these things . . . The worst crime I could think of would be to put people off by faking it, by pretending I'm having 100 per cent fun. It's better to burn out then fade away.
Words from Kurt Cobain's suicide note, read by his wife, Courtney Love, at the Seattle vigil, after his suicide had been discovered, 9 April 1994.

The death of Kurt Cobain may now be old news, but the power of that death still stings. Cobain, lead singer of the grunge band, Nirvana, wrote this note and shot himself. We will probably never know whether this action was caused by depression brought on by his drug habit, or whether he felt that he was compromising his beliefs with his success and becoming a part of the system that his songs decry. World fame had been achieved, but he ended his life at the age of twenty-seven. Yet we can see in Cobain's life some of the torment that can be traced back to childhood and adolescence, and we also see that this torment did not recede with maturity—it took him.

Cobain's death brought the subject of suicide to the headlines, yet suicide is not an 'issue' in and of itself. It is a by-product of wider issues. Suicidal thoughts should not be treated glibly, but the subject is complex—to do with personal circumstances, psychological make-up and self-esteem. Naturally, we must recognize the level of expertise required to help young people with depressive feelings. But neither should we abandon the issues to the experts. We must have a response to them, we must address this growing trend and begin as part of God's church to wake up to the needs that the statistics reveal. The statistics show that a rapidly increasing number of young people, especially males, are opting for self-destruction.

A recent article by Angus MacKinnon in *GQ Magazine*,[1] notes that by 1992, for young men aged fifteen to twenty-four suicide had become the most common cause of death after accidents. Now, an incredible 87 per cent of young suicides are male. Ten years earlier, males were only half as likely to commit suicide. The increase is staggering.

The young people in our survey were asked to mark 'agree', 'disagree' or 'don't know' to the following statement: 'I have sometimes considered taking my own life'. In fact, only 24 per cent of boys agreed with the statement, compared with 30 per cent of girls: a different response from the *GQ* survey. It means that with the two pieces of research we may be able to draw the conclusion that girls contemplate suicide more but are less likely to do it; boys think about it less, but are more likely to do it—as an impulse, without forethought.

Further crucial information to note from the Teenage Religion and Values Survey is that, of those who regularly attend church, fewer young people contemplate suicide at all. There may, therefore, be grounds for saying that Christian spiritual input gives young people more positive views about life. We must not, however, overlook the survey result which suggests that of those who have thought about taking their own lives, 23 per cent are weekly attenders in our churches! Teenage suicide is not merely an issue for those young people who are regarded as delinquent or ostracized from church.

The majority of young people who took part in this survey have not contemplated suicide. The survey was, however, conducted in school on a normal day. It therefore does not take into account the views of those young people who, on that day, were away from school with depressive feelings.

Adolescents are under enormous pressure today; they are at a stage in life when emotions are singularly significant and this can cause depressive feelings. I lead a weekly youth group in a suburban Baptist church. In it, there are about ten young people, mostly from a churched background. In working with this small group in the past year, we have discovered that two of them have been struggling with suicidal thoughts. Personal experience confirms the results of the survey: these young people are not in a spiritual desert with nowhere to turn, they are in our churches and are part of supportive families—yet they suffer these feelings. This issue is a growing one because, while there is little proof of what causes suicidal thoughts, neither our culture nor our material world help young people struggling with depression.

Mal Fletcher, in his book, *Youth—the Endangered Species,*[2] talks of several influences on the young that he believes are having a destructive impact: the music of some rock bands, the content of magazines and tabloid newspapers, even computer games and cartoons. Add to these the 'perfected', 'beautiful' people exhibited in movies and television shows such as *Baywatch,* and it is no wonder that young people are down on themselves. While Fletcher recognizes that many factors come into play when a teenager considers ending his or her life, he adds that 'the media world of young people can contribute stress to the despairing mind of an unhappy and withdrawn young person'.

The biggest mistake we can make is to dismiss these depressive feelings as a phase. Several observers have noted the upturn in teenage suicides, and suggested that teenagers who commit suicide are often reacting to a recent distressing event or problem. It may seem trivial to an onlooker, but it may well be the last straw in a long line of incidents that seem hugely important to a young distressed mind. Utter hopelessness, helplessness and loss of self-esteem are common ingredients in the adolescent suicide.

One large factor at play is the breakdown of family life. Durkheim, a sociologist quoted by Dr Tony Campolo in his article, 'The Suicide Generation',[4] concludes that psychological well-being 'requires that teenagers live in a social system that provides a clear understanding of what is required of them. When teenagers find themselves in a society that allows them to do whatever they feel like doing, they experience extreme depression and become suicidal. Complete freedom, it turns out, is more of a psychological burden than most young people can bear.'

Many parents of today's teenagers grew up in the 1960s, and experienced their own revolution in personal freedom; that revolution, however, took place *against authority*, both at school and at home. Adopting an attitude of 'complete freedom' in parenting itself does not recognize the damage that a lack of authority can bring.

A while ago, when I was regularly working in schools, I took part in a discussion with a group of teenagers about the rules their parents set for them. Some expressed frustration that their parents put a time limit on being out during the evening, whereas others complained that their parents did not give them more money. Others again were cross that they were *forced* to do their homework.

One boy, who had been very disruptive in the group, was now quiet. I asked him what constraints were put on him at home. He shrugged and said he was free to do whatever he wanted, to come in when he wanted and to go out when he wanted. His peers in the group audibly sighed with envy, yet the lad looked unhappily at the floor. I asked him if he liked this arrangement. 'No,' he replied, 'if they told me off a bit more at least I'd know they cared.' For this thirteen-year-old, the freedom that the others yearned for was the very thing that caused him to question his parents' love.

To God, each life is precious (Psalm 139:13–16; Acts 17: 25–26). God does not just create life, he is instrumental in the path life takes; and he does not just help us to survive, but he helps us to achieve great things. God said to Jeremiah, 'For I know the plans I have for you, plans to prosper you and not to harm you, plans to give you hope and a future' (Jeremiah 29:11).

Yet the Bible also shows us people's suffering and depression in the midst of difficulties. There are biblical characters who went down to the depths and wished life could be taken from them (Psalm 22). Even Jesus expressed depths of sorrow (Matthew 26:38–39).

The God of the Bible is a God who brings hope and redeems broken lives. He gives people hope and a future. In a youth and community course run recently by a local authority, the participants looked at the history of the youth service (started, incidentally, by Christians concerned about meeting the needs of deprived young people). The lecturer on the course, an atheist, was looking at the future of youth service in Britain. He had little hope of it flourishing, as the government were stripping funds. His view was that the only agent that could get involved was the church. 'Who else is there?'

The church does indeed need to equip itself to help young people who are suffering depressive feelings. This can be done in a variety of ways:

◆ Youth workers, parents and church leaders need to understand the breadth of pastoral issues involved in suicidal thoughts—reading books, becoming informed and, above all, learning from young people about how they think and feel.

◆ We all need a biblical perspective on how God views human life and potential. The desire to end a life is, as someone once said, 'a rational decision made from irrational thoughts'. Those who contemplate suicide or who commit suicide have thought through and reached decisions. This will almost certainly have meant they have strayed from, or are ignorant of, what God intended when he brought their life into being.

◆ Young people need role models who are living and believing Christians, and who feel secure about their identity with God. They need to be coached and shown how to cope with the problems that life throws at us all.

◆ Expertise is involved in these issues. The church must train counsellors to specialize in helping teenagers. Organizations such as CARE, CWR, the Samaritans, the YMCA Trust for the Study of Adolescence and several local authorities have resources and training courses.

◆ Many more young men are finding nothing to turn to. We know from other research that a large percentage of men find our churches irrelevant. We need to look at this, bearing in mind that the biggest factor in binding young people to their faith is association with other like-minded young people. Young men need a positive, relevant view of faith, that can also help them in the tough times.

The pace of change in our society separates young people from adults. Some adults fear the world of young people. As parents, teachers and youth leaders, we must learn to understand, listen to and appreciate the pressures felt by teenagers. We need to help them in practical ways to endure, persevere and cope; and those of us who claim Christ as our Lord must find a way for our faith to make sense to a young person.

The message of the gospel for today's insecure, lonely teenager needs to make sense in their setting, and it therefore needs adapting. We must also be honest about our own suffering and difficulties, rather than coming across as people for whom the love of God overrides all our problems, giving us that greatest gift of all—the 'FEG' ('fixed evangelical grin').

There is a great opportunity for the church to be involved in helping teenagers. Everyone acknowledges the pressure that adolescents are under, and if only the church would wake up to the opportunity it has, we could begin to see God touch the lives of young people in a new, refreshing way—rescuing them from the brink, and giving them hope and a future.

References

1. *GQ Magazine*, February 1994.
2. M. Fletcher, *Youth—The Endangered Species*, Word Books.
3. K. Olson, *Counselling Teenagers*, Group Books.
4. T. Campolo and others, *Collected Wisdom For Youth Workers*.

Useful addresses

CWR Waverley Abbey Waverley Lane Farnham Surrey GU9 8EP
CARE Trust 53 Romney Street London SW1P 3RF
The Trust for the Study of Adolescence (A secular organization which researches and resources those working with teenagers) 23 New Road Brighton Sussex BM1 1WZ
YMCA National Training College 642a Forest Road Walthamstow London E17 3EF
National Youth Agency 17–23 Albion Street Leicester LE1 6GD
The Samaritans For youth outreach, resources, video and literature: General Office The Samaritans 10 The Grove Slough Berkshire

I have sometimes considered taking my own life

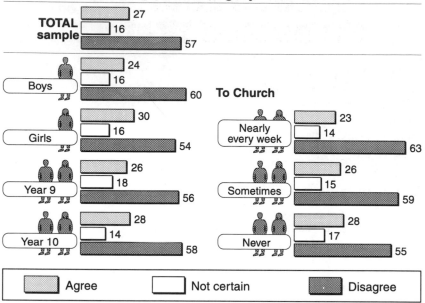

Source: Teenage Religion and Values Survey of 13,000 pupils in England and Wales. All figures refer to responses to the statement immediately above this diagram. The left hand column shows, at the top, the responses of the total sample which is divided, in the middle, into responses of year 9 and year 10 pupils. The right hand column deals only with the 11% of the total sample who attend church.

Section Four: Troubled Waters

Lyn Watson

22 An Aspiring Workforce?

It used to be said that people worked for forty-seven hours a week for forty-seven weeks for forty-seven years of their life. Multiplied out, that comes to just over 100,000 hours of employment in a working life.[1]

Times are a-changing. The thirty-five-hour week is now the norm in some organizations. With public holidays, sick leave and paid leave, some people have ten weeks or more away from the organization. With an average working life of thirty-five years, this multiplies out to just over 50,000 hours of employment in a working life. We shall soon have halved the lifetime job.[2]

As part of the Teenage Religion and Values Survey, young people were asked to respond to the statement: 'I'd rather be unemployed on social security than join the YTS' (now Training Credit Schemes).

The current feeling of moral panic would suggest that young people in Great Britain have been engulfed in a sea of apathy, low educational attainment and diminished aspirations. To compensate, they have sought solace in drugs and crime. The consequence has been that they have little collective regard for their futures. How true is this? Has Britain changed so much that young people are throwing in the towel?

The figures in the Teenage Religion and Values Survey show that about two-thirds of the young people questioned would prefer to participate in a training programme that has vocational and employment objectives, so a high proportion of young people want to work! Hasn't that always been the case? There have, of course, been huge changes in the pattern and types of work available and, accordingly, young people find that there are big differences between their expectations and what the real world has to offer.

What changes, therefore, must a young person consider when deciding on vocational training and its links with employment? The 'job' predictions for the year 2000 are:

70,000 new jobs will be created (about 1.2 million job losses in manufacturing,
    offset by 1.9 million new jobs in services);
new jobs will occur in diverse white-collar occupations;
new jobs will emerge in skills-intensive, knowledge-based occupations;
the number of full-time jobs held by women and men will decline;
the number of part-time jobs held by women and, to a much lesser extent, by
    men, and will increase markedly;
self-employment among women and men will increase.

The statistics in the Teenage Religion and Values Survey indicate that many young people (64 per cent) realize that it is more beneficial to participate in a Youth Training Scheme (now Youth Credit Scheme) or to receive relevant vocational training than it is to be unemployed. Is this because they are aware of the major shift in work patterns and occupational opportunities, or is it that firsthand experience and peer-group wisdom consider that the dole takes you nowhere?

Many young people experience a period of unemployment, and common feelings at such a time are those of low esteem, a lack of direction and a lack of confidence. Young people can also feel that that others 'look down' on them and that, therefore, they do not fit in. The normal indicators of success and individual progress, such as money and material well-being, are denied them. Consequently, frustration and alienation can cloud their decision-making.

Theological assessment

God is described in Genesis chapters 1 and 2 as overflowing with a passionate creative energy from which the whole universe has come. Unemployment deprives everyone of the feeling of importance that stems from creativity. That is why, in youth training, emphasis has to be placed on the contribution that a young person can make, whether or not it is a paid activity. It is therefore encouraging to see that the Teenage Religion and Values Survey shows that 63 per cent of young people disagree with the statement 'I would rather be unemployed on Social Security than join the Youth Training Scheme', and therefore subscribe to the notion of creativity that is part of youth training.

One of the main objectives of youth training is to provide vocational training which has national training standards recognized through the National Vocational Qualifications (NVQ) system. The activities provide the training—off-the-job workshop-based and on-the-job employer-based—which, in turn, provides the opportunity for expressing creativity. In addition, a young person is exposed to other factors that have a synergetic effect, such as team-work and collective responsibility. These skills and attributes are then transferable and useful both vocationally and socially. The dole, on the other hand, deprives a young person of these positive activities and enforces isolation.

Creativity is the key for the individual and for society. But our creative lives depend less on material gain than they do on those feelings and notions that are harder to quantify, such as self-esteem, confidence, social awareness and vision.

Many Christian organizations find that they have to become involved in tackling unemployment and its surrounding issues if they are to fulfil their mission. George Williams founded the YMCA in 1844 for the 'spiritual and moral welfare of young men in the drapers' trade' in London. It began by teaching young clerks and shopkeepers about history, politics and French, as well as about bookkeeping and shorthand, and it provided sports facilities, hostel rooms, libraries and places to relax. Today, with sustained high unemployment and with many young people needing physical and mental support, the YMCA has become deeply engaged in social and community provision. In the span of 150 years, the need for positive intervention has not receded.

Young people are becoming increasingly aware of the factors that affect their chances of work or of progress within work. They accept that world markets are both competitive and relevant to Britain's economic fortunes. By year 2000, most new jobs will be skills-intensive; working practices will require different types of skills, with a greater proportion of employees needing to hold these skills than in the past.[3] Frequent updating or reinforcing of skills will be required. The need that emerges from these employment changes is for young people to have a commitment to 'life-long learning'.[4] They will also need to have flexibility, and be supported by a portfolio of continually updated skills. This is the most fundamental change that is taking place, because it confuses the accepted distinction between education and training, bringing the classroom and workplace much closer together.

In this brief description of some of the challenges facing young people when contemplating youth training, future employment or 'signing on', it would be easy to be discouraged by the size and scope of the task. But we already know that one of the solutions is creativity. This creativity should not just be related to paid work because that would restrict its application. Nor should it be confined merely to the activities of young people with other young people. It needs a broader social brief.

No practical remedy, of course, will have an instant effect. There is, however, one path that we can follow, and that is the involvement of young people in consultation and decision-making. Creativity through involvement can take place in any organization or activity, as long as the methods of involvement are clearly signposted and access can be guaranteed. Being creative requires originality of thought, and it may be that, as those who influence young people, we need to display much more faith in their wish to shape their world.

References

1. C. Handy *The Gods of Management*, Arrow, 1995.
2. A. Rajan, *Where Will the New Jobs Be?*, 1992.
3. National Education and Training Targets.
4. National Education and Training Targets.

I would rather be unemployed on Social Security than join the Youth Training Scheme (YTS)

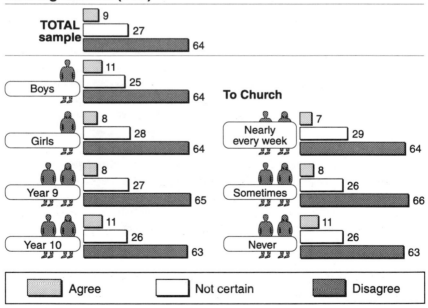

Source: Teenage Religion and Values Survey of 13,000 pupils in England and Wales. All figures refer to responses to the statement immediately above this diagram. The left hand column shows, at the top, the responses of the total sample which is divided, in the middle, into responses of year 9 and year 10 pupils. The right hand column deals only with the 11% of the total sample who attend church.

23 Elaine Williams
Anxiety

I feel permanently low, I'm not sleeping well and I'm having problems at school. I can't cope any more and no one seems to understand why.
A letter to MIZZ magazine

More than half the young people surveyed for this book reported that they often feel something like this. We should not, of course, assume that all of them are going through the depths of despair—some will be describing the troughs in mood swings which are 'part and parcel' of adolescence. Others, however, will be thinking about longer-lasting, more deep-seated feelings of emptiness, numbness, low self-worth and listlessness.

> *It was easy to see why Mark was depressed: school had always been tough for him, there had been conflict at home ever since he could remember and just recently his dad, struggling to come to terms with unemployment and alcohol-related problems, had committed suicide. But why was Alison, an academically gifted, popular, young woman from a loving family, showing all the same signs of depression as Mark?*

Clearly, depression does not just hit individuals reeling from the effects of tragedy in their lives; it is far more widespread. For most young people, it will be a kind of 'overload' reaction, a response to a mixture of problems and pressures, which they may or may not be able to identify for themselves. And before we can work out how best to help, we need to be aware of what the 'triggers' may be.

Big issues

The realization that life does not just go on as it is, indefinitely, often hits hardest during adolescence. Fear of death—of friends or family— can be very strong. The apocalyptic nature of recent reports on the 'greenhouse effect' and on AIDS, for example, have also left many young people anxious about the kind of world they are going to inherit, and feelings of depression may come with a sense of powerlessness to change things on such a global scale. Then there are key questions about personal morality: sexual awareness among young people is high—just look at out the content of magazines such as *Just Seventeen*, and the stage acts, lyrics and videos of chart groups such as Take That and Bad Boys Inc! The pressures of sexual decision making are considerable, especially if there is also pressure to stick to what everybody else seems to be doing.

This is also true of drug-taking in all its forms, including smoking and drinking. The majority of young teenagers will be aware of drug-taking, not as a remote issue, but as part of life in their town, neighbourhood or school, and home. Many will have been offered drugs. Moreover, decisions about such issues are not once-and-for-all choices; they have to be faced time and time again. Some young people in this age group will already be living with the consequences of 'bad' decisions in these areas of their lives.

A moral vacuum

Although young people have access to plenty of information about these key issues, guidance seems to be lacking for many. The approach in the media and in some educational material very often seems to be: 'here are the facts; make up your own mind'. In his book, *Getting Physical*,[1] Dr Aric Sigman from the BBC's 'Going Live' team writes, 'Many of you are probably sick and tired of being constantly told "Say no . . ." Let's face it, at the end of the day, it's really up to you what you do with your body—not parents, not teachers, not the law, not the Archbishop of Canterbury.' What a massive responsibility!

School

There is also considerable pressure in the school system. During year 9, young people will already have to think about their future careers before selecting examination courses. These start right at the beginning of year 10. In the GCSE and Standard Grade systems, continuous assessment in many subjects involves a kind of ongoing, relentless pressure which some young people struggle to cope with. I remember catching up with a colleague rushing to write something down at the end of break-time: 'I've just had a quick chat with Stephen down the corridor and I think I could use it in his English course work'! An extreme example perhaps, but I wonder how it feels to know that everything you say might be marked and assessed? Some young people will become disaffected and opt out, but most are aware that their chances later in life are largely determined by how they measure up in these few years at school—course work deadlines, exams and perceived failures are important and cause concern, disappointment and upset.

Lifestyle

Outside school, young people are heavy media consumers. As we have seen in chapters 11 and 19, the content of many teenage magazines is unlikely to make them feel more positive about themselves! Physical appearance, image and wearing the 'right' things (trends which are set mostly in the media), are very important, and feelings of depression about not looking right are common. The scenarios in many of the soaps popular with teenagers are also often fairly depressing: watching an episode of 'Eastenders' is hardly an uplifting experience!

Another favourite pastime for young people is just being with friends, and it is significant that half of those surveyed expressed worry about how they get on with other people. Popularity among peers is very highly regarded indeed, and a lack of 'success', real or imagined, can lead to anxiety and depression. People have the power to hurt us, perhaps especially during our teenage years when we tend to rely heavily on the support and approval of others as we try to work out our own identity. Some young people will suffer physical and verbal bullying. There is also a kind of cynicism, a tendency to undermine, which characterizes many relationships between young people, and which certainly will not build up an individual's feelings of security and self-worth.

The increasingly common incidence of conflict and breakdown in the family, sometimes with the added difficulties of adjusting to a 'blended' family, are also obvious sources of stress and worry whenever they occur. The relationship between parents and their sons or daughters obviously has to change during adolescence, and for most young people this process brings confrontation at some time or another. Working all this out is an ongoing 'challenge' for all concerned!

Environment

Some young people will find their physical environment—perhaps the inner city, a sprawling housing estate or a hamlet in the middle of nowhere—depressing in itself. A lack of local facilities and opportunities for young people will give rise to boredom, and a high incidence of crime and violence on the streets may also restrict what young people can do. High levels of unemployment in a region also breed a sense of hopelessness among teenagers.

Although more difficult to quantify, the priorities and values of society as a whole may also bring pressure to bear on individuals. Dr Archibald Hart, a Christian psychologist, describes our culture as 'adrenaline-addicted . . . we worship work and high-energy play; we despise rest and sleep. But we pay for this imbalance with more headaches, ulcers, heart disease and depression than most other cultures.'[2]

The antidote

So, a young person who feels depressed may be experiencing a combination of pressures and worries, and will react differently according to his or her personality and circumstances. But what about the solutions? Is the best advice: 'Hang on, don't let yourself go, 'cause everybody hurts sometimes . .

.' ('Everybody Hurts' by R.E.M.)? Dr Sigman suggests keeping a journal or talking to someone: 'brothers, sisters, parents, teachers, aunts, uncles, GPs and even your vicar(!) can be helpful in making you feel happier'.

Although such suggestions are useful, don't we as Christians have far more to offer as an antidote to depression? In a word, it is 'hope'. When everything around us is in a state of flux, our unchanging God offers stability and security. However desperate the world situation may appear, our God is sovereign. When it feels as if nobody cares for us, or that we have got to earn love and approval, our God loves us unconditionally. When society values only what we do and what we can achieve, our God values us for what we are and offers the possibility of change, not based on magazine 'quick fix' solutions, but on Jesus and the transforming power of the Holy Spirit.

God has not left us in a moral vacuum, but rather he has given us a clear framework on which to base our decisions. The statistics are a clear call to counter the popular 'whatever you decide is right' culture, by teaching God's guidelines for relationships, sexual behaviour, what we do with our bodies and so on, and by helping show our young people how to apply them to real life. One of the sobering things about the statistics is that young people who attend church regularly are also prone to feelings of depression and relationship worries. Church attendance helps, but it does not completely cure the problem. Perhaps we have been teaching what we think our church youth groups ought to know rather than finding out what they really want to know? Perhaps we have weighed our young people down with what they ought to be doing, so that they feel guilty, resentful and inadequate rather than joyful and free!

The message of this survey is surely also that we must allow space for building relationships and an accepting environment in which young people are valued and can 'grow'; in which they can share experiences and feelings beyond the purely superficial. If Dr Hart is correct in concluding that depression can be the result of an over-active lifestyle, perhaps we need to vary the pace of our programme. Is it always fast, challenging, and 'high-tech'? Or are there quieter, more reflective times? Here, perhaps, is why Taizé-style worship has become popular among young Christians.

One final question is this: as many youth leaders rush from one committee to the next and turn up at youth groups absolutely frazzled, what messages do we ourselves give about handling pressure?!

References

1. Aric Sigman, *Getting Physical—A Teenage Health Guide*, BBC, 1992, pages 79 and 86.
2. Archibald D. Hart, *Stress and Your Child*, Word, 1992, page 110.

I am worried about how I get on with other people

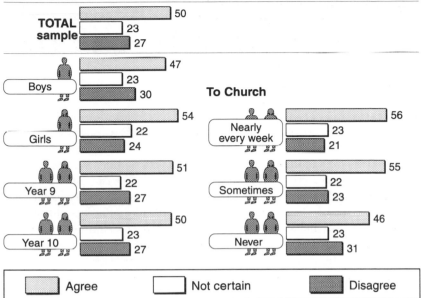

Source: Teenage Religion and Values Survey of 13,000 pupils in England and Wales. All figures refer to responses to the statement immediately above this diagram. The left hand column shows, at the top, the responses of the total sample which is divided, in the middle, into responses of year 9 and year 10 pupils. The right hand column deals only with the 11% of the total sample who attend church.

24 Maggie Everett
Someone To Call On

As a twelve- to thirteen-year-old, I remember the feelings of great anticipation on a Tuesday morning when I knew that at break time I would be very daring. Hitherto I very rarely went against what my parents said, but for the past few weeks I had succumbed to temptation. Despite being told by my mother that she did not approve, I had been reading *Jackie*, the magazine that every teenage girl had to read—and I was not going to be left out! The stories were filled with romantic incidents; but I usually left out the articles and went immediately to the ... 'Dear Cathy and Claire' problem page. There is something very appealing in reading about other people's problems. Often there are answers to questions you had yourself but were too afraid to ask; or horizons are broadened when issues are talked about of which you were totally ignorant. My teenage years are long gone, but problem pages within teenage magazines are still going strong and with them comes the realization that the desperation facing many teenagers today is due, at least in part, to a society which presents confusing messages:

> *There is an absence of truth in today's society; a spiritual vacuum in which young people are confused by the many messages coming at them within our multi-faith culture. In the face of rapid social, economic and political change, family breakdown, unemployment and homelessness, which has left a generation of young people adrift in society, the church has been seen as largely irrelevant and has not provided the role models that young people need. Instead they have turned to their peers, their idols and the video arcades. There is nothing which is giving young people a sense of purpose. Consequently a widespread personal emptiness has resulted. The vitality, dreams and exuberance of youth have been dissipated and drained by a society which no longer values them.[1]*

If this is true, then more than ever young people need to know that there is truth to be found; being loved and accepted for who they are is possible and a purpose for living can be discovered.

Suicide

Sadly, many never find this out. Statistics suggest that about 120 teenagers commit suicide each year:

Over the period of 1987–1990 in England and Wales, suicide accounted for 12 per cent of injury deaths in the 15–19 age group . . . The suicide rate for young men aged 15–19 years has climbed steadily since the mid-1970s, whereas the rate for women has remained fairly constant . . . by 1990 there were over four times as many men. The increase in suicides is thought to be related to social changes over the past two decades.[2]

Although suicide appears to be rare in children aged twelve or younger, instances begin to rise significantly after the age of fourteen. This analysis concludes that where external support appears to be weak or faltering in the life of a teenager, this can lead to suicidal behaviour:

The sources of support become shaky foundations. When the foundations become shaky, some young people turn to alcohol and other drugs for solace. These agents, when mixed with a teenager's romantic notions of death, a society which glorifies violence and easy access to the means of suicide, combine into a powerfully lethal mixture that spells death for more and more adolescents. Finally, suicide begets suicide. Suicide attempted or completed plants the idea of self-generated death in the minds of others. Also, suicide in the family especially pulls other family members to that option.[3]

While this is a somewhat simplified view, utter hopelessness, helplessness and loss of self-esteem are common in the psychological picture of the adolescent suicide. It is difficult to believe that these perspectives are arrived at overnight! Given the ready and immediate access to the larger world around them, through global communication in the developed world, teenagers are presented with a world-view which focuses on negative incidents such as disasters, which can lead to a sense of hopelessness. Believing that there is no future for them in a world where tragedy and suffering are prevalent can influence those who are already experiencing pain and struggle in their own life. Adolescence is a period of introspection, as a sense of personal identity is sought that establishes who the adolescent is as an integrated individual in each life role, someone who is separate and different from every other person. This apparent self-absorption often causes young people to shy away from the advice, opinions, values and beliefs of adults in their world, because these are counted as irrelevant and meaningless. Many struggle to work out how to respond to life, adopting values that are opposed to their parents' values, questioning everything and often developing views which underrate (or at times overrate) themselves.

Social groups

How critical it is that young people have the opportunity to see for themselves the reality of God's love in action! Where few, if any, Christian values are seen in the lives of people around them, a true understanding of the Christian faith is unlikely to be gained. The world of the adolescent is exceedingly small. The predominant influences upon their development are concentrated in relationships within the immediate family and circle of friends, and those who enter their world through school and social settings. The process of establishing committed and intimate relationships also starts during this phase of life, as adolescents begin to learn how to relate to others in their own right, based on their own judgements and opinions of others.

One of the key influences upon the teenager's development is that of his or her peers. 'Gangs' are often formed, especially among boys, and here self-esteem is related to the esteem in which an individual is held by his group. Group identification among girls is also important, although rather than a gang, which has a distinct structure, friendship between individuals takes precedence, and a group of girls may disintegrate more quickly than a gang of boys. It is often to their friends that teenagers will turn first when experiencing difficulties. Peer counselling (where older teenagers are trained to help groups of younger teenagers to talk through problems in order to find help) is one area in which teenagers could be helped to help themselves. Encouraging teenagers to take on responsibility for helping others is a positive way of facilitating their personal growth, as well as developing effective support. Where teenagers recognize that others have experienced struggles in their lives (and such information only comes through talking with others!) they are more willing to listen to ways of dealing with the issues they face.

Someone to talk to

Providing the appropriate means of support—where teenagers can feel secure, accepted, able to talk about how they feel and know they are being listened to by people who will know how to deal with the problems they express—is something which the church as yet has largely failed to do. This is often because the myth that adults cannot relate to teenagers (unless they are specifically gifted in this area) is believed! There is almost an expectation that 'no one relates to a teenager', often due to the fact that teenagers are pushing previously accepted boundaries in behaviour and questioning the *status quo*, and are no longer willing to tolerate attitudes and behaviour in others that do not match up to what that person says.

Perhaps this myth is one of the reasons why Childline is used by so many young people. Childline was launched in October 1986 and in the period between 1 April 1992 and 31 March 1993, 79,127 children and young people were counselled. Of this number, 62,989 were girls, outweighing by far the number of boys ringing Childline (16,138). This tendency for girls to verbalize their need for help more than boys is reflected in the Teenage Religion and Values Survey, where 41 per cent of the girls questioned agreed that they often long for someone to turn to for advice, as opposed to 29 per cent of the boys. The fact that Childline claims that BT figures reveal that many more attempted calls are made each day than are able to get through indicates there is a need for young people to have someone to turn to.

Many already have those people in their lives whom they trust and who are able to help; many are reluctant to turn to adults because their experience of adults is at best that they are inadequate and at worst that they are abusive. As early as 1904, G. Stanley Hall, an American psychologist, wrote that adolescence is a time of life characterized by 'storm and stress'.[4]

Identity

If the external world of today's adolescents is in a permanent state of change, this can only add to the pressure that is felt by a teenager who is undergoing extreme internal turbulence. Developing a sense of personal identity is critical to being able to develop intimate relationships with others, as well as being able to make effective decisions about life. In order to realize the potential of personal identity there are several parts to the process. First of all, there needs to be a 'self-ideal' to work towards. Children are hero worshippers and this often carries over into adolescence. As the young person matures, the object of the hero worship and the young person become more closely intertwined as those characteristics that are seen as attainable are emulated.

As the teenager's ability to assess and think in abstract terms develops, so does their sense of identity as they ask the question 'What or who do I want to be?' It is during this phase of development that Christian adults can have a profound effect upon the lives of young people. Adults displaying those qualities and characteristics to which the young person would aspire become role models. While children are enraptured by the supernatural antics of figures like 'Superman', teenagers aspire to achieving great things that will test their abilities. Many teenagers want to become the best, and will strive after attaining this. This is not confined to tasks. Values and personal qualities are emulated too.

Teenagers are looking for people who are genuine, those who have gained maturity and are the same on the inside as well as the outside! Insincerity and hypocrisy will not gain the respect of a young person who can see through the lack of reality. In a world where we talk of accepting others as they are, the reality is often far from that. It is much easier to be critical and judgemental of others because we feel bad about ourselves. Raising awareness about ourselves and dealing with those issues is the prelude to dealing with others. Where adults are prepared to be vulnerable about their struggles, the sincerity that is demonstrated will have a profound effect upon the young person, and will gain his or her respect. Where the self-evaluation of the teenager is inaccurate and negative, this is often due to a gap in their perception of their ideal self and the real self. This negative view can easily lead to turning away from life in despair, feeling incompetent and worthless, resulting in rebellious aggression or repression of these feelings.

If these negative views become resolved attitudes, this can lead to overcompensation in other wide-ranging types of behaviour. The formation of value judgements is part of the process of moral development and, whereas younger adolescents are in the phase that Kohlberg defines as 'pre-moral'—where 'right' is what I am rewarded for and 'wrong' brings punishment—many early teenagers have developed to the 'conventional or role-conformity' level. During this phase, external standards are beginning to influence decisions. 'Good' people do 'right', and obedience to the law are hallmarks of the value judgements made. It is important to note here that although during the search for personal identity the influence of parents is often rejected, the values held by the family have the greatest influence upon the moral development of the young person. For many young people who are searching for love and acceptance, the church has the potential to provide a supportive and caring environment where family, as God intends it, is demonstrated and the reality of his love is evident.

References

1. Summary, 'Strategy for the 1990s', Youth for Christ (internal document), 1993.
2. Woodroffe, Glickham, Barker and Power, Children, Teenagers and Health: The Key Data, Open University Press, 1993, pages 68–69.
3. Blackburn, 'What You Should Know about Suicide'in *Children, Teenagers and Health: The Key Data.*
4. G. Stanley Hall, *Adolescence: Its Psychology and Its Relations to Physiology, Anthropology, Sex, Crime, Religion and Education,* Volume 1, New York, Appleton, 1904.

I often long for someone to turn to for advice

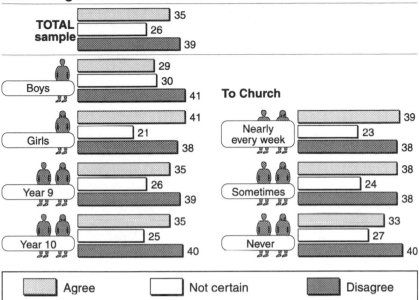

	Agree	Not certain	Disagree

Source: Teenage Religion and Values Survey of 13,000 pupils in England and Wales. All figures refer to responses to the statement immediately above this diagram. The left hand column shows, at the top, the responses of the total sample which is divided, in the middle, into responses of year 9 and year 10 pupils. The right hand column deals only with the 11% of the total sample who attend church.

25 Dave Roberts
Media Madness

Television is perhaps the most significant cultural form to have a daily impact on the lives of teenagers. As the Teenage Religion and Values Survey indicates, more than 80 per cent of those questioned watch television most days of the week. Given that the leisure time at the end of a school day is likely to be six hours, the giving over of at least two hours to television by 65 per cent clearly presents television as a primary cultural input.

These figures do not take account of the potential impact of other electronic media delivered via a screen (these might include educational materials at school, for instance, and computer games at home). They do, however, take on great significance when one begins to consider the quality of information likely to pass between the young person and their parents. Watching television and different work patterns (particularly when both parents are working) significantly affect mealtimes—traditionally occasions for family interaction and, through conversation, exerting influence on young people's views of the world. While the parent-young person communication may be measured in seconds, the young person is absorbing the values of the wider culture for two or three hours a day. This is likely to diminish a little with older teens, with sixteen- to twenty-four-year-olds being the lightest television viewers. But for the younger teenagers considered in this survey, television may be almost all-consuming. Outside the home, teenagers have more limited social opportunities in terms of public houses, clubs and so on, and they also have limited funds.

The role of television in shaping social attitudes and the young person's world-view cannot, however, be considered in isolation from the wider culture. Other cultural forms that influence young people in the United Kingdom include magazines such as *Mizz, Just 17, Viz, Sky* and *Judge Dredd*. Teenagers are also significant consumers of video games. These provide a complex culture, but there are significant sales of 'beat-em-up, shoot-em-up' games, along with the role-playing 'dungeons and dragons' activities. Games such as 'Mortal Kombat' have earned their reputation through their explicit electronic visual gore. The role-play genre often has explicit occult themes and will familiarize users with occult folklore, possibly prompting further exploration. Television is also a carrier for two other key youth interests, sport and music.

While some readers of this book may value a detailed analysis of the content of contemporary youth culture, it may serve us better to equip ourselves with the tools of discernment and to pass that understanding on to the young people we deal with. Three questions need to be asked. How do these media convey their key messages? If this media culture changes or shapes attitudes, how does it do so? Is there a broad principle which helps us understand the ideas of contemporary culture?

The dominant method of communication in youth culture is through parable or story. Avid consumers of peak-time dramas such as 'Neighbours', 'Emmerdale Farm' and 'Brookside' see groups of fictitious people in artificially dramatic lifestyles. These television characters may, however, be in similar social situations to the viewer and facing similar problems in terms of relationships or jobs, and confronting similar major life-issues such as abortion or sexual orientation. Exploration of a lesbian sub-plot in widely-viewed soap operas such as 'Emmerdale Farm' and 'Brookside' powerfully legitimize a similar choice by a teenage viewer. The parable form is also strong in role-play games, and in comics such as *Viz* and *Judge Dredd*.

Another mode of cultural interaction involves the 'eavesdropping' syndrome. In the problem pages of *Sky* and *Just Seventeen*, the reader 'listens in' to the problems of others and may find them relevant to his or her own everyday struggles or questions. Many girls, particularly, obtain a good deal of their sexual guidance from these pages, together with peer-group conversations.

In a visually literate age, symbolism and imagery will often convey a wealth of non-verbal messages to the viewer. Much popular video culture is not so much orientated towards story as towards the most vivid representation possible of signifiers—items of clothing, hairstyles, backdrops, absurd images. Behind a haircut or a shirt style often lie several other attitudes or cultural habits. U2, a leading rock band, worked hard with photographer Anton Corbijn and various image consultants to develop the visual aspect of the heroic pilgrimage that was at the core of their album, *Rattle and Hum*. Their own questions about life, knowledge, image and meaning are reflected in random, disjointed imagery—from their *Achtung Baby* album onwards. It is possible to connect up clothes, drugs, politics, and eating habits if you are knowledgeable enough. Think of several band or youth culture movements, then go through the list above for each one.

With these varied routes for cultural messages in mind, the Christian youth worker will want to face the tough question: does culture affect people's attitudes and life decisions? This is not a question which one can do justice to in a few hundred words. Suffice it to say that a simplistic analysis that suggests there is a widespread cause and effect relationship between television and crime, for instance, is not very satisfactory.

It might help if we regard the role of media through an advertising metaphor. Television helps create brand names for certain types of behaviour. These can be for good or bad attitudes. Television has created a strong 'premarital sex' brand. When people have the chance to sample the brand, their choice has been legitimized by the understanding that what they are doing is culturally normal. Watching television has not caused them to sin, but it has reinforced their choice to sin. The spark of human sinfulness becomes a flame of personal rebellion as the paraffin of social revolt is poured onto it.

If we are to understand the power of the media to affect young people, we must look beyond a correlation with anti-Christian values; we must question the root impact of the vivid lifestyles the media portray.

The concept of idolatry may be helpful here. At the root of the biblical picture of idolatry lies the idea that something that is innocent and neutral, a part of God's creation, becomes an object of worship. People who have turned their back on God will seek to find their security, joy and meaning elsewhere. Innocent elements, such as creative dress, good food, the joy of sex with a life-long partner, the blessings of hard work, money, or good stewardship, become obsessions. The values associated with idolatry are to do with a perverse non-Christian perfectionism—perfect body, sex, home, clothes, and relationships. The tele-evangelists of secular revolt batter the fragile identities of their teenage audience with invitations to come to the altars of consumerism, to drink of the waters of the beauty myth and worship at the altar of sexual gratification.

The trouble is, the people remain thirsty. The Christian youth worker, working with both the churched and the non-Christian young person, will want to help others learn to discern and to find their ultimate security and value systems in their acceptance by God, through the work of Christ.

Making sense of faith in a mass-media age means that more than ever there must be a deliberateness about our youth work. A responsible Christian ethic will seek to affirm God's good creation, while acknowledging that it can be corrupted by sin and rebellion. The young Christian, aware of the broad sweep of Christian truth, can then engage the culture, using the media to express different aspects of the Christian world-view which permeate every sphere of their thinking.

We should be in no doubt that those who have a Christian world-view are more than capable of being culture-formers, telling their own parables and helping Christian truths trickle down through society, just as the grassroots Christian community complement it with the 'trickle up' work of local relational evangelism.

Some will have a subversive, underground input. Manchester's Christian house band, World Wide Message Tribe, has seen 1,000 young people commit themselves to explore the Christian faith in the past twelve months. They are virtually unknown outside Manchester. Others will have international recognition, such as Nick Park, the creator of the Oscar-winning 'Wallace and Gromit'. The Scottish music scene is dominated by bands with Christian members. These include Runrig, Proclaimers, Deacon Blue and Wet, Wet, Wet. The media is not an evil place. It is often dominated, however, by people with idolatry on their minds. Young people with biblical vision can learn to reject its blandishments and create alternative ways to reinforce truth, goodness and patience—even in an age of 'I know what I want, and I want it now!'

Last week, how much television did you watch?

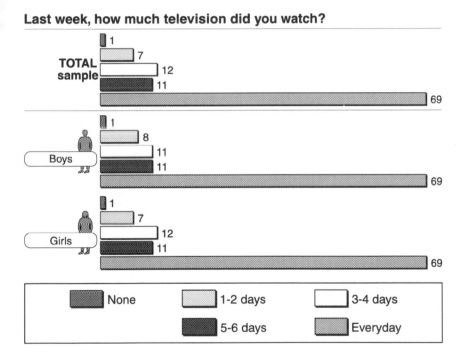

Source: Teenage Religion and Values Survey of 13,000 pupils in England and Wales. All figures refer to responses to the statement immediately above this diagram. The left hand column shows, at the top, the responses of the total sample which is divided, in the middle, into responses of year 9 and year 10 pupils. The right hand column deals only with the 11% of the total sample who attend church.

26 John Allan
Happy Families

Well, I knew that he was mine, so I gave him all the love that I had. And someday soon I'll take him home, to meet my Mum and my Dad.

So sang the Crystals in 1963. If things were getting serious with a boyfriend, the family had to meet him. Even if you defied them, your parents remained an important, reassuring, stabilizing force in your life.

Thirty years on, everything has changed. In the United Kingdom, according to J. Haskey's 'Children in Families Broken by Divorce',[1] one child in four experiences family breakdown before turning sixteen. Some sixteen-year-olds leave home as soon as possible anyway, while others are forced out by economic pressures. Most are simply seeking independence. But each year, 80,000 young people affected by divorce also lose their relationship with the 'non-custodial' parent.

For those who stay at home, life is often far from peaceful. More than a quarter of parents think their children are 'out of control'. A third of the parents questioned said that they had difficulty in coping with their children's disobedience.

When advertising executives from the agency Gold Greenlees Trott examined youthful consumer trends in order to predict the spending patterns of the 1990s, they soon became convinced that they were dealing with a different kind of young person from anything that had been seen before. The reason, they said, was that they were 'the children of the most divorced, least child-oriented generation of parents ever':

> *People who have gone through emotional traumas in their lives bring a more realistic, down-to-earth approach to the problems of life. They don't fall in love easily, and they are cautious about entering into new relationships.*
>
> *Their attitudes towards other people are reflected by their attitudes towards the products and services they consume . . . The emotionally scarred children of the 1980s are growing up into the 1990s with a similar, once-bitten twice-shy attitude to life.*

The same research showed that young people are becoming more concerned

134

about personal success than ever before. More than half of the boys interviewed wanted to have more money than their parents; and 49 per cent of both sexes believed that 'looking after number one' was the right philosophy of life.

At the same time, researchers from another advertising agency, McCann-Erickson, were asking 8,000 young people from ten different countries to pick the three things they felt 'most important in people's personal lives'. The United Kingdom results showed that 'success' had reached the top five for the first time (in the 1970s, 'health', 'honesty' and 'kindness' had all been more important), and 'money' was firmly lodged in third place.

Perhaps it is not surprising to see a developing concern with personal success and survival, in a society where the family is notoriously failing to provide a stable centre to life. When the magazine *The Face* brought together some of the latest wave of British rock performers to discuss serious issues, this was part of the conversation:

JUSTINE:

I don't know anyone our age who believes in marriage any more.

SONYA:

People our age seem to get divorced after their first major argument. On the other side of the world, marriage is expected to be for life.

HOOLIGAN:

I'm a bit vague on things like marriage. My parents are separated, so marriage has never been a big part of my life. I just think it's nice to have sex with someone. Commitment's a bit of a nightmare. It's hard enough to get your own shit together. I can't think of the future in that way.

RICK:

I'm the same. I've never really had a proper, serious relationship with anyone. I don't know how I'd act in that situation. I don't really want it.

A quick straw poll at this point revealed that, out of a panel of eight, four had divorced parents.

But before we conclude that the family is finished forever, and that young people today are totally alienated from their parents, we need to look at the other side of the picture. Research is also showing that today's young people feel closer to their parents than those parents felt to their own. When girls were asked to nominate the person whom they most admired, the most popular answer by far was 'my mum'. Even in the McCann-Erickson survey mentioned above, British teenagers put 'a happy family' in second place; it was behind 'health', certainly, but ahead of 'money'.

Why is this? Perhaps it reflects the fact that the family is becoming more greatly valued, just because it seems so much more fragile. Young people do not want to be abandoned to their peer group; instead they want a reliable relationship with parents who are happy to be adults, rather than constantly attempting to stay young themselves and evade the responsibilities of maturity.

In the Teenage Religion and Values Survey, young people were asked to agree or disagree with the statements 'I find it helpful to talk about my problems with my father' and 'I find it helpful to talk about my problems with my mother'. Mothers came out better—51 per cent compared with 31 per cent for fathers—which clearly reflects the fact that the mother still tends to be the constant presence in the household. Absent fathers (whether divorced, overworking or just down at the pub) continue to present a major problem for British families.

Churches should be concerned. If 47 per cent of the young people who are in church every week do not find it helpful to talk about problems with their father, and a further 23 per cent are non-committal about it, then there is a major defect in the parenting which Christian families are providing for their teenagers. (Ironically, those who *never* go to church reported a slightly better relationship with their fathers.) Youth workers are keenly aware how limited their chances are with teenagers compared with the influence the parents of teenagers have. Unless the church is able to persuade parents to *parent*, there won't be much its youth workers can do.

Sue Slipman, of the National Council for One-Parent Families, believes that society's changing expectations are intensifying the problem:

> *Women's aspirations have changed but these have not been matched by changes in male patterns of parenting . . . In many families men are no longer breadwinners and there is little prospect of permanent jobs for young men. They have not found a new role within the family as joint carers and are not getting the message from their fathers that this is a desirable or do-able development. They have none of the traditional routes into adulthood—and have not developed any new ones.*

It is interesting that more boys than girls would talk to their father, and more girls than boys would talk to their mother. Perhaps it shows that teenagers do want a model, rather than just a confidante. In a world where growing up is complicated by more choices and pitfalls than ever before, young people need a living demonstration of how to make those choices and survive well.

Teenagers were also asked to respond to the statement 'My parents do not agree with most of the things I do in my leisure time'. More than half of both sexes disagreed; there was little difference between boys and girls, or between older and younger teenagers. But a sizeable proportion (including, alarmingly, one-third of those who go to church every week) were just not sure. Perhaps parents are not giving as clear signals of their approval or disapproval as they should.

Teenagers still want to shock; the generation gap is not yet dead! In a recent television programme in which a large group of teenagers had been assembled to talk about sex, several of them explained (with no dissenting voices) that to have sex before sixteen was very important—because it was illegal. After that, it was 'no big deal any more'. And just as many older people seem finally to be realizing that smoking is dangerous, only one group in British society is actually smoking *more*: those aged between fourteen and twenty-one.

But teenage rebellion is only part of the story. At heart, teenagers still want to be respected and esteemed by their parents. They want to be given a pattern they can follow and principles they can test out. Not many are so isolated or alienated that they have lost sight of that desire.

What implications does this have for churches? First, it is important that Christians should give the family the importance that God does. A good deal of the Old Testament laws were devoted to facilitating and regulating relationships inside families; and the New Testament treats the family with no less respect and attention, even if its primary focus is God's new family, the church. Ever since creation, said Jesus (Matthew 19:4), marriage and the family have been at the heart of God's matrix for human life and relationships.

Our youth work must therefore strengthen the family. Youth work must not be left to a few specialists, who take the teenagers off on their own until they grow up and become human beings again. Instead, it must involve growing relationships of respect and appreciation between teenagers and people of every age group in the church. Furthermore, the youth worker must do everything possible to strengthen teenagers' appreciation of, and contribution to, their own families. (All too often, it is the opposite: a lively youth group becomes a refuge from quarrels at home; a youth leader becomes a sounding-board for irritations with Mum and Dad which really ought to be faced up to by the family concerned.)

This means that we need to come alongside Christian parents who are clearly not doing their job—to confront, if necessary, but most importantly to communicate the fact that both youth worker and parent are doing the same job. Both want the same good things for the young people. By cooperating, rather than competing, they are more likely to see results.

It also means that our busy, overburdened churches must not be allowed to destroy family life by sucking adult free time into endless committees and interminable meetings. It means that the structures of our churches have to give a responsible place to young people, and reflect the importance we truly believe they have. On the other hand, it means that we must not worship young people either, and put them on a pedestal, but expect them increasingly to accept the disciplines of responsible, mature, Christian living.

So much for families within the church. But what of young people who come from families over which we have no influence? We need to be prepared for the fact that many young people today have very little grasp of 'relational grammar': they just do not know how to behave in a close relationship with an adult. The only real relationships some teenagers enjoy with adults are commercial ones.

137

Sue Slipman also said:

There is a need in the modern world to develop the emotional literacy of the young. They need to understand what is happening to them to absorb the changes in their lives and overcome their pain . . . Life skills may well now be the most valuable thing we can give young people.

Today, as never before, youth work is more about building friendships, winning confidence, and dealing with the individual, than it is about running programmes or teaching Bible lessons. The massive youth groups of the 1960s are (with some honourable exceptions) a thing of the past. Youth work tends to be small-scale, less programmed and much more intimate.

Don Posterski, whose observation of Canadian teenagers is noted for its shrewdness, has remarked that young people today tend to relate to one another in 'clusters'—small groups of two or three very close friends—rather than in a large group. This is probably a reflection of the fact that many are searching for trusting relationships among their peers because they cannot find them in their own families. Whatever the reason, the phenomenon is real, and we need to take note of this in the way we shape our work.

Calling a young person to follow Christ as an individual, without paying attention to his or her closest cluster of friends, may be asking him or her to pay an unacceptably vast social price. Winning clusters, rather than individuals, may be a much more rewarding strategy. And because we need to see young people in context, we need to know about their families as well as their 'clusters'; without prying, the more we can gain a picture of their home life, the more appropriately we will be able to offer friendship.

In some cases, our youth work will need to provide something of what is lacking in the family. Jay Kesler has told how, back in the 1950s, Youth for Christ USA discovered that there were three kinds of teenagers they were trying to reach: 'A kids' (churched teenagers with whom they were very successful); 'B kids' (friends of the churched teenagers, close in outlook and social world, and also very successfully contacted); and 'C kids' (teenagers outside the kind of social environment which Christians inhabited, and out of touch with the church). YFC was having little success with 'C kids' because its whole strategy was 'teen on teen'—using Christian teenagers to reach others—and that worked well with 'Bs' but not with 'Cs'.

We then tried to find out how we could go about reaching 'C' kids. We discovered one very interesting result in their survey. They indicated that the special group of people to whom they go when they want an answer to a question are what the survey called 'empathetic, caring young adults'. So we began to take our staff, most of them raised in the evangelical hothouse, and try to get them to go and reach such high-school-aged kids with the gospel. They found this very threatening. But eventually we invented some vehicles . . . We saw many 'C' kids come to Christ, but it was not through our method of youth to youth. Rather they came to Christ as 'caring young adults' related to them.

In the United States in the 1950s, 'C kids' were a minority. In Britain today, 'C kids' represent 90 per cent of all teenagers; and they are looking for precisely the same qualities in us as their forerunners looked for in Kesler's day. This asks a great deal of a youth worker—much more than organizing an exciting term's programme, or putting together the perfect house party. But if we are to serve British young people effectively, nothing less is adequate.

References

1. J. Haskey, 'Children in Families Broken by Divorce', in *Population Trends*, 1990.

I find it helpful to talk about my problems with my mother

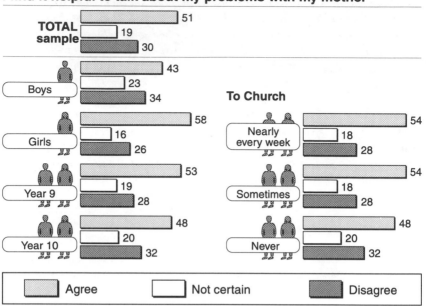

I find it helpful to talk about my problems with my father

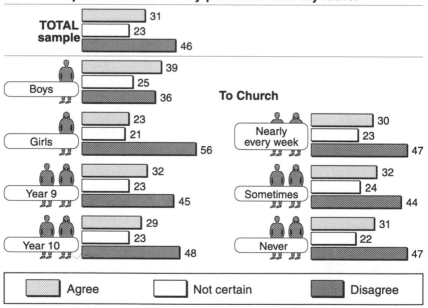

My parents do not agree with most of the things I do in my leisure time

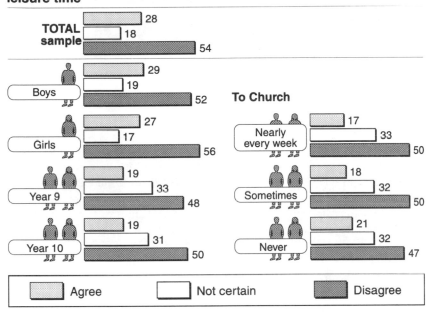

TOTAL sample
- 28
- 18
- 54

Boys
- 29
- 19
- 52

Girls
- 27
- 17
- 56

Year 9
- 19
- 33
- 48

Year 10
- 19
- 31
- 50

To Church

Nearly every week
- 17
- 33
- 50

Sometimes
- 18
- 32
- 50

Never
- 21
- 32
- 47

| Agree | Not certain | Disagree |

Source: Teenage Religion and Values Survey of 13,000 pupils in England and Wales. All figures refer to responses to the statement immediately above this diagram. The left hand column shows, at the top, the responses of the total sample which is divided, in the middle, into responses of year 9 and year 10 pupils. The right hand column deals only with the 11% of the total sample who attend church.

141

27 Phil Wall

The Question of Abortion

If you are reading this chapter and were born in the United Kingdom after 1967, you are part of what is increasingly known as the 'abortion' generation. The abortion generation is characterized by something that has not been true of any other generation of people: you are only alive because someone chose to let you live. Prior to the Abortion Bill in 1967, the number of abortions per year both in hospitals and back-street clinics had been estimated at 2,200 in England and Wales. Since then, the floodgates have opened and more than 3.7 million abortions have been conducted—the vast majority of which have had very little to do with the health of mother or child.[1]

One point about this article is that it is written by a man. So often throughout history, decisions have been made by men that have had far-reaching consequences on women. Many of those decisions have been made in ignorance, often with prejudice, regarding the welfare and well-being of the female population. Consequently, I am very aware of the sensitive caution needed in a limited male perspective. Nevertheless, it is total nonsense to say that men have no right to comment on an issue they cannot directly experience. It makes about as much sense as saying that people who are not South African have no right to comment on the injustice of the previous apartheid system in South Africa.

Another point concerns the direction of this chapter. At the end of the chapter, there are addresses of organizations that can provide medical and legal information; and there are details of in-depth, expert analyses of abortion issues. The focus in the next few paragraphs will therefore be on the thinking processes and world-view of most young people questioned in the Teenage Religion and Values Survey. This mind-set is rarely dealt with, but it must be addressed if we are going to equip young Christians to think intelligently, and help them challenge other world-views on abortion in the market-place of faith and ethics.

Where are we?

Until the philosophical period known as the Enlightenment (in the eighteenth century), the authority of the Bible—and more specifically the teaching of priests regarding the Bible—went almost unquestioned within European society. To secure your authority in any discussion or debate, you referred to the Word of God and the perspective of those who studied that Word. One of the results of the Enlightenment was a revolution in thinking which began to strip biblical thinking and biblical characters of that previous authority. This occurred for a number of reasons, not least of which was the previous abuse of power by religious institutions to enforce beliefs and protect the *status quo*. The religious establishment had vigorously persecuted those like Galileo, for example, who argued for a completely different working of the solar system.

During the period of the Enlightenment, people began to question previously-held absolutes and to strip religious dogma of its authority. This began in earnest a process of secularization of prevailing religious beliefs. For example, prior to Enlightenment thinking and the onset of secularism, any debate regarding abortion and the sanctity of life would have been quickly dealt with by a pronouncement that 'the Bible, or church, says such-and-such'. This would have been followed by a theological exposition of God's view on the sanctity of human life, and the discussion would normally have ended there. In modern, post-Enlightenment thinking on this subject—and any other regarding ethics— biblical authority is far from being the greatest authority within our secularized culture. To claim that it is can actually be the quickest way to lose an argument. A politician recently commented that the easiest way to lose a debate in parliament is to give it moral and ethical overtures. There is today a secular mind-set that causes people to question previously held absolutes dictated by the Word of God.

Another key influence on the modern world-view of abortion has been existentialism. Existentialist ideas were particularly advanced by the French writers, Sartre and Camus. A brief definition of existentialism states that 'existence precedes essence'. In other words, nothing has any meaning or purpose in itself other than that attributed to it by somebody else. Existentialism stresses the fact that things exist without essence (hence the technical term) or meaning. Human life, for instance, has no value until that life is in full existence and can bring meaning to its essence. The individual's opinion and perspective on life and the universe have therefore become the highest authority that there is. The right of an individual woman to an individual choice about her individual body has, it appears, become unquestionable, there being no higher authority than the individual on which to call. Along with the impact of secularism on religious dogma, existentialism has stripped us of moral and ethical absolutes. In other words, there can be no such thing as an absolute right or wrong for an individual other than that which the individual chooses. It follows that this may be different for every individual, and that an absolute morality or ethic regarding the sanctity of life cannot exist. It is up to every individual to move from 'inauthentic existence' to 'authentic existence'.

The consequence of these two key influences—secularism and existentialism—is first that, when considering the issue of abortion, there are no religious, ethical or moral absolutes that most people in Britain can call on to give them guidance. All of these have been stripped of their authority. Second, freedom of individual choice has become the ultimate plumb-line by which all such issues are judged. In the lives and thinking of young people, this works itself out along the lines of, 'it's up to her', 'she must do what she feels is right', and 'nobody has the right to tell anybody what they should do'. Listen to any conversation on abortion among young adults, and the same comments will be heard.

Before moving to a critique of these philosophies, however, we must step back to look at the results and the confusion that they bring. The following is not a justification of actions taken by individuals but purely a comment on the confusion that so many young people feel. Recently, a doctor from an abortion clinic was killed by pro-life campaigners for taking the life of thousands of children via surgical removal. The following public outcry was significant as people from both sides of the debate condemned such violence. Knowing this, young adults may well be excused for their confusion living in a country like Britain or America who, with limited hesitation, committed billions of pounds and the lives of many thousands of forces personnel to protect the freedom of a relatively small number of Kuwaiti citizens from abuse and domination by an alien power seeking to limit their choices of self-determination. With the presence of such confusion, and with so many young adults within our culture holding such diverse opinions, it is now important to bring in a rational and biblical critique of the modern world-view behind it all.

The challenge

We must be equipped to challenge the secularism which has stripped biblical belief of its authority. This may be done in a number of ways. First, if someone claims to have the authority to dismiss biblical authority, an obvious question to ask is by what authority do they make that claim. Nine times out of ten they will say the Bible is not true or that it is historically inaccurate. These statements must be challenged strongly, and in any discussion on the issue we must ask people to wrestle with their authority for their belief. We must also challenge the reasons for dismissing the Bible's validity. At this point we will have done, and have encouraged other young people to do, the hard work of having a strong Christian apologetic for scripture. Of course, some people reading this chapter may not use the Bible in this way. If so, they, too, need to examine the unique authority of the Bible, constantly reinforced as it is by new historical and archaeological evidence.

Many people make huge 'authoritative' statements regarding the Bible's inaccuracy. It is important to encourage people to articulate the reasons for such views and tease out the actual depth of their objections. All statements are made from some kind of authoritative base, and we must challenge people to justify theirs and identify the validity of such authority.

Another area of existential thought also needs challenging. It is one expressed not only in the lives of young people but of many older Christians as well, and it concerns how people 'feel'. In so many situations today, how an individual feels about life or a certain course of action appears to be the strongest influence in the decision-making process, rather than the absolute of God's word—for example, 'I don't feel like witnessing' or 'I don't feel like caring for the poor and the needy'. Since when was how you feel about something relevant in obeying the commands of God? Too often, many of us slip into existential theology which we claim as our own, rather than discipleship. Mature people live by their responsibilities, not by their feelings.

The greatest challenge, however, concerns the issue of absolutes themselves. I was once in a university speaking with the head of the philosophy society prior to a debate he and I were going to be having the next day. I commented to him that I thought the field of philosophy was crucial in the area of ethics, because so often the absence of absolutes left people swimming around in a sea of relativism with really no idea of where to go. He turned to me with a wry smile and commented that I had identified the weakest problem with Christianity, in that we believed in absolutes when there actually was no such thing as an absolute and that was our problem. 'Are you saying to me there is absolutely no such thing as an absolute?' I asked. I wasn't trying to smug or clever, and we were able to talk quite seriously about the difficulty of claiming there is no such thing as an absolute, which in itself is an absolute statement.

For abortion on demand to be justifiable, there must be shown to be no absolute morality banning such actions. This view is held by many, dismissing the existence of absolutes as Judeo-Christian legalism. The problem is that such statements are in themselves absolutes, the very thing many people seek to deny. So often, female abortion on demand is justified on the grounds that it is the absolute right of the individual to make a choice; and it is at this point that we need to challenge the authority of the statement and, having established the existence of absolutes, begin to encourage people to discover what the real ones are and who made them.

The above is in no way a definitive response. But if it is taken seriously, and some hard work is done in study, it can provide not only security for the young Christian in believing what to do about abortion, but it can also stand in the market-place of beliefs as a viable challenge to so much of what is believed in our culture. Hard work has never been that popular, but let us never forget that this is an issue of life and death.

Finally, we must always remember that in dealing with this important subject we are not concerned with some empty philosophical debate, but the lives of real human beings. If people choose to reject the 'pro-life' perspective and go through with abortion, we must consider their viewpoint, not their worth as individuals. It is often after someone has actually had an abortion that they are is most in need of the love of Christ and his people. Moreover, if we are going to teach and defend certain ethics we must be willing to support those who are persuaded by it and who subsequently face a lifetime of bringing up a child on their own. Too often, our commitment to an intellectual ethic is greater than our commitment to the action it requires of us. May I also add that I hope and pray that my words have not caused injury or hurt to those reading this, knowing that the question of abortion is far more than a chapter in a book.

List of resources

CARE Campaign 53 Romney Street London SW1P 3RF
Society for the Protection of the Unborn Child 7 Tufton Street Westminster London SW1P 3QN

References

1. Statistics from *OPCS Monitor* AB 94/1, 'Trends in Abortion' No. 64, and *Population Trends No. 71.*

Abortion is wrong

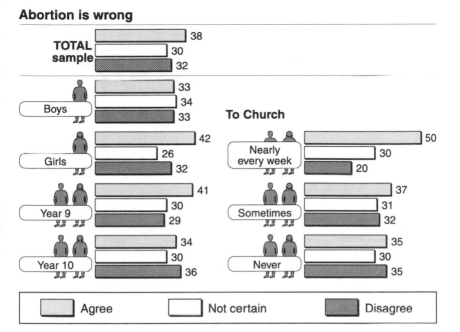

TOTAL sample
38
30
32

Boys
33
34
33

Girls
42
26
32

Year 9
41
30
29

Year 10
34
30
36

To Church

Nearly every week
50
30
20

Sometimes
37
31
32

Never
35
30
35

▨ Agree   ☐ Not certain   ▨ Disagree

Source: Teenage Religion and Values Survey of 13,000 pupils in England and Wales. All figures refer to responses to the statement immediately above this diagram. The left hand column shows, at the top, the responses of the total sample which is divided, in the middle, into responses of year 9 and year 10 pupils. The right hand column deals only with the 11% of the total sample who attend church.

28 Dave Roberts
The Wider World

Before the modern age, people knew little of the struggles, pains and pressures of their fellow human beings in other lands. Their primary concern was to ensure that the local despot did not exploit them mercilessly. The problems of the world as a whole seemed remote. The advent of fast travel, the invention of the printing press and the eventual arrival of the electronic media have shrunk the world. These days revolutions are televised. In our own front rooms, we can sit and watch our bombs dropping on someone else's high street.

Curiously, the knowledge of the complexity and brokenness of human life all around the globe seems to paralyse us rather than galvanize us. The Teenage Religion and Values Survey addresses two key responses and illustrates one major facet of the youthful-minded. First, whereas one in four feel powerless to help change the world's problems and one in three are uncertain, 44 per cent are idealistic enough to believe they can change them. Idealism, untainted by cynicism, is alive and well.

What are the roots of the uncertainty among the rest? Some would suggest that in a large, complex society, run by experts and socially fragmented by career mobility, family breakdown and corruption at every level, many individuals feel powerless and alienated. People have no sense of 'ownership' and are at the mercy of socio-economic forces. They can barely change their own private world, let alone help solve the problems of nations. There may also be an element of social Darwinism in their response, a kind of perverted Western version of the Hindu Karma doctrine: if you are in a mess it must be your own fault and, anyway, charity begins at home.

It is significant that the regular church attenders among those surveyed are markedly more hopeful about change. The roots of this must lie in the basic presupposition of active Christianity about the possibility of personal transformation. The potential for change is inherent in the Christian faith. This then trickles over into an idealism about the possibility of change on a larger scale and a sense, derived particularly from the minor prophets in the Old Testament (Amos, Hosea, Micah), that it is part of the church's responsibility to call for change. As church young people become acquainted with church history, it becomes clear that the church and its representatives can bring about change, both by campaigning and through the phenomena of redemption and life! This comes about when large numbers of individuals become Christians and their influence 'trickles up' through society.

A brief look at the social history of the nineteenth century reveals that figures such as Wilberforce and Shaftesbury, both evangelicals, helped bring about an end to slavery, penal reform, and child labour. A host of other socially responsible institutions came into being and their influence trickled down through society.

Contemporary social historians are also suggesting that the growth of evangelical Christianity in Latin America and the lifestyle changes that flow from it are creating a new breed of socially responsible citizens, who will impact the politics and economics of the region for decades to come.

Armed with idealism and stories of past success, and aware of the need to empower others to help themselves discover solutions to political, social and economic woes, there is every reason for the young Christian to be optimistic about his or her contribution to the righting of worldwide wrongs. A theological underpinning is found in the tension or paradox that the young believer understands is at the heart of the Bible. The scriptural descriptions of inhumanity are found in the stories of murder (Cain and Abel), jealousy (Saul and David), and abuse of power (Ahab and Jezebel); and they alert us to the need for realism about the propensity of humankind for evil. A naive idealism about perfectibility through education withers in the face of the biblical record and the brute realities of everyday life.

Wedded to this realism, however, is biblical hope. The Pharisee, Saul, a bitter opponent of the church, changed his ways and his name, and became a pillar of the early Christian community. Josiah, the young but godly king of Israel began to reform the nation at the age of sixteen. Peter, a fallible person who denied his closest friend, became a foundation stone of the worldwide church.

An understanding of the realism-idealism tension spurs on hope, and perhaps also patience and perseverance. Wilberforce worked for forty years to see slavery abolished. The Baptist missionary pioneer William Carey laboured for eight years before seeing significant conversions in India. He spent that time learning about the culture and establishing schools and hospitals that were a 'message' in themselves.

Two tenets underpinning any Christian response to world problems are found in Isaiah 61 and Matthew 25:31–46. The Isaiah passage was cited by Christ and underlines the liberating message of Christianity. The Matthew passage indicates that feeding the hungry, clothing the naked and visiting the prisoner are all aspects of a life of worship. The Christian working with young people is faced with a dual task: how are we to motivate the young Christian, and how do we respond to the pessimism of some unchurched young people alongside the idealism of others?

For the young Christian, we must present a biblical-historical model of local, national and global concern. There is no shortage of material which will aid this process and provide practical hands-on involvement in compassionate acts and campaigns for change (see Chapter 48). For some, involvement comes in projects such as the Christmas Cracker aid and relief project, or the Whose Earth? environmental initiative. With their up-front appeal to act and to change specific situations, these projects can lead them from instinctive compassion into educated action.

Such projects are also a window on the church for the idealistic but unchurched who are challenged by the ethical and spiritual concerns at the root of Christian action. Moreover, they can be a challenge to ethically blunted and pessimistic young people. In a local situation, only the hardest of hearts will refuse to participate in something that will aid others who are suffering. Although some may salve their consciences and soon forget, others may grow to be more sensitive. Projects that give young people responsibility in compassionate service draw on the 'whole person', and can be the means of a shift in their world-view—possibly encouraging them to an exploration of faith.

We need to be clear, however, that the roots of any significant Christian response to youthful passion is through a holistic approach to ministry. The old 'one-note' solutions will not work. It is simply not enough to 'save' or 'fill' young people and hope that everything will flow from there. Although conversion experiences and spiritual hunger do much to motivate, a renewal of the mind is vital. In the case of the unchurched, challenging the popular mind-set is also vital. In terms of world problems this means that any youth programme or dialogue must challenge the fatalism, nihilism, and social Darwinism that is the focus of much popular culture. The average rock music fan will not be entirely optimistic about life, if he or she has drunk from the well of despair so prominent in the lyrics of this musical genre. Invitations to 'Rape Me', celebrations of drug-fuelled escape and disparaging references by such groups as Guns 'n' Roses to 'niggers' and 'faggots' (in their album, 'Use Your Illusion') are hardly calculated to promote positive social attitudes. The explicit violent sex of much rap, particularly NWA's catalogue which often has a four-times-a-minute use of the 'f-word', help to create an egocentric, non-compassionate attitude.

The creation of a mind-set that believes that addressing the world's problems is both right and indeed possible can only be rooted in a willingness to unfold creatively the 'whole counsel of God'. In our youth programmes there must also be a willingness on our part to do the detective work and address the attitudes, both positive and negative, found in popular culture. Nihilism—the philosophy of despair and hopelessness—is simply an abstract philosophical word, until its prominence in popular culture is revealed in the songs of the Rolling Stones or punk rock or, more recently, grunge music. When the young people see how this attitude affects everyday life and the attitudes of peers, they are better equipped to make choices or to respond when they see that attitude in action.

For the young Christian, the wisdom of God can then start to come alive. The positive, life-affirming, realistic but idealistic Christian moves out from a purely individual understanding of faith and can begin to see how God's guidelines for relationships and community are a powerful antidote to all self-centred philosophies. The tasks of the youth leader and the church pastor are clear. If Christian young people are to be world- changers, they must have a broad Christian education. If the non-Christian is to be challenged by the cross, he or she will often need their lifestyle challenged by the ethics of Jesus, creatively applied to contemporary cultural situations.

There is nothing I can do to help solve the world's problems

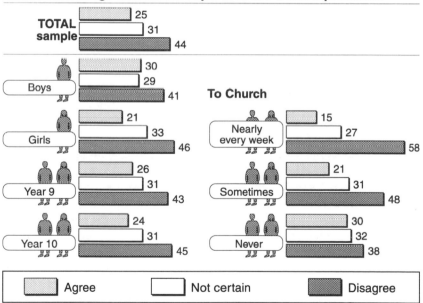

Source: Teenage Religion and Values Survey of 13,000 pupils in England and Wales. All figures refer to responses to the statement immediately above this diagram. The left hand column shows, at the top, the responses of the total sample which is divided, in the middle, into responses of year 9 and year 10 pupils. The right hand column deals only with the 11% of the total sample who attend church.

29 Sue Eccleston
Fantasy

'Tinker, tailor, soldier, sailor, rich man, poor man, beggar man, thief . . .' we chanted as children, pushing our plum-stones across the plate one at a time, trying to find out what type of profession we would have when we grew up!

According to the Teenage Religion and Values Survey, today, 10 per cent more girls than boys agree that fortune-tellers can tell the future. It seems to be generally accepted that girls, on the whole, are more inquisitive than boys about the future and do tend to spend more time thinking about who they might marry or what kind of career they might have. There is an urge within all of us, to a lesser or greater degree, to know what the future holds. There is also a fascination with what we know is there, but know very little about.

The word 'occult' means 'hidden' or 'secret', 'only for the initiated', and 'not known about'! In other words, the occult is not out in the open for all to see, investigate and question. There are a number of different aspects to the occult, and some are seen as less harmful or dangerous than others. Yet they are all part of the dangerous, deceptive, and damaging occult world.

Horoscopes

Horoscopes are probably the most popular aspect of fortune-telling, and probably the most ridiculous! Horoscopes are all about self, what will happen to me today, or this month. Will I be happy? Will I meet Mr or Ms Right? Will I pass my exams?

But although God created stars and planets as part of his design and purpose, to be enjoyed by us, he never intended that we should attempt to consult them about our future. And although there are some very caring people who believe that they are 'helping' others by 'reading' things in the stars, the fact is that this is a major con trick which millions of people have fallen for. Those who profess to tell the future by reading the stars are paid a lot of money to write their predictions for popular papers and magazines. If they sometimes appear to 'get it right', it is only because their predictions are so vague and general that they could mean almost anything! Furthermore, the implication of astrology is that one twelfth of the planet are having a similar sort of day, each day. This is because one-twelfth of the population is born under each star sign. It is clearly ridiculous to think that an Australian Aborigine and a French stockbroker who share the same birthday have anything meaningful in common other than their humanity before God.

If God created the stars and the planets, it must follow then that *he* is the best one to consult about our futures. If you want to know what the finished building will look like, consult the architect not the bricklayer!

New Age

Another aspect of fantasy is demonstrated in New Age philosophy. Again, this philosophy is all about self-awareness and self-fulfilment, and it seems to promote the idea of becoming one's own god: self-worship and self-orientated creations becomes ends in themselves.

Technology games

In technology games, the players become the masters of their own destiny, dictating, by their actions and responses, what will happen to themselves and those around them, all in the name of having fun.

Black magic

Black magic concerns the use of curses, evil spells and developing relationships with evil spirits to produce evil results.

White magic

White magic is used to undo evil spells and curses, and to call up occult powers for one's own good.

Nearly half those surveyed either agree that fortune-tellers can tell the future, or are not certain one way or the other. This is a large number of young people. These young people are the ones who are in danger. They are likely to look further into the claims and promises made by the occult world, and could find themselves being dragged into things which both frighten and, ultimately, destroy them. Of those surveyed, 12 per cent who believe in fortune-telling go to church nearly every week! Youth leaders and other adults with leadership responsibilities within the church should take note of this figure.

Ask yourself what you are doing to help your young people learn about the dangers of the occult and all its related activities. Do you regularly include teaching, discussion and question time in your programme about issues relating to the horoscopes, ouija boards and the like? It is not enough to say that these things are wrong and dangerous without discussing the reasons for—and consequences of—dabbling in them. Young people need to know, and if you don't tell them, who do you think will?

The Bible uses a variety of different words when describing occult practices, including 'sorcery', 'magicians', the 'witch of Endor' (who was a medium), the use of mandrakes to ensure conception, curses and the wearing of charms. The Bible tells us very clearly what God thinks about people who get involved in things of the occult. The Old Testament book of Deuteronomy, chapter 18:10–12, says, 'Let no one be found among you who sacrifices his son or daughter in the fire, who practises divination or sorcery, interprets omens, engages in witchcraft, or casts spells, or who is a medium or spiritualist or who consults the dead. Anyone who does these things is detestable to the Lord, and because of these detestable practices the Lord your God will drive out the nations before you.' Strong stuff! God wants us to know just how strongly he feels about people who get involved in these things, not because they do not exist, nor because they are 'just a bit of fun' but because they do exist and are dangerous and damaging, and in the end destroy those who become involved.

The New Testament also carries a warning in Galatians 5:19–21, where Paul says that anyone involved in witchcraft and idolatry will not inherit the kingdom of God. In the book of Acts, we read about a young girl who was earning money for her masters by fortune-telling. Acts 16:18 says that Paul became so troubled by this girl that in the end he commanded the spirit to leave her. It did so and she was no longer able to tell fortunes. Her masters were very angry because their source of income had gone. If these things were harmless fun we would not read about such radical reactions to them in the Bible.

Devilish practices distort the truth and ultimately destroy us. How Satan goes about this task is both varied and creative: making things *look* harmless, fun, colourful and beneficial to the user are the main avenues he uses to draw people through their own natural curiosity into his web of destruction. His methods are varied and numerous and are taking on new aspects all the time. When we start being interested or curious about these elements of the future, or ways of predicting it, we make openings in our lives through which Satan can enter and wreak havoc. Satan is no gentleman: he sneaks or pushes his way in as soon as he sees even the slightest gap made by our inquisitiveness! He will not seek your permission, or say, 'Excuse me, do you mind?'

Jesus is full of love, compassion and mercy. If we are caught up in evil practices, he can set us free. Jesus is infinitely more powerful than Satan. He showed that on the cross and by rising again, and he has God's resources at his disposal. When we come to him truly sorry for the things we have done, he forgives us and wipes the slate clean. Jesus can set us free from any involvement we may have had, no matter how trivial or how deep. All we have to do is admit we have done wrong and are in need of his forgiveness and he does the rest. John 8:36 says, 'So if the Son [Jesus] sets you free, you will be free indeed.' That is a fact, not a 'maybe' or 'perhaps'. It is important that we put our trust in the Creator and not the things he created. Surely the one who created the world is the one most worthy of our trust, faith and love.

If young people admit to having been involved in one way or another in evil activities, listen to what they have to say. God can deal with their admission very easily and can forgive their involvement. They may need your help to know how to repent, and your prayer, support and encouragement to stay away from these things in the future. It is important that you are informed about this issue, and are able to talk about it and answer questions when asked. Do not ignore it and hope it will go away. It will not; and because it is there, young people will be interested in it!

I believe in my horoscope

	Agree	Not certain	Disagree
TOTAL sample	35	31	34
Boys	24	30	46
Girls	46	31	23
Year 9	34	32	34
Year 10	37	30	33

To Church

	Agree	Not certain	Disagree
Nearly every week	23	28	49
Sometimes	38	32	30
Never	36	30	34

Source: Teenage Religion and Values Survey of 13,000 pupils in England and Wales. All figures refer to responses to the statement immediately above this diagram. The left hand column shows, at the top, the responses of the total sample which is divided, in the middle, into responses of year 9 and year 10 pupils. The right hand column deals only with the 11% of the total sample who attend church.

Section Five: Lifeline

30 Heather Evans
Youth Events

In 1979, 13 per cent of teenagers went to church. Ten years later, according to the Church of England census, the figure had dropped to 9 per cent. If we go by the statistics, God is dying out!

Attendance at church is dropping and young people are not experiencing anything religious, so have no desire to do anything religious. Our society has become indifferent. Christianity is one of many religions on offer. In many ways it is the least attractive as it seems to have rules, regulations and involves going to church which, of course, falls into that well-known teenage category, 'boring'.

Many churches, however, are waking up to the need for specialist youth initiatives. More and more advertisements are appearing in the Christian press for full-time youth workers. Nevertheless, the church in Great Britain is not even holding on to its young members, let alone reaching young people who never come near a church.

Christians would wholeheartedly agree with the statement that 'Christianity is about a relationship with God'. Yet we also know that this implies working out relationships in God's family, the church. Are the depressing statistics regarding teenage attendance at church transferable to the same issue of teenagers' religious experience? In today's culture it may be easy to feel that the church is failing young people. But is God failing them too?

In the Teenage Religion and Values Survey, teenagers were asked if they had ever had anything that they would describe as a religious experience. Seventy per cent said that they had had no religious experience, which confirms the judgement already made. However, more than 25 per cent had had what might be described as a 'religious experience', and 6 per cent said that they had definitely had a religious experience.

In his book *Reaching and Keeping Teenagers*, Peter Brierley discusses this issue of teenage experience. He finds a similar conclusion in his survey of schools: 26 per cent agreed they had had a religious experience, and although 58 per cent of these had said that their experience was about becoming a Christian, yet only half of these described their commitment as strong. His research goes further and asks those who have had some sort of experience to categorize it in one of the following ways:

Type of religious experience per cent 'yes' per cent 'not sure' per cent 'no'
Becoming a Christian 58 34 8
A feeling of peace 53 35 12
The presence of God 50 37 13
Conversion 25 16 15
To do with healing 20 69 11
Something else 9 87 4

Reaching and Keeping Teenagers.[1]

What comes through in Brierley's survey is the high level of uncertainty among teenagers on this issue. The 87 per cent who said 'something else' often experienced something to do with the Holy Spirit (see Brierley's book for more detail). These experiences should not be dismissed.

But what needs highlighting is that around 25 per cent of young people are experiencing 'something religious' that they do not know how to explain. For the teenager, experience and action go together. It is obvious that young people are experiencing something but that they do not know how to respond to it. Obviously we cannot assume that all these experiences are Christian, but we can assume that God is always potentially active in the lives of young people. They may simply have no framework to discuss or experiment or find out more. In John 4:35, Jesus said, ' . . . look at the fields! They are ripe for harvest.'

The lack of certainty young people feel about spiritual concerns comes from the intellectual fashion of the day. 'If it works for you, it's OK for you'—today's ruling philosophy. School, home and friends are generally highly secularized and dismissive of religious experiences, so there is little guidance for youth on what they may be experiencing. Yet many young people are sensitive to spiritual issues because they are open to new ideas. They are not set in their ways.

But how many teenagers in our society experience any religious input, Christian or otherwise? Religious education is incredibly varied in the United Kingdom, and is rightly and primarily about understanding facts rather than experiencing 'religion'. There may also be little religion experienced at home. There is, however, one area where interest among young people is growing: the occult (see Chapter 29). Mainly among young people, the occult seems to be a 'credible' way of exploring the spiritual. There is an obvious link between interest in the occult and experimentation. Once teenagers start looking for occult spiritual experiences, it is hard for them to stop.

To understand more about the link between experience and action, we must also look at the reasons why young people have lost interest in, and have stopped, going to church. Brierley found that two reasons stood out clearly. First, going to church was boring. Second, there were few other people of their own age. Brierley goes on to point out that 'boredom and loneliness are correctable problems.'[2]

If young people are having a bad 'experience' of church, it will result in only one action: leaving. As Christians, it is right that we talk about belief and truth, but we often neglect the experiential side of our faith. Or if we do discuss it, it is in terms of the rights and wrongs of the charismatic. Yet experience has as much to do with the social and practical as it does with the spiritual and the supernatural. If we are to meet teenagers' needs, we must link together experience and action.

Teenagers are very susceptible to spiritual experiences, but by very nature of being adolescent they are prone to placing more importance and significance on experience than doctrine. This needs to be recognized, and churches must provide a balance, with opportunities for experience and good teaching!

But what are young Christians experiencing? In 1991, Lion Publishing published a book entitled *Teenage Beliefs*. Interviews were held with teenagers who had recently become Christians. They were asked about their experience and, when asked if becoming a Christian had changed their behaviour in any way, they said it made them more self-controlled and tolerant. They would try to obey the ten commandments. 'It [my faith] makes you think much more about what you are doing.'[3]

Christianity also offered young people someone to turn to—youth leaders. These are some of the qualities that the young observed in such leaders: love, care, warmth, sympathy, understanding, openness, self-sacrifice.[4]

He was very understanding and patient. I felt he was really interested in me as a person.[5]

Many of them speak of the hope for the future that they experience:

Melanie, a former glue sniffer, when asked if being a Christian makes a difference to the future, replied, 'It's made a big difference, because I never thought I had a future. I'd never look to the next week or even tomorrow 'cause I was so scared of what if held for me.'

Brierley, in his research, found that churches that were seeing growth in their youth work had an 'emphasis on relationships, lively worship, relevant activities, and a strong sense of identity and belonging'.

Jesus' statement, 'The fields are ready for harvest and the labourers are few', could sum up our conclusions. It would be easy for the church to give up and concentrate on what it is good at—perhaps work with children or the elderly—because such projects see material results quite quickly. But youth work is just as important!

Indeed, the youth work of a church can be used as a 'thermometer'. If a church has a growing and integrated youth programme, it will reflect a growing church. In our 'stay young and with it' society, a church that can communicate with young people in a relevant way can also communicate to the wider populace.

In order to give young people the opportunity to explore and experience the living power of Christ and a knowledge that they have eternal life, we must look at targeting young people in outreach. We therefore need more specialized, thought-through evangelism. How might we do this?

First, the church family needs to be educated about how it needs to reach out to young people in order to offer relevant activities and helpful advice. We need to break down the stereotypical idea of what a youth worker is. We need youth leaders to take on parent and grandparent roles with young people, as well as to embrace the 'all fun and ideas' characteristics that 'give the kids a good time!' Churches need to look at starting relevant youth services, that offer young people a place to mix, with relevant worship.

Full-time youth workers need to link up with local schools either informally or formally (see Oxford Youth Works for more details), taking lessons and assemblies, or assisting Christian Union groups in schools. Churches need to work towards opening youth advice centres, which in turn should offer trained advisors for young people to discuss emotional, spiritual and practical matters. Churches also need to give young people the opportunities for practical service. This will help to prevent introverted spirituality.

Too often, full-time youth workers spend their time maintaining a church youth programme which exists primarily for the children of church members. Radical new models are needed, so that churches become lively, active members of the community—and especially the community of young people—offering social activities, resourcing local schools, and providing advice, help and guidance to young people.

Is this a naive dream? There are signs of hope. There are churches in Britain that are stepping out in this way. It is risky, but the church must move away from 'keeping up the maintenance' of those who come along on Sunday. Instead, it must face outwards to those who are in need, who may be experiencing God at work in their lives. Isn't this what J

References

1. Peter Brierley, *Reaching and Keeping Teenagers*, MARC, 1993, page 119.
2. Brierley, *Reaching and Keeping Teenagers*, MARC, 1993, page 124.
3. P. May and D. Day, *Teenage Beliefs*, Lion Publishing, 1991, page 15.
4. May and Day, *Teenage Beliefs*, page 74.
5. May and Day, *Teenage Beliefs*, page 75.

Have you ever had something you would describe as a "religious experience"?

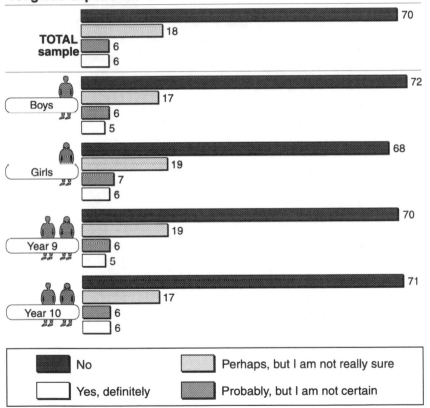

Source: Teenage Religion and Values Survey of 13,000 pupils in England and Wales. All figures refer to responses to the statement immediately above this diagram. The left hand column shows, at the top, the responses of the total sample which is divided, in the middle, into responses of year 9 and year 10 pupils. The right hand column deals only with the 11% of the total sample who attend church.

31 Phil Moon
I Believe in God

Does it or does it not matter what we believe? And when we talk about belief in God, can we be sure what we believe anyway? How can we know? The prevailing attitude among many young people is that it does not matter too much what we believe, and there is a growing feeling among some that not only does it not matter what we believe, but it cannot matter, because we cannot know.

This is all somewhat curious. We live in a world where it does matter what we believe. That is abundantly clear from everyday life. For instance: you are on a train; you believe it is going to Glasgow. If it is not, you are not going to get to the party, and that matters. If you are sitting down while reading this, you believed that whatever you are sitting on would hold your weight, and then you acted on that belief. Belief changes actions. If you believed otherwise, you would have acted otherwise.

But when it gets to religion, it is somehow different. 'You believe what you want to believe and I'll believe what I want to believe. You believe in God if you want to. That's fine, but when you tell me about the gospel of Jesus' death and resurrection, I'll simply say "So what?" It doesn't matter what you believe,' so they say.

As a result, a lot of young people are unsure now whether they believe in God. In the Teenage Religion and Values Survey, one-third of the boys agreed with the statement 'I believe in God', one-third disagreed with it and a further one-third just did not know: perhaps they were confused or, more likely, just could not care—the 'so what?' syndrome.

Girls are more positive than boys, with 44 per cent agreeing with the statement. But note that the statement 'I believe in God' presumes no need for actual commitment, merely mental assent: it merely requires people to say whether they believe that God exists. This in itself hides the fact that for the great majority of young people, God is a huge irrelevance; and these days the irrelevance is not even necessarily that huge.

What is more, there is a fall-off in belief in God from year 9 to year 10; 79 per cent of year 9 pupils (boys and girls) agree with the statement, 'I believe in God', but this drops to 73 per cent of year 10 pupils. Correspondingly, the percentage of those who disagree with the statement rises from 11 per cent to 14 per cent from year 9 to year 10. And the decline in belief in God will continue (on the evidence from other surveys) in later teenage years.

Church attendance does help young people to be clearer about their belief in God. Of those who go to church nearly every week, 84 per cent agree with the statement, 'I believe in God', and only 2 per cent of those disagree with the statement. But as church attendance becomes more sporadic, so does firmness of belief in God. Half of the young people who go to church 'sometimes' agree with the statement 'I believe in God', and 23 per cent of those who never go to church still believe that God exists. Conversely, the degree of certainty about the non-existence of God increases as church attendance falls: 2 per cent of those who go to church nearly every week and 40 per cent of those who never go to church disagree with the statement, 'I believe in God'.

These statistics reveal two interesting points. First, they give some force to the earlier assertion that, for many young people, God is irrelevant. The 23 per cent of those who never go to church who agree with the statement along with the 37 per cent of those who never go who aren't certain about it suggest that the 'so what?' syndrome is alive and well. They agree that God is there, or that he might be there, but don't see the pressing need to do anything about it. This suggests that the church is failing them. We are failing to communicate that belief in God is not merely mental assent. We are failing to communicate that belief in God must result in action. Belief in a divine being who makes such claims on our lives must result in more action than a mere nod of the head. Or to put it the other way, if you believe you can just nod your head in the direction of God, it is not God you are nodding at.

Second, the fact that only 84 per cent of those who go to church every week agree with the statement 'I believe in God' raises an interesting question. Does this show that churches are actually quite good at evangelism, drawing in young people who aren't yet sure of their faith? That would be good, and in some cases that is happening. There are some churches which are very good at attracting young people because their activities are interesting and relevant for young people. But for the majority of churches, this is probably not the case.

It is possible that relativism is now inside the church as well as outside it. It is reflected in a certain kind of apathy. There is apathy about lifestyle. Young people often do not appreciate that *how* you live matters, so there is no discernible difference between those who are Christians and those who are not. And if it does not matter what you believe, why should what you believe affect how you live? So what can be done?

If we live in a 'don't know, don't care' generation, and if adolescent society frequently asks 'so what?', the Bible provides a completely opposite statement. The Bible is a 'do know, do care' document. It is the antithesis of the shrug of the shoulders, the 'so what?' response.

In a world where lack of certainty is normal, Christianity claims to have clear answers and it claims to be founded on the actions and teaching of a person who was certain and who spoke with clear authority. Moreover, the Bible itself claims to be a reliable, certain document and a record of the life of Jesus of Nazareth. The Bible also claims to portray an authoritative revelation of what God is like. It has been written so that all people, whatever their age, can know and be sure about belief in God. The Bible is the main way that God reveals himself to us. Of course, God can and does do that in other ways, but we must not ignore or avoid the Bible. That has happened in the past, and that is one reason for the rise of the 'so what?' generation.

We need to have a thorough, rigorous belief in the Bible, which sees the Word of God as it really is—itself important news for today's young people. Then, having confidence in the Word of God, we need to teach it, imaginatively and carefully—believing that the Bible, taught well, is all that young people need in order to understand the gospel and start heading for heaven, and all they need in order to learn and grow in their faith.

For the church though, teaching the Bible to young people, any young people, has been an area of stultifying weakness. We seem to have lost our faith in the Bible, and our methods of teaching it have not kept up with the changing culture of young people. But it is still possible to teach the Bible to young people; it is still possible to teach it in ways which young people find interesting, relevant and enjoyable. We need not be intellectual or academic about this. Instead, we need to work hard to find ways of communicating the Bible appropriately to young people so that it is easy for them, in their culture, to understand what it is saying.

The Bible is a book and, for most youth leaders, reading the Bible is an easy thing to do. Because of the way that we have been brought up, we naturally tend to communicate it to young people in ways which appeal to our minds. It may be, however, that there are other, more appropriate ways of communicating the Bible to young people. We have to make sure that it is the Bible that we are teaching, for we are not at liberty to tell our young people any old thing. We must tell them what the Bible is saying, and not tell them what it is not saying. We must tell them about God's Word. But we must tell them about it with a communication which is clear, relevant, attractive, stimulating, funny and enjoyable.

Teaching the Bible is so often a turn-off. Yet the Bible itself cannot be uninteresting. How can something which is God communicating to humanity possibly be a turn-off? How can something which is 'living and active, sharper than any two edged sword' be boring? Yet we make the Bible boring by the way we misunderstand it, and by the dull way in which we communicate.

Teaching the Bible should not, and need not, be boring. When we make it so, we insult God. If we can regain our confidence in the Bible and in our methods of communicating the Bible to young people, we can all begin to see that relativism is a 'no-no'. Of course, merely teaching the Bible is not enough. We have to live it out as well, and we have to encourage our young people to live it out too.

Leaders and teachers need to live it out in every way they can. Their lives need to adorn and illustrate their message, because young people need to see that Christianity works. If they teach one thing and then live another, which side of the contradiction are our young people going to believe? Lifestyles are terribly important.

This in turn means that young people need to see youth workers as they really are. If everyone involved meets for no more than two hours on a Friday night, inadequate youth work will be the result. Young people need to see how faith works out in normal, everyday lives. That means investing huge amounts of time, getting to know each other, letting them into each other's lives and allowing them to see how Christians live.

On a personal note, I learned more about Christianity as a teenager from my youth leader's driving habits, and from the fact that he had verse cards in his loo and a Bible in his living room, than from any of the excellent youth meetings that he spoke at. It was not that those were not important, but that his daily life showed me how what he spoke about worked out in practice.

Most young people do not know what they believe, and they often think that they do not care, because they do not think it matters. They may believe in God. They may not. 'So what?' In fact, nothing could be more important.

I believe in God

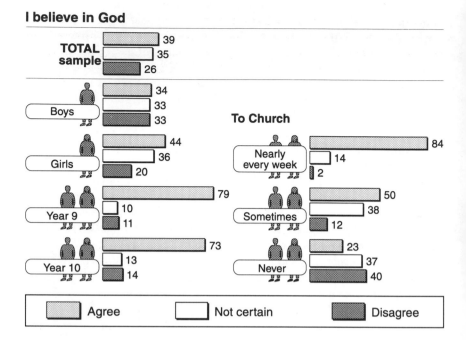

Source: Teenage Religion and Values Survey of 13,000 pupils in England and Wales. All figures refer to responses to the statement immediately above this diagram. The left hand column shows, at the top, the responses of the total sample which is divided, in the middle, into responses of year 9 and year 10 pupils. The right hand column deals only with the 11% of the total sample who attend church.

32 John Buckeridge
Church Membership

The vast majority of young people rarely, if ever, attend church. Three recent surveys have put the percentage of regular attenders as 13 per cent[1], 9 per cent[2] and 14 per cent (at least once a month).[3] The Teenage Religion and Values Survey found that 11 per cent of teenagers aged thirteen to fifteen attended church or another place of worship each week.

The second of these figures, 9 per cent, is most likely to be the closest to actual attendance at a church-related activity on a typical Sunday. What is not in dispute is the continuing decline in church attendance by children and young people throughout the twentieth century. The third survey mentioned above, by Crusaders, also reveals that 14 per cent of girls compared with 9 per cent of boys attend weekly worship—a difference of 5 per cent. Adult church attenders also show this imbalance of the sexes. Why? A pragmatic view might identify the range of outreach options which appeal more to women or are scheduled at times of the day or week less likely to attract men. But the gender-disparity among teenage church attendance is more likely to caused by the image and impact of church than by the timing of its events.

By the age of thirteen, most adolescent males want to impress their peers and conform to the majority view. Attending church, which has the image of being irrelevant, out of touch and boring, may be just too 'uncool' for some males. Unless Christianity can be communicated as being manly, tough and relevant to modern living, young men will continue to marginalize church. Hymns, liturgy, sermons and visual images of Jesus have tended to play up his feminine qualities and play down his masculine strengths. This is not to advocate a Schwarzenegger-type Jesus, merely to redress the balance.

The survey in *Reaching and Keeping Teenagers*[4] found that the main reason teenagers gave for stopping church attendance was that the worship service was boring. The second reason was a lack of other people of their own age. Churches of some denominations appear to be more successful than those of others at attracting young people to their worship services. The new house churches have a far higher percentage of teenagers attending their services than do churches of other denominations.

The 'new church' style of charismatic worship which uses modern music may well attract teenagers. But the emphasis on feelings and experiences may be a more important factor in the popularity of these services. Most young people are interested in spirituality; it is formalized religion which tends to put them off. New churches, which often meet in non-religious buildings and offer a 'feel it' faith of spiritual gifts and an acceptance of the reality of the supernatural, appeal more obviously to the average teenager. These churches are also less bound by tradition and more open to modern influences. But even in a more traditional, formal church, if a group of fifteen or more young people attend regularly, a positive group identity can form which transcends the problems of a boring service or an unfriendly clergy. The positive pleasure of belonging to a group which enjoys being together can be enough to withstand a less than ideal church setting. This is especially the case in rural areas, where people do not enjoy the luxury of choosing a different church down the road. Young people want to be part of a group and churches which fail to attract enough young people will probably struggle to keep the few they have. Many Christian parents of teenagers choose to change churches to ones which do attract a reasonably large group of teenagers in an attempt to meet the legitimate needs of their own children.

Many churches have responded to the overall decline in church attendance among teenagers by appointing full-time youth workers. Although these probably number fewer than 300 in England and Wales, the figure is rising. Youth work is enjoying an increased status and there is a growing proliferation of resources.

This trend could, however, be temporary. Much of the effort and many of the resources appear to be directed at the minority of young people who already attend church, rather than the majority who do not. Since the people paying the wages of full-time church youth workers are often the parents of teenage or pre-teenage children that attend church, it isn't too surprising that churches direct most effort towards churchgoing children!

But these young people may have become hardened to the Christian message through continuous exposure to a one-dimensional presentation of biblical truths. Our communication to these young people needs to emphasize the relevance and application of faith in the modern world, and to turn mere hearing into active listening and then active participation.

For unchurched young people and those who have virtually no understanding or knowledge of the gospel, we have to discover a way to communicate the good news in a culturally relevant way to teenagers unused to doctrinal language and culture. It is vital that churches regularly review their youth ministry programmes, both in content and in style. They need to match their communication according to the trends and culture of the Nintendo generation.

However, one area of youth work which may have a universal appeal to Christian and unchurched young people alike concerns alternative youth services. These youth-friendly worship services are a deliberate attempt to encapsulate Christian worship and the heart of the gospel in popular youth culture. Using the current popular musical genre (in 1994 it was 'rave'), a mixture of dance, live and recorded music, liturgy, visual images and the spoken word are mixed to form an act of Christian worship. In some locations these alternative services have spawned youth churches, but most commonly they are held as supplementary to family or adult worship services.

Nevertheless, before we get carried away with culturally relevant, big budget programmes, it must be remembered that in the United States, where big bucks have been thrown at youth programmes for more than fifteen years, a truth has been rediscovered: youth work and integrating youth into the wider worshipping community of Christians will be ineffective unless they are built on human friendship. And although we certainly need a professional approach to youth work, we should beware the spread of 'professionalism'. Instead, we must model our efforts to reach out to teenagers primarily on Jesus, whose ministry in the Gospels can be summed up in the word 'incarnational'. In other words, he lived with, and got involved in, people's lives.

Incarnational youth work—being there for young people—must be at the heart of our ministry. People are more important than programmes.

References

1. Gallup.
2. Peter Brierley, *Reaching and Keeping Teenagers*, MARC, 1993.
3. Crusaders.
4. Peter Brierley, see 2. above.

Do you go to a church or other place of worship?

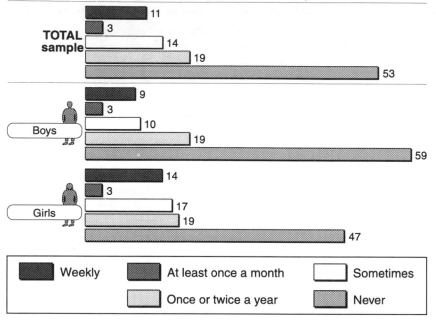

TOTAL sample
- 11
- 3
- 14
- 19
- 53

Boys
- 9
- 3
- 10
- 19
- 59

Girls
- 14
- 3
- 17
- 19
- 47

Weekly	At least once a month	Sometimes
	Once or twice a year	Never

Source: Teenage Religion and Values Survey of 13,000 pupils in England and Wales. All figures refer to responses to the statement immediately above this diagram. The left hand column shows, at the top, the responses of the total sample which is divided, in the middle, into responses of year 9 and year 10 pupils. The right hand column deals only with the 11% of the total sample who attend church.

33 Dave Fenton

What Keeps Teenagers?

There is a saying that 'young people are not the church of tomorrow, but they belong to today'. But does the grassroots situation live up to this optimistic statement? If it does, then we should be able to find churches all over the country with vibrant youth groups. These groups should not only have independent social and learning programmes, but they should also be fully integrated within each church congregation.

We must ask why, where significant youth groups exist, they are rarely integrated in this way. There is much current concern about the exodus of young people from church. Our response to this, as youth leaders, has been to look primarily at the culture of young people, not at the state of the church. If our aim is to integrate, then we must give at least half of our attention to the body which we are attempting to graft onto, and we must consider how it needs to prepare for this operation. The approach to youth work which only considers young people in their cultural milieu creates an appealing programme without considering the connection to adult ministry; as such, it is never going to achieve integration. It will only achieve polarization.

In many of our major Christian events the same effect is achieved. The aim is to provide a relevant youth programme with music that is contemporary, and the programme is culture-driven with more energy given to copying *The Big Breakfast* than to giving Bible teaching applied to the real world.

It is rare for these events to provide a way of bringing youth and adult programmes together. Admittedly, such events have been a major factor in changing church life in recent years, but they have only aided the separation of youth and adult programmes. It could even be said that these youth programmes contain some 'anti-adult' concepts. Words like 'wrinklies' abound and again the effect is polarization not integration.

Is the answer to reject all forms of structure and liturgy and replace it with 'hip and trendy' services, where the sermon is said to be 'cool'? In fact, young people themselves would say 'no'.

Only a quarter of Free Church young people think their church worship is not up-to-date. The high proportion of uncertain responders would suggest either that many lack the ability to make a judgement, or that they do not see style of worship as an issue. It may not be the service which is the major factor in the integration of young people, and it may be that the desire we have to 'appeal' to the young has been our undoing. If we are just another part of the adolescent's social round, when our appeal fades he or she will be drawn to pubs and clubs which in terms of appeal knock most youth groups out of sight.

Of course, no youth programme should be ancient and tedious, but the primary aim of our events should not be so much to appeal to young people as to provide an environment within which the gospel of Christ can be communicated in its fullness.

Understanding the target

As a local church worker, I am sometimes mystified by the training that is given to youth workers. It is vital that we understand the culture that surrounds young people today, but there are many strands running through this. Music tastes are very broad and it is 'cool' in my local area at the moment to accept a wide taste. But culture is only a façade for the processes through which a child seeks to become an adult in a very few years. Culture is a sociological phenomenon, with little to say about physical, mental and spiritual development. Church youth leaders need to understand adolescent development more, and worry less about culture or programme planning.

Teaching the Bible as God's Word

In trying to make the Bible relevant, we may have lost our courage in teaching its eternal truths. Our desire to be culturally relevant may have made us reluctant to attempt to teach the Word. God's revealed truth cannot be exclusive to adults, so there has to be a way of teaching it for God to be relevant to young people. Perhaps it is because the Bible has some hard challenges, and demands repentance, that we fear to teach it. Nobody wants to call anyone a 'whitened sepulchre'; but Jesus did.

If, however, we teach with love as our motive and with room for the questions that young people have, we will produce 'fruit'. We must help people to understand the culture and background of the Bible if they are to understand its message; washing feet *is* relevant if it is understood correctly. We need to apply contexts, not merely give illustrations. 'God is like a mountain stream' is an illustration because, on its own, it does not apply the Word to our culture. 'Washing one another's feet' becomes an application when young people see that they should be aware of each others needs and serve one another. When the Bible is taught with a serious attempt to understand its background, its message, and its relevant applications, then young people will stay around for more.

Discipleship

Discipleship has the same root meaning as discipline, and is a key element in any church's programme. As Jesus taught his disciples, the question came: 'How can a person be born again?' We must be prepared to give 'a good account of our faith' as young people seek answers which fit their world. This may be achieved best in small groups where there is freedom to talk. It is here, within the context of loving fellowship, that discipline based on love can be given. 'Those whom I love, I rebuke', reads Revelation 3:19. Again, we must not allow prevailing culture to take over. It is good that teenagers are given ways to express themselves but there must be boundaries; that is the way we all create stability in our lives.

In a youth group, someone who constantly interrupts needs to be removed and talked with, one to one. The group member who treats his parents like hotel staff needs your words to support those parents and to give the young person a chance to improve. No correction at all means not helping the spiritual growth of such a person.

In discipleship, it is equally important to be positive. It is good to give young people creative and definitive outlets of service. Many teenagers like working with younger children, or visiting elderly people, or even helping to dig over the church garden (sometimes!).

Leadership is another issue in keeping teenagers. 'We don't have anyone in our church willing or able to do youth ministry' is so often the heartfelt plea of churches who search in vain for youth leaders. But if we want youth work to survive, leaders must be found and will need all our support and prayer. Leaders need not be 'trendy'. They just need to like adolescents for themselves. They need not be under twenty-five to be effective with young people, nor need they emulate their ways.

After all, our greatest leader is Jesus. Although clearly relevant to his culture, he attracted people by revealing to them a radical new way of life. In a large team of youth workers, balance is the key. The last thing we need in such teams is a gaggle of young up-front posers, who cannot talk through problems in any depth because they have little experience of life. It is surely no accident that Jesus' team of twelve is not evenly reported in the Gospels. Peter, James and John were key talkers but what does Bartholomew ever say? Jesus must have chosen him for a purpose, and not merely to make up the numbers. In any leadership team, there should be a balance of single and married people (with and without children), students and older individuals. Everyone can be effective!

Services of worship

Another issue is that of worship services themselves. It seems that young people will put up with quite a lot if they feel involved in the church community. Some have responded to 'boring services' by setting up youth churches, which may be

173

effective—except that they prolong integration. Special youth services can be held to attract young people, but if they deviate too far from the norm, many people will not return.

There is a middle road which most young people are happy to accept, and that is one in which they are involved in the service as much as any other section of the congregation. Family worship really should be just that, not merely a children's service. Young people need to be involved in all aspects of the service from welcoming to counting the money—even if, at times, they make mistakes.

This has to be very much a church policy decision. When we have major events, such as the carol service, our young people need to be involved. We should be delighted if they read lessons or lead prayers, and it can be a blessing to many of the congregation. The best approach is not to polarize age groups but to encourage acceptance, both by what is said and by what is done, even if it means telling your pastor now and again what is of current interest to the youth group.

Structures

In terms of structures, most churches have something for children—a crêche, a Sunday school— and, because children are still under parental authority, they keep on coming. In the earlier years of secondary school, however, independent thought is encouraged and children begin to develop intense loyalties, mainly to people of their own sex. This is normally the stage when lines such as 'church is boring' or 'none of my mates go' begin to be heard and, when left unanswered, result in young people leaving the church. Most Christian parents respond by giving their children the choice of whether to attend church or the youth group.

In many churches, the alarm bells then start ringing: 'We're losing young people! What can we do to help them?' is the sad cry. Some churches have tried to hold 'open' youth groups but, unless well staffed and resourced, these have limited success. We may try working in schools, in assemblies or lessons, but how often do we plan what to do next if pupils do respond? It may be that we are event-orientated rather than process-orientated. If we hold a concert, for example, then we are providing for our young people, but what comes after the lights have gone down? It could be that our alarm bells are ringing too late and that the problem needs to be addressed when children are much younger in age.

In other words, we need a whole ministry, from babyhood to the day we can vote, which also provides ways for others to join along the way. No Sunday school teacher or youth leader has the right to see their work as independent; instead, he or she needs to be responsible about receiving and passing on children to other groups. However small the church, the appointment of a coordinator who is part of the church leadership team is key. This may be, in larger churches, a more key appointment than a 'youth' worker. Of course, such a model may not be appropriate for all to follow; but it may provide a catalyst for rethinking.

It would be easy to conclude that youth work in some churches is thriving and totally successful. Although some teenagers do choose the clutches of the secular world, others stay with their discipleship to make further progress in adult areas of ministry. But youth ministry is not easy, nor has it ever been. The paradox is that it still targets the age at which many people are most spiritually aware, and most ready to receive the gospel.

Notes

1. All ages are calculated as from 1 September, so that children are in school-year groups.

2. The passing of names from one group to the next is vital, as also is giving children social activities to bond them as a group long before the teenage years. If you leave social activities until the children becomes adolescents, they will probably bond to groups outside church. Children understand sin if it concerns their world, and they can and do respond to the gospel. If we leave social events, evangelism and group bonding until the teenage years, youth leaders (full-time or voluntary) may well give up the unequal struggle. But if they are handed a well-bonded group, many of whom have heard and responded to the gospel, they will, perhaps, be encouraged to keep going.

The Sunday worship of my church is up to date

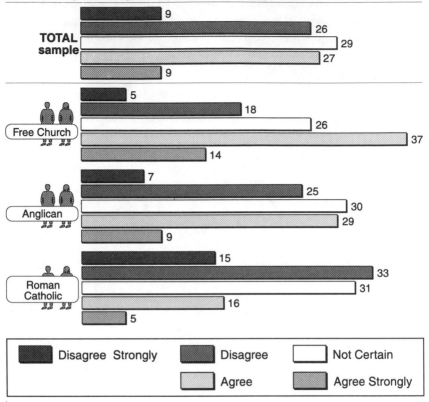

Source: Teenage Religion and Values Survey of 13,000 pupils in England and Wales. All figures refer to responses to the statement immediately above this diagram. The left hand column shows, at the top, the responses of the total sample which is divided, in the middle, into responses of year 9 and year 10 pupils. The right hand column deals only with the 11% of the total sample who attend church.

34 Phil Wall

Youth Evangelism

As part of the Teenage Religion and Values Survey, young people were asked to respond to the question: 'Have you experienced anything that could be called "conversion"?'. The word 'conversion' can mean so many different things. To some people, it may apply to a new room at the top of a house, or to changing from four-star to unleaded petrol; to others, it may apply to some kind of religious experience. Consequently, it is essential that we define the term as we seek to interpret the survey.

As a member of the Free Church in the form of The Salvation Army, I am deeply committed to the view that the Christian faith begins with an individual commitment to a relationship with God. Not everyone is dependent on a crisis experience, however. My wife, for instance, has always wanted to follow God as long as she can remember. Yet there has to be that point when a person recognizes his or her need of God, turns from sin and, having been transformed by the Spirit of God, seeks to follow and serve Christ. This point of view may not be shared by all, but it is a starting point from which the rest of this chapter will flow.

The statistics would seem to support the different perspectives expressed by the historic theological positions of church traditions. Hence, those from the two main church groupings—those who are church members and those who are confirmed— are taken to be of the Christian faith. A key feature of the statistics is that less than one quarter of all questioned church attenders claimed a conversion experience. Even among the very committed questioned by Peter Brierley, only 58 per cent claimed to have had a conversion experience.[1]

Many youth workers, parents, ministers and others concerned for young people have been rocked by the haemorrhage of young people from the church over the last few decades. Barring the occasional exception in the historical denominations and the more effective Free Churches, we have been largely unsuccessful in reaching young people. In light of this, it is imperative that we look at the reasons, and take some steps towards some of the answers.

Ask the average teenager to describe the church and the common response is a militant 'boring', expressed either with frustration by church attenders or with incredulous disbelief that you even asked the question. The fact of the matter is that to the most visually-literate and experience-orientated culture of all time,

177

most church services certainly are boring. Any attempt to reach and keep teenagers must take this criticism into account and begin to address it.

Not only do teenagers find church boring, but they also find it incredibly irrelevant when wrestling with issues of self-identity, masturbation, sexuality and environmental catastrophe. Hearing a sermon on the eschatological significance of Melchizedek's sandals may not be the most helpful thing a young person hears that week. It must be something that relates to their everyday life.

Two other key reasons for non-attendance at church that are given by young people are that church brings loneliness and a lack of involvement. These are issues that must be dealt with at local church level because so much is linked to forms of worship and structure. Rather than read how some people are successful at 'being' a church, go and see some of the places listed at the end of this chapter. The key aim of the text is to look at how we actually communicate the Christian faith. Unless we address this, it will be virtually impossible to make any changes.

Let us look first at the culture and context in which God speaks. When God created a people, he raised up a nation from among the nations (Exodus 19:5). Its job was to fulfil and live out the eternal truth of God and provide a visible expression of God's society in the context and culture of the day. Consequently, when God spoke to Moses it was not on a ROM drive laser disk but on tablets of stone, in the Hebrew language, appropriate for that culture and context. To speak directly, within the prevailing culture, has always been the way that God has spoken. He did so most specifically in the incarnation of Jesus, who came and lived where we lived, spoke as we spoke, and fleshed out the character and will of God in the way of that time.

If the omnipotent God of creation considers culture and context to be important in seeking to communicate effectively, then so must we. Paul, preaching to the Athenians on Mars' Hill (Acts 17:23), made allusions to contemporary culture. We must use our culture to help us communicate in the most effective way. At a time when 91 per cent of teenagers do not attend church, we need a fresh look and some fresh perspectives. As with the people of Issachar (1 Chronicles 12:32), we need to be like them in understanding our times, so that we will know what to do in our own day.

This current generation of young adults has received many labels—the cyborg generation, the lost, the fatherless—and it is essential that we seek to understand something of its make-up if we are to reach it.

Space does not allow a full analysis of the current youth culture, but three key characteristics must be considered. First, ours is a generation without a great deal of hope. The idealism of the 1960s that sought to change the world has all but been lost. Ask most young adults why they won't vote or get involved, and they answer, 'There's no point, nothing will change'. We now have a generation characterized by the philosophy of Nihilism (literally, 'nothing'), powerfully expressed in the music of bands like Nirvana. The futility of the music is agonizing and at times becomes too much for people to cope with. The band's leading member, Kurt Cobain, was called *the* rock musician of his generation; his suicide made the greatest statement of all: money and fame do not produce happiness.

Second, ours is a generation without purpose: it seems to have neither ambition nor any focus on the future. In a Western culture like our own, where purpose and value are largely measured by our ability to contribute and receive from the materialistic pie, many young people lack a sense of purpose and ownership. They should be snapping at the heels of the older generation; instead, most of them sit whimpering apathetically in the corner.

To quote the sociologist, Tony Campolo,[2] we have the 'not needed, not wanted' generation. Young people feel unneeded for the reasons stated above, and they feel unwanted because that is the normal emotional response of those who lack a sense of purpose or function. This is the most needs-orientated generation of all time and, if our gospel is seriously influential, then these needs must be addressed.

The third key factor that must be considered is how people receive information and how they learn. The previous 'chalk and talk' style of education, where one speaks and others listen, is no longer adequate for everyone—some educators would say it never was. These days, the experiential method of learning while doing is seen to be the way that information is most effectively communicated—more 'caught than taught'. The same may well be true of how many young people come to faith.

Current evangelistic methods

We desperately need to move from sole reliance on the previous didactic method—'one talk, many listen'—to the process of 'dialogue'. So often our communication misses the mark as we seek to answer questions not being asked. 'The gospel is true' we cry, when the question being asked is, 'Does it matter?' The gospel is 'public truth', as declared so clearly by Bishop Lesslie Newbigin,[3] and in our day it needs to stand alongside all other world-views to be seen as such. This will require much work on our part, to understand contemporary thinking, if we are to dialogue effectively. The evangelist Nic Pollard[4] has done a great deal of work on this issue.

We also need to stand in awe of great preachers such as John Wesley and William Booth, who could keep thousands spellbound in the streets with their communication. Yet although open air preaching was obviously very effective a century or two ago, it has become an inadequate evangelistic method for reaching the current generation. Young people who are not yet Christians will not come to our events just to stand and listen to preachers. We need to reassess our current ethos and methodology.

Learning

How do people learn? What is the philosophy behind learning? Most Western thinking about education has been greatly influenced by the philosophy of Plato. He suggested that our learning was a process which started from intellectual awareness and proceeded to action. The working out of this theory in evangelism among young people is as follows: we seek to educate young minds about the facts of the gospel; through the work of the Spirit this academic knowledge moves from the intellect to enflame the emotions; then, when people really have taken everything 'to heart', they become 'Christian' disciples and change their behaviour.

The influence of this philosophy can be seen throughout Christian publishing: a wide variety of Christian evangelistic resources is now available to take people through the mental processes mentioned previously. It is fervently believed that if you give young people a tract which will challenge their thinking and which, by the work of the Spirit, will change their heart, they will then become disciples. This is how most of us try to evangelize among young people. But frankly, Plato's philosophical model is not working that well.

Karl Marx, however, believed that we learn, and change behaviour, in a totally different way: 'We think in the context of action'. In other words, if you involve people in what you actually want them to learn, this will change their mind and consequently their behaviour. Commenting on revolution, Marx stated that it was little use merely talking about revolution. Instead, involving people in the process and context of being a revolutionary would, he said, bring their souls to the revolution. This process he called 'praxis'.

If it was applied to evangelism, this philosophy would enable us to involve young people in the work of the kingdom, alongside the people of the kingdom. Through the context of doing the work of the kingdom alongside the people of the kingdom, young people would then come to understand what the kingdom is all about and commit themselves to the King of the kingdom.

Now, before everyone starts screaming 'Heretic!', let us ask the honest question: which of these, if either, are biblical models? In the Gospels, Jesus not only gives us the theology of mission but also the methodology for mission. Using ideas with parallels in the two philosophies above, Jesus employed one of the following strategies.

The first of the strategies fits in with the philosophy of Plato. Jesus talked at very great length with his disciples, and he made them read the Torah until they became convinced he was the Messiah. Then he called them to follow him. But is there also a second strategy at work? Jesus called the unregenerate disciples to follow his example, to watch what he did, to get involved in what he did, and then to do the things that he did. And in the context of watching, being involved and in doing, they came to understand who he was and followed him. Which of these do you think most reflects the model of Jesus?

In fact, Jesus obviously did teach and preach to the disciples. But the methodology of Jesus better reflects the praxis model, which is rarely used today in our evangelism among young people. What we often say is that before a young person can become involved in living as a Christian, they must first jump numerous hurdles—of theological understanding, belief and commitment. The creation of these unnecessary barriers is possibly quite unbiblical.

A practical example of this process is the charitable project, Christmas Cracker. In essence, this is a social action programme but, as young people get involved in this work of the kingdom alongside the people of the kingdom, many hundreds have come to faith in Christ. This is not to deny the use of cerebral communication and education; because when young people seek to ask questions, how else are they to know the answers? Our problem has been that this is where we have started, before questions are even asked. Instead, the future of outreach to young adults is wrapped up in the application of the praxis model, running social action projects; it is here that we can begin to get prospective Christian young people involved.

This will be successful for the following reasons:

◆ First, the praxis model is the most biblical for our context, as it reflects closely the example of Jesus. In fact, Christ himself stated that it was in the 'doing' of God's will that the confirmation of its truth would be found (John 7:17).

◆ Second, it puts people where they are actually challenged to ask the big questions of life. The middle name of our culture is 'superficiality', an attitude that continually avoids the real issues of life. Yet when faced with major questions, young adults usually respond positively, with questions and searching of depth. Social action projects that seek to care for the poor and marginalized are particularly powerful in drawing out this kind of response.

◆ Third, we must remember that this is the most needs-orientated generation of all time. Consequently, our outreach must address the needs of the 'not needed, not wanted generation'. Through the praxis model, we are able to stress that every person has an important function and is very much needed. To those who are not wanted, we are saying a very big 'Yes, you are very much wanted'. Rarely will young adults take even a look at something that doesn't meet their felt or perceived needs.

Finally, the praxis model smashes the commonly held view that the Christian faith is all talk and no action. It demonstrates the transformational nature of the gospel, which meets the whole needs of the whole person. There is, however, an important question which must be addressed no matter what model we choose, and that is: what kind of gospel and faith are we calling young people to? A

181

religious lifestyle which is largely identical to that of the average Western middle classes, with a few Jesus-flavourings, will in no way invite the commitment of young people; and we should all ask ourselves to what extent our lifestyle and message reflects the radical call of the gospel. Too often, young people have left the comfortable institution of the church, which appeared to them about as threatening and radical as Mothercare, only to join far more militant secular organizations focused around a particular cause. There is nothing more militant than a God of heaven who kissed a broken world with love by sending his own son to be butchered by people who did not ask for that love but who were so desperately in need of it. As Martin Luther King once said, 'A man or woman has found nothing worth living for until they have found something worth dying for.' Only the gospel provides that, and we must ensure that this is what we live and communicate.

References

1. Peter Brierley, *Reaching and Keeping Teenagers*, MARC, 1991.
2. Tony Campolo, Interview with Phil Wall, 1991.
3. Lesslie Newbigin, *The Gospel in a Pluralist Society*, SPCK.
4. Nic Pollard
Solent Christian Trust PO Box 200 Southampton Hants SO9 7LX

Helpful models

Stopsley Baptist Church 36 St Thomas Road Luton Bedfordshire
Revelation Fellowship PO Box 58 Chichester PO19 2IO

Have you experienced anything that could be called 'conversion'?

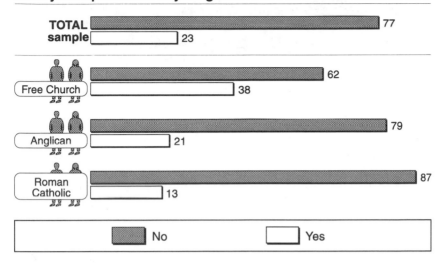

TOTAL sample	No 77 / Yes 23
Free Church	No 62 / Yes 38
Anglican	No 79 / Yes 21
Roman Catholic	No 87 / Yes 13

No   Yes

Source: Teenage Religion and Values Survey of 13,000 pupils in England and Wales. All figures refer to responses to the statement immediately above this diagram. The left hand column shows, at the top, the responses of the total sample which is divided, in the middle, into responses of year 9 and year 10 pupils. The right hand column deals only with the 11% of the total sample who attend church.

35 Bill Hogg
Youth Ministry

As part of the Teenage Religion and Values Survey, young people were asked to respond to the statement: 'I would be reluctant to discuss my problems with a youth club/group leader'. The resulting statistics hold no surprises whatever, even for the newly appointed 'wet behind the lugs' youth worker! Youth ministry does not happen overnight. Trust, respect, patient listening and open hearts do not happen just because you grin and say, 'I'm Alice the youth worker at St Frederick of Bedrock's'. Indeed, only about one-fifth of the total survey sample expressed a willingness to discuss their problems with a youth leader.

If trust and respect do not come with the job, how can we influence young people for Christ? How can we communicate effectively with our audience, whether a large group of young people or one hurting adolescent perched on a wall by the chip shop? How can we get the message across? Mark Ashton tells it straight:

The first aim of Christian youth work must be to present a young person with the claims of Jesus Christ. It is only by an encounter with the living God that a young person's deepest needs can be met. Youth work is not 'Christian' if it is not true to Jesus Christ in facing young people with this gospel and warning them of the consequences of not accepting it. It is this message that distinguishes Christian youth work from secular youth work. If we abandon it, we are discarding the most important contribution that we as Christians can make.

We need to recognize that communication is more than the words that come out of our mouths. Jesus calls us not just to deposit a few pearls of wisdom in the adolescent minds around us. He calls us to share our lives. Paul could say in 1 Thessalonians 2:8, 'We loved you so much that we were delighted to share with you not only the gospel of God but our lives as well . . .' This means that we have to invest blood, sweat, tears, and time to be available. We have to allow people the time and space to find out if our faith is real.

In Ezekiel 3:10–15, the prophet gives us an inside look at an amazing encounter with God. He recounts his commissioning by God to declare God's message; he testifies to the power of the Spirit coming upon him and speaks of 'the strong hand of the Lord' being upon him. He concludes his spine-tingling experience with the words, 'And there, where they were living, I sat among them for seven days—overwhelmed.'

Ezekiel's call has at least two implications for every youth evangelist bursting to share Jesus. First, we need to know the power of the Holy Spirit. This compendium is full of analyses and ideas but God does not necessarily call you to be a technician executing a stack of clever ideas. The call to make young disciples involves preaching treason in the devil's ranks, and setting the captives free. We need to be filled for the fight. We need to be open to and soaked in the Holy Spirit (see Zechariah 4:6; Acts 2).

Ezekiel, however, did not then start his ministry immediately. He sat among his audience in complete silence for a whole week. He was committed to observation and listening, as we, too, must be. We must know God and understand our audience. The apostle Paul charged his apprentice, Timothy, with the words, '. . . do the work of an evangelist' (2 Timothy 4:5). God calls us to biblical thought through youth evangelism. So the youth worker should be the one who stands with a Bible in one hand, and a copy of *Smash Hits* or a computer magazine in the other.

As the *Willowbank Report on Gospel and Culture* states, 'The process of communicating the gospel cannot be isolated from the human culture from which it comes, or from that in which it is proclaimed.' We should take our cue from 1 Chronicles 12:32 which describes the 'men of Issachar, who understood the times and knew what Israel should do . . .'

What are the trends in youth culture that affect young people in your area? What makes them tick? What are the pressures they face? What are their fears, hopes and ambitions? We need to understand young people and be students of youth culture if we are to share good news effectively.

Paul was committed to the proclamation of the gospel. However, his communication of that message was markedly different in Acts 17:16–34 from his preaching recorded elsewhere in Acts. Why? The answer is that Paul's audience was different. Most of Paul's recorded sermons were addressed to a Jewish audience, but in Acts 17 Paul was talking to the Greek population in Athens. So he identifies a beachhead in their Athenian culture for his message—the monument to the unknown god. He even quotes a love poem to the god Zeus! Paul was convinced of the authority of the gospel, but he was also committed to understanding his audience.

Our problem is that church life is based on a book culture, yet most young people are post-literary. According to an NOP poll for *The Independent on Sunday*, 55 per cent of eleven- to sixteen-year-olds have their own television, and 10 per cent of eleven- to sixteen-year-old males have their own video recorder. A study published by the University of Exeter discovered that a third of young people watch more than three hours of television a day, and that one in ten are glued to the box for more than five hours a day!

185

We are called to reach a visually-sophisticated MTV generation. Television, video or Nintendo addicts do not cope well with lengthy linear monologues. This means we must work hard at involving our audience in our communication.

A school teacher was asked to describe how children and young people are taught. He answered:

Children are taught and learn in a variety of situations using a range of methods. Through experimenting, hypothesizing, investigating, drama, problem-solving, story and discussion, they develop their skills, attitudes, knowledge and conceptual understanding.

Very few lessons are based on the old method of chalk and talk. Through structured programmes of work which involve repetition, consolidation and development of concepts, children are able to increase their knowledge and understanding of the task in hand.

Does that description of teaching sound like the typical methods of youth evangelism currently used? Preachers need to understand their audience and use that information to communicate effectively.

Jesus' style of preaching would go down well with the teenager of the 1990s. His sermons as recorded in the Gospels were full of word pictures, and the parables were powerful stories which often shocked his listeners. The Sermon on the Mount consists of 2,320 words and contains 348 visual images and nineteen direct questions. Jesus uses 'you' 221 times in a direct, personal and immediate approach. We need to learn from the master communicator.

If you are speaking to a group, it would be helpful to know as much about them as possible. Jesus' communication was shaped by his audience and his sermons often sprung out of the questions people asked him. Today's preachers need to ask: How many will be there? What is the age-spread of the audience? Are they committed Christians? Are they unconverted? Do they have much of a religious heritage? What issues are they facing?

It will also help a great deal if you know what you are talking about. You may be very comfortable if you are invited to speak to a group on 'the influence of Eastern pantheistic monism in pluralistic Britain'. But if you're not *au fait* with the suggested topic, you only have two options: do a lot of homework or decline the invitation.

You have to fight for the right to be heard, and work at gaining your audience's attention. It is surely a sin to be boring when God has entrusted us with such an exciting message! Just imagine the following:

You are at Saint Hilda's Church on Sunday. A tired pastor has mounted the pulpit steps and speaks from his wooden castle, six feet above contradiction. A glazed look uniformly envelops the congregation. You find yourself debating whether or not to employ some of the tactics suggested in '101 Things To Do

During a Dull Sermon'.

But only twenty minutes previously, the congregation watched with rapt attention. Why? One of the Sunday school teachers was delivering the children's address. The children were down at the front for this part of the service but the lights stayed on across the church because the children's talk is always, at St Hilda's, visual, involving the group in participation and feedback. This week, the teacher made one point and made it well, and she was unpredictable.

In stark contrast, the good church members are now, during the main sermon, too polite to stray from their pews. But their minds are elsewhere. The minister is familiar and therefore, perhaps, predictable; he is also physically removed from his audience.

We must have something to say, and we must say it well! Teenagers today are not impressed by guru-based communication: 'I'm the vicar so you'll listen' doesn't work. Most young people wouldn't be impressed even if you managed to book the Pope to speak on 'Why I am a Catholic'.

Mean what you say and say what you mean! Be direct and to the point. A good dose of enthusiasm helps. If you are talking about joy and you are as miserable as someone who has been baptized in vinegar, do not expect to impress your audience.

The Bible has a rich tradition of communicators who used visual imagery and object lessons. Ezekiel repays careful study. He lay on his side for 390 days to symbolize the 390 years of captivity for the northern kingdom. He also lay for a slightly less excruciating forty days to symbolize the impending forty-year captivity for the southern kingdom. He walked about with a frying-pan in front of his face, prophesying, 'A siege like iron is closing in on you.' Did Zeke realize that people retain more of what they hear and see than just of what they hear? He was certainly committed to a multi-media approach. He even scalped himself and barbecued a meal over cow dung to get his point across!

Jesus' use of parables, stories and analogies show that he was a superb communicator. And even Paul used object lessons, using a visual object—for example, by referring to a religious monument to illustrate his sermon on Mars' Hill (Acts 17).

Remember the KISS principle—Keep it Simple, Stupid! Purge your speech of religious jargon. Once, when I was doing some street evangelism training, I introduced Joe, who was to tell people in the shopping precinct how he became a Christian. 'Well,' he said, 'it's better felt than telt . . . one day the Holy Spirit fell on me.' Another young evangelist informed the Catholic youngsters who had gathered around them, 'Your problem is you don't believe in justification by faith alone through grace alone'.

John Wesley used to practise his sermon on his maid. If she couldn't grasp all that he was saying, it was changed. Similarly, Billy Graham says he targets his evangelistic addresses at the level of a twelve-year-old. That way, everyone can understand!

We must rely on the Holy Spirit for illumination—only he can bring light into people's darkened hearts and minds (2 Corinthians 4:4). We must also be committed to explanation. One Ethiopian treasury official in Acts 8 was poring over arguably the most Christ-centred passage in the Old Testament, Isaiah 53. However, he still required an explanation, and it was Philip who gave it and lead the man to Christ.

Be natural; be yourself and maintain good eye-contact with your audience. If you use notes, do not be chained to them; or use little postcards with bullet points. Your posture, clothes and appearance also send signals to your audience. Keep your group on its toes! Use objects and illustrations. Humour, too, can be a great arrow to have in your quiver; it can relax and disarm people and open them up to you and your message.

Of course, if you are sitting with an adolescent who is pouring out his or her problems, the key thing to remember is that God gave you two ears and only one mouth. In the end, listening to God and listening to the person, it is the good listener who will get to the heart of it all.

I would be reluctant to discuss my problems with a youth club/ group leader

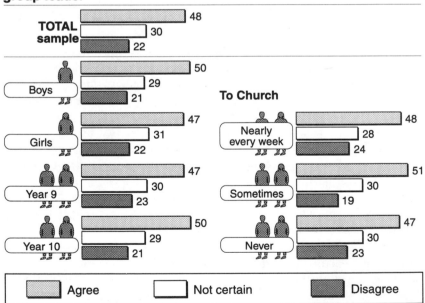

Source: Teenage Religion and Values Survey of 13,000 pupils in England and Wales. All figures refer to responses to the statement immediately above this diagram. The left hand column shows, at the top, the responses of the total sample which is divided, in the middle, into responses of year 9 and year 10 pupils. The right hand column deals only with the 11% of the total sample who attend church.

36 Grahame Knox
Christian Groups in Schools

Viewed quickly you may feel that the Teenage Religion and Values Survey on attendance at school Christian activities just reflects the reality of living in a largely godless society, where God's name is just another swear-word and where Christian faith and morality are viewed as irrelevant by many young people. As part of this survey, young people were asked if they attended Christian meetings/societies at school. Only 8 per cent of boys and 9 per cent of girls indicated that they ever attended such an activity and, for half of the boys and one-third of the girls, that was perhaps only once a year. Regular weekly attendance at such groups was even lower.

However, the poll results can also be interpreted more positively. They help to reveal that nationally, across years 9 and 10, many thousands of young people are meeting in Christian groups for fellowship, or inviting their friends and peers to hear more about the good news of the gospel. Agencies such as Crusaders, Scripture Union and Youth for Christ can confirm that throughout Britain each week, hundreds of groups, large or small, are providing a powerful and effective witness to the rest of the school community. The existence of a Christian group is a reminder to the whole school that some young people believe that the Christian faith is important. For young Christians it can be an exciting and challenging opportunity, and many have found that living for Jesus at school brings a greater sense of purpose and responsibility to their Christian experience. Although they may be teased by some people for belonging to the 'God squad' or the 'holy huddle', and opposed by others, many teenagers have discovered that in being a witness their faith becomes stronger, not weaker.

Christian groups in school are significant. In the experience of many people, such groups help them grow in their faith. They help people to apply Christian belief to real-life situations and to learn more about what it meant to be a witness, to be 'salt and light' to their friends and peers. Christian groups have also been a training ground for many who are now in Christian leadership. Young people have come to faith through school groups. Brought by their Christian friends, they have found a bridge between their culture and the church.

Where churches have realized the importance of school groups and the role they play in ministry and outreach, they have actively supported those groups and exciting opportunities have opened up. In my own town the churches together support a Youth for Christ schools' worker. As a result there are school groups in every secondary school and, with the help of volunteers from some of the churches, exciting and challenging activities take place throughout the year. Similar situations exist across the country. Many more groups could be developed and supported but, sadly, some groups do still struggle, or never start, because of lack of support from their local churches.

How, therefore, can the church respond positively and creatively to the school community on its doorstep? To begin with, the church must realize that voluntary Christian groups in school are a part of the church's mission and outreach. These groups are an oasis for young Christians under pressure from the morality and values of their peers. They provide a chance to pray together, to share and to have fun, and to help people realize that they are not alone. They also serve an important role as a 'halfway house', where interested young people can come to hear more about the Christian faith.

Where do you start? First, establish the facts. Is there a Christian group in your local school? Who leads it? Do any young people from your church go? Are young people from other churches involved? Are other churches supporting the group? Are any Christian teachers you know involved? Find out and encourage your church to pray for the school and the group. Be an encouragement to the young people from your church and beyond, by your interest and your commitment to support them in prayer. There are lots of ways the prayer support in your church can be developed. You can, for instance, ask for information about the group to go in the church magazine. You can invite prayer requests from the young people or interview a group member or Christian teacher during a church service.

If no group exists, pray about starting one. Discuss it with the young people in the church. Talk to Christian teachers at the school. Local schools' workers or agencies like Crusaders, Scripture Union and Youth for Christ can give advice and support. Be prepared to offer practical support with ideas, or to offer time or financial help—to produce publicity or pay the travelling expenses of a guest speaker or hire a Christian video.

In encouraging the development of Christian groups in school, the church youth leader also has an important role to play. Often Christian young people are not encouraged to support the local school group, and many who are committed members of the Sunday youth fellowship nevertheless keep a low profile on Monday morning! The youth leader can profile and promote a school group with regular information spots. Teaching on evangelism and sharing your faith could be related to activities in the school group. If the school group is run by young people themselves, the youth leader can help with ideas for Bible studies, games, or videos. Invest in the potential of young Christian Union leaders, and spend time training them to lead small Bible study groups or times of prayer; be prepared, too, to offer pastoral support when everything just seems to be going wrong. Obviously, the young people in your group may come from different schools. Talk to other local youth leaders and share your vision of actively supporting and promoting different school groups.

Christian groups in school are important. You can make a difference in your local school by actively supporting an existing group of young people seeking to be 'salt and light' where God has placed them, or by encouraging the start of a new group.

Do you go to Christian meetings/societies at school?

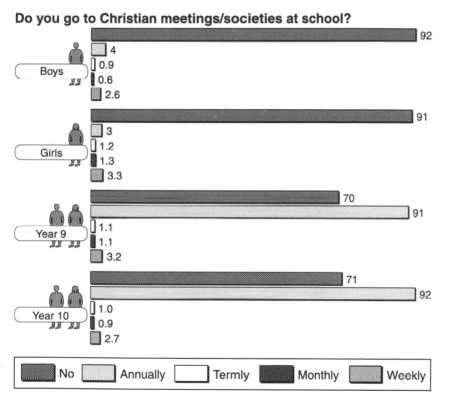

Source: Teenage Religion and Values Survey of 13,000 pupils in England and Wales. All figures refer to responses to the statement immediately above this diagram. The left hand column shows, at the top, the responses of the total sample which is divided, in the middle, into responses of year 9 and year 10 pupils. The right hand column deals only with the 11% of the total sample who attend church.

37 Olaf Fogwill

Church and 'Parachurch'

It takes two to tango or so the saying goes! But is it possible for more than two to tango without becoming a tangle? A vexed question perhaps, but this question of partnership between church and 'parachurch' youth organizations must be addressed if this generation of young people are not to be separated from Christian teaching by a horrendous communication chasm of our own making.

Leading youth workers were asked to share their experiences—twenty-four responded from twelve different youth organizations and denominational backgrounds. There was disagreement about the term 'parachurch', so it is not surprising that there is so much confusion in the use of this term. The interpretation is key to the positions on partnership held by many who would traditionally be labelled as 'parachurch'.

A useful paper was written by the Rev. David Howell MA for Youth For Christ (YFC), entitled, 'YFC's Relationship to the Church',[1] which defines 'parachurch' as 'a structure which stands alongside of, by, near or parallel to the church and any specialist body which seeks to fulfill a particular activity on behalf of the church but which is not seeking to be a church in its own right'. Acknowledging the fluid meaning of 'parachurch', YFC prefers to position itself as an 'inter-church organization'—a part of the church, accountable to the church, serving the church and networking together those committed to youth evangelism. This was a position favoured by several youth organizations, but it hinges on what is understood by 'church'. Howard Snyder argues persuasively that the so-called 'parachurches' are church in its mobile flexible form.[2]

For the purposes of this contribution, 'parachurch' is taken to mean any agency providing a specialist service for the local church but which is centrally managed outside of the local church. All Christian activity is part of the 'church'—although this chapter does not seek to argue for or against 'parachurch' bodies, it clearly recognizes the many benefits they provide. This is endorsed by Peter Brierley in his book *Reaching and Keeping Teenagers*[3].

Views of parachurch organizations

In a survey carried out by Crusaders[4], findings from twenty-four parachurch organizations show that:

82 per cent had experienced increases in their youth work in the past five years;
92 per cent believe that there is scope for partnership between church and parachurch for youth outreach;
83 per cent have been involved in cooperative ventures; and
92 per cent say that church and parachurch are complementary ministries.

Perceptions of parachurch youth organizations

Forty-three per cent believe their ministries to be an integral part of the church, but 13 per cent observed the danger of working independently of the church. John Marshall of Scripture Union (SU) notes that there is more commitment to relational work with less 'hit and run' evangelism and more diversity. Michael Eastman of Frontier Youth Trust adds, 'as a rough generalization ministries among the disadvantaged young of necessity have developed outside and beyond the narrowing scope of much "church-based" youth work. Without new initiatives by non-congregationally based agencies, these cultural and class barriers cannot be overcome.' Note some other comments: 'a strategic arm of the church'; 'at the cutting edge of youth outreach'; and 'a desire to implement locally what is successful nationally'.

Perceptions of youth work within local church

Fifty-two per cent said that the local church needs more support in training and resources because youth work is now complex and demanding. Iain Hoskins of the Baptist Union points out that 'youth work is inadequately organized, resourced and delivered by local people high in commitment, but receiving little in support or sense of direction'. Paul Franklin, National Youth Secretary of United Reformed Church, adds that there is quality at the national level but there is a need for this 'to be maintained at regional and local level'. Nigel Taylor, team leader of Ipswich Christian Youth Ministries, notes a 'lack of youth leadership to take up the challenge of developing a youth work for non-church youngsters.' The Rev. Jonathan Sewell, Diocesan Youth Officer for Winchester says, 'volunteers need training and support'.

Advantages of partnership

Fifty per cent stressed the benefit of combined skills and expertise. Thirty-six per cent mentioned extra resources and staffing. Twenty per cent saw the advantages as being two-way in that youth organizations provide resources and expertise, and churches give support in finance, prayer and personnel. Also mentioned was the avoidance of wasted resources in duplication, playing to each other's strengths and strategies to reach the unchurched. Some local churches have combined with the help of 'parachurch' agencies to develop new ministries, for example, SU and Crusader projects with schools, and detached youth work with the unemployed. Ken Argent, Director of Campaigners, states 'programmes and resources to enable local "average ability' to achieve above-average work'.

Drawbacks of partnership

There was less unanimous comment here, with 8 per cent believing that there are no drawbacks. Twenty-one per cent felt that there was a problem in the area of control and direction. Eighteen per cent noted the difficulty of clashing rather than complementing objectives with the risk of losing a cutting edge. Thirteen per cent were worried about extra time for meetings and the extra pressure on leaders already struggling with internal organizational priorities. Parachurch organizations must take care not to come across as arrogant!

Examples of partnership

These were at three levels. Many had been involved in one-off national events, for example, Fired Up, Yes 91, Feet First, Brainstormers and Mission England. Others are involved in regular meetings of national bodies, such as English Churches Youth Service, Quo Vadis and National Youth Agency. The majority have partnership with local churches in helping youth work, training leaders, running holiday clubs/missions. The third type of partnership is where two or more parachurch organizations form a loose coalition for the purposes of producing joint teaching materials, putting on roadshows (Campaigners, Covenanters and Crusaders), prayer or to meet a specific need. Examples of thriving partnerships include Brainstormers (a training event for youth leaders pioneered by Alpha, YFC and Oasis) and Spring Harvest. There is a downside for organizations which are often unable subsequently to join a healthy partnership for valid reasons but ones which could be debated *ad nauseam*.

More general partnerships

Alpha magazine posed the question 'Did Jim fix it?' in its July 1994 edition. An objective critique of the 'Jesus In Me' (JIM) and 'Minus to Plus' campaigns reveals that many local churches participated in these high-profile national events but that, for differing reasons, their high expectations were not met. Despite the lower numbers involved in the Elim-led JIM project, the great strength was a 'mobilization of grass roots community-based evangelism', writes John Buckeridge. Some 15,000 churches registered for the 'Minus to Plus' campaign, but it was fraught with logistical problems of getting the mailing out. 'The project's overall impact has been diminished as a result of unreal expectations in pre-launch publicity,' comments Mr Buckeridge.

Personal experience

As Public Relations Support Manager for Crusaders, I have worked for partnership to achieve common goals wherever possible. At an Intra-Organizational level, Crusaders' Youth Group Model relies for its success on partnership between churches and Christians of different denominations. Beyond that, we have tried to form partnerships at an Inter-Organizational level for prayer initiatives, for international youth outreach, for work with disadvantaged young people and for the sharing of resources. These have been varied in their success, from high flyers to dead ducks, not to mention dodos! This book, *Fast-Moving Currents in Youth Culture* is one of the positive examples of partnership for encouragement. While still committed to a supra-organizational goal for partnerships that build God's kingdom rather than empires, I have gleaned material for tongue-in-cheek 'principles and laws of partnership between Christian agencies'.

Reflections on the Teenage Religion and Values Survey

As part of the Teenage Religion and Values Survey, young people were asked to respond to the questions: 'Do you go to/belong to the Boys Brigade?' and 'Do you go to/belong to the Crusaders?'.

Boys Brigade: of the 91 per cent of boys who have never belonged, it would be useful to know the percentage that had been linked to other parachurch organizations, and to compare it with the penetration ratio of Scouts. The retention ratio is a vital indicator of the relevance of an organization. Did the 8 per cent stop attending due to age, perceived irrelevance or the boredom factor? Should it consider becoming a 'mixed' organization?

Crusaders: although only a 3 per cent contact was recorded, the retention rate was better, at 50 per cent. In the sample, it was notable that no boys had left.

Both organizations act as services to churches, but for Crusaders this is not exclusive because they have many independent groups. If the parachurch organization is closely reliant on the local church, then it will be linked to the overall pattern of membership experienced within church denominations.

Principles and laws of partnership between church and parachurch

1. Remove rose-tinted spectacles, that is, be realistic.
2. Agree and accept common goals with clear timetables.
3. Look for those things which unite.
4. Recognize and be faithful to distinctives.
5. Consider how action may affect supporters' perceptions.
6. Accept that there may be times when partnership is not possible, even if it is preferable. The footballer and the swimmer do not have much to offer to each

195

other unless a new game is invented.

7. *Two plus two can sometimes equal five, but it can also sometimes equal three.*
8. *The more partners, the less chance of success.*
9. *The more partners, the longer the time to achieve objectives.*
10. *The more partners, the greater the potential for frustration.*
11. *All partners must contribute something if they are to receive anything.*
12. *All partners must receive benefits if it is to be worth joining in the partnership.*
13. *Make it work with one partner first, and then add slowly and selectively.*
14. *Is there ideological agreement?*
15. *Are the personalities going to clash?*
16. *Be clear who can negotiate for the organization.*
17. *Ensure that the top person is committed to partnership as well as the appropriate committees and communicators, otherwise volunteers will not catch the vision.*
18. *Do not operate closed networks—keep an open mind, tempered by a practical diary.*
19. *Sharing resources and avoiding duplication makes sense, but it can be threatening.*
20. *There must be agreed action, accountability and ownership.*

Conclusion

The real church is a classic example of partnership with the creative tensions between the denominations, but surely it should be a more united body. Sometimes it seems as if it has five legs, two arms and four heads, so it is not surprising when it struggles to communicate the gospel effectively.

Partnership can and does work between church and parachurch. Ken Argent, Director of Campaigners, adds 'I know of many "go it alone" initiatives that have started with enthusiasm but failed through lack of continuity and ongoing programme resources'. Alan Hewerdine of Covenanters points out that 'youth work is essentially the responsibility of the church—parachurch organizations have a role to play in helping churches face up to the responsibility and equipping them to accept it'. Liz West of YWAM Youth Department wants to encourage churches to put resources into youth work. Simon Parish of Oasis emphasizes the value of networking between parachurch and denominational groupings—do not offer a confusion of similar options to the local church. Iain Hoskins of the Baptist Union believes in the complementary ministries whereby the parachurch implements work in new areas quickly and churches maintain the ongoing support. He stresses the need for a long-term approach which is not reliant on short-term initiatives. Paul Franklin of URC and Phil Pittard of Crusaders look for increasing partnership at the local level between churches and parachurch youth organizations.

There is a general commitment to partnership and both sides stand to benefit in the achievements of a common goal: bringing young people to Christ. It is not to be entered into lightly, because broken partnerships are both a bad experience and a poor witness. Now, I am not a theologian but if the whole church is to make real progress, the different parts of the body must do more than pay lip service to the concept of partnership which is, after all, a voluntary choice and one that honours God.

Postscript

Since writing, there have been two proposed initiatives which reinforce the call for partnership with greater urgency. Martyn Lewis of BBC fame has launched the Youth Network, which has the stated aim of cooperation among disparate groups working with young people. 'Partnership and cooperation—on a scale that many have hardly dreamt of, and which some may resent and oppose—are the key words that will shape and guide the successful charitable projects of tomorrow.'[5] Recognizing that some have a sense of personal pride and possession that goes with each piece of territory, he claims that wise charities have nonetheless begun moving in that direction. Mr Lewis points out that this will only be successful where the leading personalities are 'of the less-abrasive kind' and 'prepared to put the grand vision above narrow interests'.[6]

These obstacles could surely not apply in the world of Christian youth work, could they?! A further proposed initiative is for a new Youth Outreach Forum (YOF) to be established, which will be taken seriously for all 'parachurch' youth organizations and denominations. YOF will look at prayer, evangelism, spiritual priorities, integration of young people into churches, finance and partnership in the light of the findings of this book, for a far greater impact with young people than the 15 per cent we collectively achieve at present.

The church is an armada. If we recognize the one flagship, the common 'pirate', the rich diversity and capacity of vessels in the fleet, and if we set our sails to catch the same wind, then we will move forwards at great speed without collision. At stake is the survival of many perishing young people, so there is no room for outmanoeuvring, mutiny or ignoring signals of the day, which lead to self-inflicted damage. Let us celebrate the distinctives, enjoy teamwork and sail in the same direction.

References

1. Rev. D Howell, MA, 'YFC's Relationship to the Church', (YFC internal paper), 1994.
2. Howard Snyder, *The Problem of Wineskins*, Marshall Pickering, 1977.
3. Peter Brierley, *Reaching and Keeping Teenagers*, MARC, 1993, page 87.
4. Olaf Fogwill and Gill Meredith, 'Findings from 24 Parachurch Organizations', 1994. Including: Crusaders, Mission Aviation Fellowship, Campaigners, Scripture Union, Cove-

Do you go to/belong to the Boys Brigade?

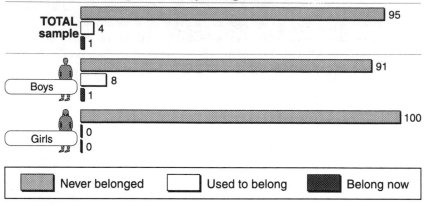

nanters, Church Pastoral Aid Society, Frontier Youth Trust, YWAM, Oasis, Youth Alive
Ministries, Baptist Union of Great Britain, United Reformed church, Ipswich Youth

Do you go to/belong to the Crusaders?

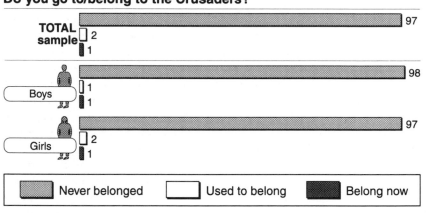

Source: Teenage Religion and Values Survey of 13,000 pupils in England and Wales. All figures refer to responses to the statement immediately above this diagram. The left hand column shows, at the top, the responses of the total sample which is divided, in the middle, into responses of year 9 and year 10 pupils. The right hand column deals only with the 11% of the total sample who attend church.

Ministries, Winchester Diocesan Youth Office, Youth For Christ.
5. Taken from *The Observer*, 2 October 1994.
6. *ibid.*

Section Six:
In the Boat

Sue Rinaldi

38 A Christian Lifestyle?

The English Church Census published in 1991 revealed a startling statistic: 1989 ended with 155,000 fewer teenagers attending churches across the country than 1979. It represented an average loss of 300 teenagers per week! The main reasons given for not attending church were that church was boring and irrelevant: 'Going isn't the done thing', said many of those questioned, along with, 'none of my friends go'. The figures sadly reflect the fact that many have abandoned churchgoing and, as a consequence, rejected the Christian faith as a valid foundation on which to build their lives. The church, however, should be the most dynamic, radical and relevant organism in existence.

For many people, church is a window onto the Christian faith. If churchgoers meet only with lifeless irrelevance in the form of a boring meeting, out of touch with reality, then the conclusion must be that Christianity is also boring and equally out of touch with reality. (It must be noted, however, that an increasing number of churches *are* effectively communicating the truths of Christianity to all ages.) Churches should be places where life issues are tackled with honesty, where there is support and care, and where people can develop a relationship with a living God. Churches should be outward-looking and actively involved in the local community, seeking to represent fully the attributes and teachings of Jesus Christ. More importantly, churches should be enabling and equipping people to live out their faith on a daily basis at home, at work or at school. The existence of such churches will have major repercussions for young people. Teenagers will come to feel understood rather than patronized; they will feel valuable rather than accommodated.

An alternative lifestyle

The same census disclosed that 14 per cent of church sixteen-year-olds have lost their virginity, as have 43 per cent of nineteen-year-olds. In a culture where 41 per cent of non-churchgoing sixteen-year-olds have done likewise, it is vital that issues relating to morality are discussed and that practical help is given. Young people need to be able and motivated to stay celibate. Failure to include appropriate topics at church will result in casualties. The embarrassing silence within church life about many of the more worldly issues must end in order to facilitate a new generation of radical disciples, modelling an alternative lifestyle based on biblical ethics.

If societies are denied guidelines for living, they reap the dire consequences of moral decline. However, according to Janet Street-Porter, head of BBC youth programmes, young people are 'increasingly turning to ways of disciplining their lives. Far too much attention has been paid to the material world they inhabit.' A spiritual search has, it seems, begun, and churches must rise to meet the challenge for people's attention. A positive message based on biblical truth and common sense must be communicated in today's language. Young people, if given sufficient support, can become role models for their own generation, reclaiming a way of life that advocates virginity until marriage, and treasures commitment for life within the context of a life-long relationship.

Overcoming peer pressure

Without doubt, the temptation to conform to peer pressure is enormously strong. Values and conscience are discarded, in order that people may be accepted and approved by their peers. In today's pluralistic culture, owning up to being a Christian is often embarrassing. Christianity is considered old-fashioned and irrelevant, with society opting either for hedonistic pleasures or, more recently, one of the many New Age spiritual offerings which are considered to be more fashionable and worthy. Society, with the constant help of the media, has openly embraced a multiplicity of unbelievably weird doctrines and practices which purport to give spiritual enlightenment by tapping into the divine energy of the individual and the vibrations of the universe. Belief in a creator God, who offers everyone a personal relationship with him, has been hijacked and sacrificed on the altar of irrelevance.

A reasonable faith

It is therefore imperative for each Christian young person to know what they believe and why they believe it. It is vital to be able to ' . . . give the reason for the hope that you have . . .' (1 Peter 3:15). If we know that the claims of Christianity are historically true, and we are able to explain the unique message of the Christian faith, we will begin to raise again the profile and validity of Christianity and the universal church.

Churches are responsible for training and equipping young people to explain their faith and effectively communicate the life-changing good news. Young people need the confidence to admit and explain belief without feeling ashamed or embarrassed, in the full knowledge that they have the right to believe what they believe without apology. Facts and figures are obviously not enough; knowledge must go hand-in-hand with a lifestyle that reflects the ethics of the Christian faith. Various organizations, such as Youth with a Mission, British Youth for Christ and Pioneer have responded to this need for training and have provided long- and short-term courses.

Living the Christian life is not easy. Young people are required to make tough choices in a world where the softer option of compromise seems more immediately attractive. In order to maintain Christian witness, it is imperative for individuals to be active members of a church or fellowship group, where support and understanding, motivation and stimulation are tangible ingredients. Churches should provide environments of teamship and family, where young people feel sufficiently secure both to contribute their services and to accept responsibility.

Pass it on

Christianity highlights the importance of having a personal friendship with a living God as a basis for individual faith. It is imperative that once this good news is received and experienced, it is passed on to others. By the process of communication, all people everywhere can have the opportunity to accept or reject the message of the Christ. The process of witness that influences people to consider the claims of Jesus can be embodied in the word 'evangelism'—from the New Testament Greek *euvangelion*, meaning 'life-changing good news'. The messenger or proclaimer of this news would be the *euvangelistes*, from which we derive the word 'evangelist'.

Friendship evangelism

The process of communicating the good news can be split into two main parts. The first is 'friendship evangelism', and the second is 'programme- or event-based evangelism'. Friendship evangelism relies on genuine love and concern on a long-term basis, where profession of faith has to be consistent with lifestyle. It involves people in having the confidence to explain their personal faith to friends and colleagues at school, often in a hostile environment where the Christian viewpoint is held by the minority. Effort and persistency are also required and, in order to avoid inflicting intolerable and unwanted pressure, sensitivity is equally necessary for knowing when to speak and when to be silent. In a survey conducted among 10,000 Christians, 80 per cent were converted through friendship evangelism.

Events

Programme- or event-based evangelism is designed to create opportunities for aiding and enhancing friendship evangelism. It should not, however, act as a replacement. Church strategy for growth is dependent on both, with events that are relevant to specific target groups. Unfortunately, an adventurous programme of events can sometimes act as an excuse for neglecting friendship evangelism. Events such as the 1994 JIM campaign did increase many people's awareness of God and raised the profile of the church. These gains were vitally important, but events themselves must be built on the foundations of friendship evangelism if they are to be truly successful.

The Teenage Religion and Values Survey asked church members if they attended an evangelistic group. The answers revealed that 97 per cent of them did not. This indicates that only 3 per cent consider themselves part of an evangelistic group. One could surmise that the majority of young people are therefore uninterested in communicating their Christian faith to others, seeing church as a cosy club for friendship rather than a stimulant for action. The 97 per cent could be comprised of three possible groups:

those for whom evangelism is outside their concept of church;
those who do not understand the term 'evangelistic group', and therefore said 'no';
those who did understand the term and honestly replied 'no'.

It could be, however, that many of the 97 per cent of respondents are involved with friendship evangelism but simply do not attend an evangelistic group.

Although it is true that many churches are introspective and thus failing to influence the community through either category of evangelism, it is also true that the 1990s have seen significant advances across the spectrum of denominations. Throughout the initial four years of this decade of evangelism, emphasis has indeed been laid on training young people to communicate their faith, alongside events such as Jesus In Me, Fired Up, March For Jesus and Minus To Plus.

What's in a word?

There are, however, many adolescents people who, at the very mention of the word 'evangelism', react with fear and embarrassment. Attached to this word are certain methods that make some people feel uncomfortable. Door-to-door witnessing, leaflet-distributing, talking to strangers on the streets, second-rate stage presentations in half-empty marquees—all these leave many young people cringing with embarrassment at the cultural irrelevance of it all.

It is not surprising, therefore, that a total of 57 per cent of churchgoing young people said 'no', when asked if they wanted their church to give more time to conducting evangelism. Of this 57 per cent, Roman Catholics were the most likely to want evangelism, followed by Anglicans and then Free Church members. The Teenage Religion and Values Survey also revealed that of the 30 per cent who responded 'yes', but who did not want to get involved themselves, only 14 per cent said 'yes' to more church evangelism as well as 'yes' to personal involvement. Of this last small percentage, Free Church members were the most enthusiastic. These figures may indicate the low priority that young people give to evangelism, or they may refer to the stigma attached to the phrase 'conducting evangelism'. There is a glaring need to provide cringe-free events that relate to youth culture! Events to which young people can go without embarrassment are usually those which they help to organize and run. Willingness to be involved will increase if people are given the responsibility to organize and influence programmes. Bringing friends along will become a lot easier!

The church is often said to be the only organization to exist for the benefit of its non-members. Therefore, the importance of communicating personal faith should never be underestimated. Young people must be encouraged to be confident and unashamed about their beliefs, and church strategy for growth must continue to emphasize the importance of friendship evangelism alongside event-based evangelism, motivating young people to adopt both.

Do you attend an evangelistic group?

Source: Teenage Religion and Values Survey of 13,000 pupils in England and Wales. All figures refer to responses to the statement immediately above this diagram. The left hand column shows, at the top, the responses of the total sample which is divided, in the middle, into responses of year 9 and year 10 pupils. The right hand column deals only with the 11% of the total sample who attend church.

39 John Buckeridge
Discipleship

Learning what it means to become a Christian and then living it out takes a lifetime, not a moment. Even people who can point to a time and place when they made a definite decision to follow Christ find that discipleship is a continuous process.

Within the past fifteen years, there has been a growing effort to teach and to disciple young people more effectively in the Christian faith. This has resulted in an explosion of teaching resources. A major reason for this spurt of activity is the realization that the church has often failed to communicate the basics of the faith in a way which keeps the attention of young people.

One of the pioneers of youth ministry resources in Britain has been Bob Moffett. In 1980, *Buzz* magazine (the predecessor of *Alpha* magazine) began publishing a monthly youth-group meeting-plan written by Moffett. He was keenly aware of the wide range of youth resources available in the United States, but in the 1980s the books and magazines of the Youth Specialties Group were virtually unknown on this side of the Atlantic.

Moffett's 'Power Page' columns were published by Scripture Union, and became best sellers. Since then, there has been an ever growing list of books and curriculum videos, and in 1992 there came the launch of the first inter-denominational youth ministry magazine, *Youthwork*.

To date, these materials have catered mainly for churches who work with churchgoing young people and there is still a lack in Britain of resources to help disciple non-churchgoers of the same age. Nevertheless, there have been some fundamental changes in the way British evangelical churches are grappling with the task of teaching young people about the faith.

The majority of churches no longer expect new converts, adult or teenage, to be assimilated immediately into church life without specialized help. There are now nurture groups to introduce recent converts to the basics of the Christian faith, replacing the 'drop them in at the deep end' approach. In the past, this has resulted in a high fall-off rate, with many young people failing to learn to 'swim'. Small groups of young people who are new in the faith are likely to understand the specific needs of new teenage converts better.

Church growth experts refer to these small groups of people from similar backgrounds as 'homogeneous'. The level of openness and practical encouragement the group members can offer each other is always likely to be deepest if the group come from a similar background, social sector and are of a similar age. Many thriving churches worldwide use homogeneous small groups to build a grassroots kinship and group identity within the larger (sometimes very large) church.

Advocates of specialist or homogeneous small groups sometimes find themselves in heated disagreements with those who point to scriptures which call for the church to be a mixed community. But it is surely arguable that every Christian should have the opportunity to be part of a small group of people that he or she can relate to easily.

At times, the lack of person-power and other resources mean that younger and older teenagers may have to be put in the same nurture or youth fellowship group, but this is not ideal. Having a group with which they can identify, and to which they can belong, is particularly important to young people. Learning together about the Christian faith is hard enough without putting twelve-year-olds in the same groups as seventeen-year-olds.

In our 'post-Christian' British culture, knowledge about the basics of the Christian faith is thin. In past generations children learned scriptures from the Old and New Testaments in school. Now the demands of a wide-ranging curriculum have rendered religious education to status of a poor cousin and Christianity is just one of several religions taught. There is now widespread ignorance about even the basics of the faith. It makes little sense to mix churched young people, who have a good knowledge of Christianity, with unchurched recent converts who do not. Their needs are very different. By putting like-minded young people together in small groups, an overall group identity can naturally develop and positive peer pressure can encourage cohesion. Another key factor in helping young people to grow in their faith is amply illustrated by the statistics in the Teenage Religion and Values Survey.

Three-quarters of the churchgoing sample who attended Anglican or Free churches said they wanted their church to devote more time to learning what it means to be a Christian; and a large majority of that group wanted to be involved in the learning process. Learning involves more than just listening or talking, it requires action and involvement.

Peer education among young people is enjoying growing popularity. In the United States, studies have shown that young people taught by properly trained peers have a higher level of understanding and recall of a given subject. Today, large numbers of American teenagers receive AIDS-awareness education from people of their own age. Peer counselling programmes exist in half of the schools in the state of California. In Britain, too, peer counselling and peer listening programmes are becoming more common in the secular workplace. Although they have yet to find a toe-hold in local churches, it is probably only a matter of time. The survey certainly suggests that many young Christians want a more active role in learning their faith.

Practical projects like Whose Earth? and Christmas Cracker help young people to see that their faith is not a collection of words, but consists of action and involvement—in short, it is a new way of living.

Dr Tony Campolo, author, popular speaker, sociologist and a professor at Eastern College, Philadelphia, refers to this learning-in-action process as praxis. (See also chapter 33.) 'In simplistic terms praxis is a special kind of reflection that occurs in the context of action', writes Campolo. Living out the faith requires those in all levels of church leadership to give young people meaningful responsibility. Acts of compassion, service, witness and worship are all required. A church needs to allow young people more than a mere token involvement in church services. It should be prepared to let young people lead worship and preach, as well as to give them the lower-profile, lower-risk opportunities.

Charles Spurgeon, the great but admittedly exceptional Victorian Baptist preacher, was the pastor of a London church at the age of nineteen. How many churches today would let a nineteen-year-old near a pulpit?

Interestingly, the Teenage Religion and Values Survey reveals that Roman Catholics are less likely than Protestants to want their churches to give more time to learn what it means to be a Christian. Three in ten answered 'no' to the question, 'Would you want your church to give more time to learn what it means to be a Christian?'; 44 per cent answered 'yes', but wanted no part in that process; and only a quarter said 'yes' and wanted to be involved. Why the difference between Roman Catholic and Anglican or Free Church young people?

A key factor may be the formalized catechism classes that most Roman Catholic churches use. Before they can participate in the Mass, young Catholics attend classes where the foundational doctrines of the Roman Catholic Church are taught. It could be that having attended these classes, the Catholics surveyed thought that this provided adequate instruction and therefore they did not need to learn more about what it means to become a Christian. Or it could be that this process was a dull one which they do not want to repeat!

The passive style of learning that Catholic children are used to may also explain the low percentage who wanted an active learning style. Many churches are using mentoring as a form of teaching and discipling young people. This can be especially effective when working with young people from a difficult or disturbed background. Indeed, the emotional and psychological problems that some young people bring into their new faith make an 'under-the-wing' style of apprenticeship essential, with support constantly available, if a real change in lifestyle is to occur.

We all need heroes and heroines, people we can look up to. So many of the heroes of young people are negative figures. Paul told Timothy: 'Copy me'. Members of the Christian community need to be prepared to give of their time and live a life worth copying. That is the challenge.

Looking to the future, would you want your church to give more time to learn what it means to be a Christian?

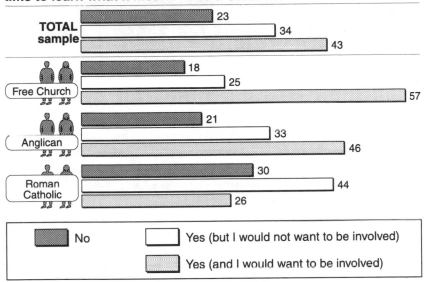

TOTAL sample
- 23
- 34
- 43

Free Church
- 18
- 25
- 57

Anglican
- 21
- 33
- 46

Roman Catholic
- 30
- 44
- 26

▓ No	☐ Yes (but I would not want to be involved)
	▒ Yes (and I would want to be involved)

Source: Teenage Religion and Values Survey of 13,000 pupils in England and Wales. All figures refer to responses to the statement immediately above this diagram. The left hand column shows, at the top, the responses of the total sample which is divided, in the middle, into responses of year 9 and year 10 pupils. The right hand column deals only with the 11% of the total sample who attend church.

40 Maggie Everett
Picking Up the Pieces

The Old Grey Donkey, Eeyore, stood by himself in a thistly corner of the Forest, his front feet stood well apart, his head on one side and thought about things. Sometimes he thought sadly to himself 'Why?' and sometimes he thought 'Wherefore?' and sometimes he thought 'Inasmuch as which?'—and sometimes he didn't know quite what he was thinking about. [1]

While most of us would not necessarily choose to stand in a 'thistly corner of the Forest,' I am sure that we have at some time or other been in Eeyore's shoes: needing the time and space to think and reflect about life, and not knowing quite what to think! As adults we have (or certainly should have) developed the skills to reason, predict and plan ahead in the context of comparing the reality of the world around us with ideals. This ability to think in abstract terms and to reason and reflect is a major change that teenagers undergo.

It is widely accepted that the stages of intellectual development identified in the work of Piaget (and others) are accurate. Piaget claimed that the thinking processes undertaken by the child begin to change from about the age of eleven or twelve. Before this age, the child is locked into thinking that is based on their handling of concrete facts and situations. As this begins to change, the young person moves into the beginnings of abstract thinking, using abstract concepts, symbols and propositions. At this stage, young people are earning to reason about hypotheses and deduce conclusions without the help of concrete objects.

The maturing teenager thus begins to become more adept at imagining alternatives, identifying possible consequences of the choices, and systematically reasoning through tasks that require the skills of problem solving and decision making. In order for the teenager to be able to function effectively in this way, it is important that an adequate framework of security—where there are boundaries, and where parameters of acceptable behaviour have been clearly and fairly laid out—has been in place. Where no such effective discipline has existed, the ability to make choices becomes impaired because the foundation of facing the consequences of one's actions has not been put down.

Blaming circumstances, other people and often God for what has happened can at times shield the individual from addressing a situation where it is they who need to accept some responsibility for what is happening. Taking control, initiative and responsibility in situations requires the maturity to which teenagers aspire but which, sadly, many adults do not fully attain.

The abstract thinking abilities which have begun to emerge in early adolescence enable most thirteen- to fifteen-year-olds to imagine ideal possibilities and to compare these with the reality of the world around them. However, it needs to be said here that while many thirteen- to fifteen-year-olds are working this through internally, learning to express their thoughts and conclusions in an articulate way is another part of the developmental process. It is one thing to know what you think about something and quite another to express that in a way that can be fully understood by another!

In addition to the development in the teenager's thinking processes, physical developments during this period often effect his or her emotional state. The ability to articulate feelings that have not been previously either felt or labelled is something with which many struggle as they begin to assess their feelings in the context of the world around them. Teenagers often worry about what they believe they *should* feel.

By the time she was thirteen years old, Tracey had experienced a continuously stormy home life. Over the years, her parents—both Christians—rowed increasingly and with greater ferocity, frequently resulting in violent outbursts and in one or other of them leaving the house. Tracey had begun to assume responsibility for her younger brother and sister, often trying to calm them when the arguments woke or frightened them. An essentially gregarious girl, Tracey had begun to withdraw from others and had become rather aggressive towards others in her class who disagreed with her.

Talking with Tracey one day, I asked how she was: 'OK' came the reply. 'How are things at home?' she shrugged in response, 'same as usual'. 'How are you coping?', I asked. Tracey shrugged again: 'OK'. 'Do you want to talk about it?' Another shrug. I tried again: 'How do you feel about what's going on?' Another shrug. 'Do you want to talk to me or is there someone else you feel you'd rather talk to?' 'I'll talk to anyone . . .' Learning how to draw from teenagers their thoughts, feelings and problems takes time and usually greater effort than asking an adult to do so. Allowing them to explore and examine what is going on internally, as well as how they interpret what is happening around them, is critical for their personal development. It should also be remembered here that expressing thoughts can be very easy. Young people often enjoy stimulating discussions in which they can express their opinions. Sharing feelings and problems is another matter. Positive feelings are relatively easy to talk about, but allowing others to know that what one is feeling is 'negative' or 'difficult' is not so straightforward. It is usually the case that such feelings and resultant problems are only expressed in a situation where the young person wants to and is able to find possible resolutions to the issues. (Unless, of course, they are desperately seeking some attention.)

It is also during this phase that many begin to criticize those around them, as they begin to evaluate the personal qualities they might or might not wish to develop. This critical stage is not simply applied to those around them, or to the wider world that impinges upon their horizons, but is also applied to their perception of themselves. Additionally, there can be a tendency to believe that others are thinking the same things as they are! Consequently, when a teenager at this stage of development experiences self-doubt or negativity about themselves, they will expect others to think the same way and react accordingly!

As the process of developing their sense of personal identity continues, their willingness and ability to articulate their thoughts, feelings and problems should begin to emerge. It is important for us to realize that as teenagers begin to establish their personal identity they often feel insecure about how well they will be received. Self-consciousness, and the fear of being unacceptable to those who are important to them (whether that is someone they look up to or their peer group) will have a bearing upon their desire to express themselves.

It must also be recognized that there is a difference between being the only one to express an opinion and to state how one is feeling, and being within a group where that is a common occurrence. Sharing feelings and problems is not always something at which the church as a whole excels. Cultural perceptions that it is inappropriate for men to express emotion and problems, especially in public, are present within the church as much as outside it. Because the leadership within many churches is predominantly male, an environment can result where teenagers perceive that such expressions are just as inappropriate within the church.

Is anyone listening?

It is evident from the research conducted among the sample of the group who feel that they belong to a Christian church that 29 per cent of these thirteen- to fifteen-year-olds did not want their church to give more time to sharing thoughts, feelings and problems! It is interesting to note that the highest occurrence of those young people (both male and female) who stated definitely that they did not want their church to do so hailed from a Roman Catholic church. Obvious generalizations could be made, but it would appear that an apparently more formal approach to expression of faith does not appear to encourage those young people questioned to share with others their feelings and problems. While the practice of confession provides one environment in which issues can be shared, this gives little room for debate or for a mutual sharing of feelings and problems. Taking this further, it is interesting to see that of the 71 per cent who said that they would want their church to give more time to sharing thoughts, feelings and problems, the highest ratio came from those aligning themselves with the Free Church, as opposed to those who came from a more formal tradition. It might be fair to reflect that within the Free Church there are perhaps more opportunities for and greater emphasis laid upon sharing through discussions, and the experience of God as being an integral part of faith.

Expressing what is happening internally is often difficult for adults, let alone for teenagers who are struggling to understand what is going on inside. The Teenage Religion and Values Survey does help to reinforce the picture of a church that is not used to articulating and giving room to expressing the inner turmoil that many experience. A great number of life experiences are not easy to deal with within a Christian framework, and side-stepping issues and trying to provide 'pat' answers only heightens the perspective that Christian faith is naive, inadequate and consequently irrelevant, and that Christians are hypocritical. Christian leaders who are willing to be honest about their own struggles and to acknowledge that things do not always go right, rather than to impose upon others the 'right Christian response' (whatever that might be!), are those who enable their 'followers' to face the reality of life and to see God both involved in and capable of dealing with all circumstances. This maturing process is hard work and, unfortunately, many give up along the way often because it is threatening to have to face situations with which we feel inadequate to cope.

Paul wrote to the Corinthian church:

When I was a child, I talked like a child, I thought like a child, I reasoned like a child. When I became a man, I put childish ways behind me. Now we see but a poor reflection as in a mirror; then we shall see face to face. Now I know in part; then I shall know fully even as I am fully known.[2]

Putting childish ways behind us does not mean that we lose all our thoughts feelings and problems (although we might well wish that to be true and often act as if it is!); understanding how to face them and deal with them is a process with which, as adults, we often need help ourselves. It was not until I was well into my twenties that I began to recognize how my life experience had affected my thoughts, feelings and attitudes which subsequently caused me to have problems in my perception of both myself and the world around me. The fear of rejection makes the prospect of being 'fully known' by anyone other than God (who loves us and accepts us anyway) very threatening, and there are many of us who even struggle to accept that to be true.

An attitude of openness and honesty, and a willingness to listen to the perspectives and experiences of others in a non-judgemental atmosphere, is essential if young people are to feel accepted and to have the confidence to express those issues with which they are struggling. Problems are not likely to surface until there is security within relationships and an environment where they can feel confident that they will still be accepted whatever they might say.

A church community where those of all ages are free to share in a supportive atmosphere does not precipitate a situation where problems abound. It is one where each person will be able to make choices and assume responsibility for their own actions. Surely this is following not only the example of Jesus who continued to accept Judas as one of the twelve disciples even when he knew what he was like and what would happen, but truly putting 'childish ways' behind us.

References

1. A. A. Milne, *Winnie the Pooh*, Methuen and Co. Ltd, 1966, page 39.
2. 1 Corinthians 13:11–12.

Looking to the future, would you want your church to give more time to sharing thoughts, feelings and problems?

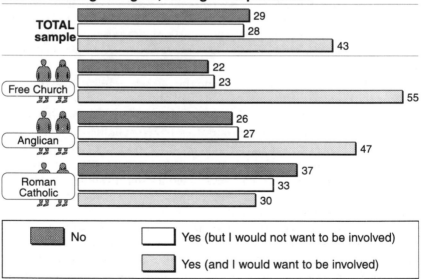

Source: Teenage Religion and Values Survey of 13,000 pupils in England and Wales. All figures refer to responses to the statement immediately above this diagram. The left hand column shows, at the top, the responses of the total sample which is divided, in the middle, into responses of year 9 and year 10 pupils. The right hand column deals only with the 11% of the total sample who attend church.

41 Pete Ward

Teaching Young People

Should the church change in order to keep young people coming to services? This is the question which is in the forefront of most people's minds when we discuss youth ministry. All around the country, churches are setting up worship services which take account of the needs and interests of young people. There is a general feeling that young people are finding little within normal church life which suits them.

Change, it would seem, is in the air and young people are right at the heart of these developments. In part, it would appear that this change is coming about because churches are afraid that young people may depart from their pews forever if something is not done to keep them involved. This, if you like, is a pragmatic movement, but it is motivated in many cases by Christian parents and youth ministers who are in close relationship with young people, and who are listening to what they have to say. Change, however, is not just motivated by the needs of young people who already belong to a church.

Many feel that the church needs to take more account of youth culture because they are engaged in outreach to those who currently do not attend the church. This force for change in church services arises from mission. In my own case, I realized that many of the young people I had recently seen coming to faith would never feel comfortable in the services currently happening in the local churches. Rather than see these young Christians slowly lose interest in spiritual things, I felt that the way forward was to set up a service which was designed for them and by them. The service, which is called JOY and happens in a local Anglican church, is still running.

Given this general background, the results from the Teenage Religion and Values Survey, indicating that only 25 per cent of young people who attend church find sermons to be less than helpful, is curious. My first response to these data is: 'Can this be true?'. I am even more nonplussed when I find that 43 per cent of the sample felt that sermons were either OK or very OK. There is something here, to my mind, which needs some investigation. After all, the sermon must be the most inaccessible part of a regular church service for many young people: words with no pictures!

I find some solace in the realization that these young people are a relatively small subsection of the entire sample, that is, those who feel they belong to a Christian church. There is something of the 'eight out of ten cat owners who expressed a preference said their cats preferred Kiticat' about this statistic. In other words, the group is already self-selected, in that they are already regular churchgoers. In this sense, it is understandable that a good few feel that there is something to be gained from going to church. While this may be the case, a sizeable proportion (32 per cent) are not at all sure that the sermon has much in it for them. If the 'not sures' are put together with those who disagreed or disagreed strongly with the statement, we are left with more than half of the young people being left at the end of a sermon either confused, bored or well and truly fed up.

There are a few ecumenical points which can be reflected upon in the split which we have in this particular question. While those who are not sure of the value of sermons remains a constant 32 per cent across the denominations, roughly double the number of Roman Catholic to Anglican and Free Church young people find little of value in sermons. There are three ways of looking at this response. It could be argued that in the Protestant denominations, a more lively approach to church worship has begun to prevail, particularly in more evangelical churches. The use of illustrations, overhead projectors and drama has probably gone some way to making sermons more endurable for all pew-dwelling folk. In contrast, some might feel that the Roman Catholic Church is lagging behind in this respect. It could also be said that the young people who attend non-Roman Catholic churches are likely to be more committed in general to the Christian faith. The Roman Catholic Church, some might say, has a more nominal membership. While these arguments may have some truth in them, they fail to take account of the changes in the Roman Catholic Church since Vatican II.

Since the upheaval of the 1960s, the Roman Catholic Church has seen the advent of folk and rock masses, a widespread renewal in the Holy Spirit and a fresh emphasis on the ministry of the word. All of this has done much to brighten up Roman Catholic worship. It should also be said that in many Roman Catholic services the sermon is much shorter than those in Free Churches, taking the form of a very short homily. With the emphasis on the sacrament, it could be said that Roman Catholic young people would experience the sermon as a much less of a focus of the service than would their Free Church brethren. This may also go some way to explaining the difference in figures.

Given all of this, there still remains the question of what the church should do about the sermon in worship. Clearly, the figures would point us to the fact that at least some of the young people who come to church find something in the sermons they hear which can help them in the faith. We should not underestimate the importance of this to the ongoing encouragement of a good many young people in our churches. At the same time, however, there is little, if any, room for complacency in these findings.

A good few clergy would say that the sermon is a God-given method of teaching, to be abandoned at our peril. In support of this general position, I would like to say that my own experience is that there really is a power in speaking about the gospel to young people in a formal, up-front way. At the same time, however, I have usually found this to be most effective when I am sharing the story of Jesus with young people who are from outside the faith community. Speaking about Jesus in this 'gospelling' kind of a way has unique power, but it needs to be done with sensitivity and with the utmost brevity.

When it comes to the preaching of sermons to those who regularly attend church, I am less convinced of the long-term value of this approach outside of a small proportion of the population who, through education and cultural conditioning, are able to assimilate information which is given in lecture format. For the majority of young people, most sermons probably go in one ear and out of the other.

The key question we need to ask is: 'How do young people learn?' In particular, how do they learn the practice of the Christian faith? For the most part, being a Christian is not about knowledge alone—it is also about values and behaviour. These things are best learned on the hoof through experience. Experience alone is not enough; we need to reflect on the events of life in the light of the scriptures and we need some space to discuss what has been happening in the experience. This, to my mind, is the way that Jesus went about teaching his disciples. In most instances, Jesus did not plan to engage in lengthy formal teaching sessions. Most of his messages arose from events that come up as he and his disciples went about the kingdom business. Take, for instance, the teaching on fasting and the Sabbath in Mark 2:18–28 and the teaching on prayer in Luke 11:1–4. In both these passages, and in many others, Jesus' teaching came about because of a question which arose from his lifestyle.

Informal teaching, which comes about when young people's interest or curiosity is raised by the lifestyle of the youth minister, is a much more effective and life-changing approach to discipling young people. In the first instance, it takes seriously the role of the adult who is in relationship with the young people as a model and an example of the way the Christian life should be lived. It also takes as its starting point the felt need or prior questions of the young people. To teach the content of the faith from such a place is not only to follow the example of Jesus—it also has much greater chance of being seen as relevant by young people.

References

1. Leslie Francis 'Believing Without Belonging' The Essex Hall Lecture, Unitarian Information Department, 1994.
2. Peter Brierley *Reaching and Keeping Teenagers*, MARC, 1993.

I find sermons helpful

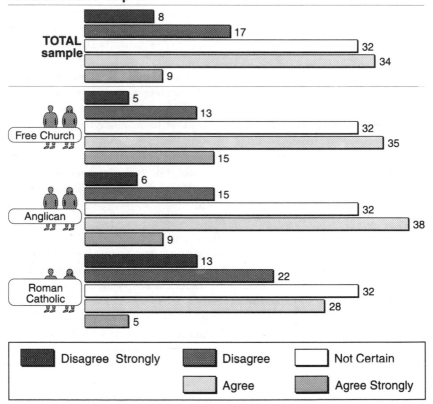

Source: Teenage Religion and Values Survey of 13,000 pupils in England and Wales. All figures refer to responses to the statement immediately above this diagram. The left hand column shows, at the top, the responses of the total sample which is divided, in the middle, into responses of year 9 and year 10 pupils. The right hand column deals only with the 11% of the total sample who attend church.

42 David Bruce

The Isolated Christian

Why should there be so much teenage apathy towards praying together, working in the community and having fellowship? Of course, young people aged between thirteen and fifteen have many commitments during the evenings when fellowship groups often take place. They have homework and sports activities, not to mention an escalating social life. But is this sufficient explanation?

It is probably true that most young people look on church as more of a social opportunity than a serving opportunity. This in itself need not be a bad thing as young people need to socialize: the making and developing of friendships is crucial to their future maturity in relationships. But it can lead some people to the view that teenagers have a superficial attitude to organized religion, and this is not always so.

As part of the Teenage Religion and Values Survey, young people were asked to respond to the following questions: 'Looking to the future, would you like your church to give more time to attend prayer groups?.. community service groups?.. informal house groups?'

Prayer groups

Why, therefore, should it be that churchgoing young people generally do not want to allot more time to meet together to pray? In fact, most teenagers find it difficult to pray anyway. This is partly because self-discipline is involved and thirteen- to fifteen-year-olds are only starting to develop skills in this area. More fundamental, however, is the disconcerting fact of what prayer is and how it cuts across the culture of teenage life. Ultimately, prayer implies that a person is helpless, and there is no one who dislikes feeling helpless more than a teenager. Why do we pray? We do not pray because we may but because we must. One Bible teacher, the late Dr Alan Flavelle, once said, 'The greatest reason for Christians not praying is that they think they don't need to'. People who pray articulate their helplessness. Older people gather the experience to prove the necessity of this in their lives, but teenagers have difficulty believing it because everywhere they look in their media-driven world they receive messages telling them that they have the power within themselves to do anything they want.

Helplessness is the last idea in contemporary youth culture.

There is more than a hint of this in many churches, too. The importance of prayer as celebration has happily been growing, with approaches to intercession such as that taken by 'March for Jesus', but this is not the whole story. Jesus sweated drops of blood in Gethsemane as he prayed before his crucifixion. Whatever else that may say, it certainly indicates that he was engaged in a task which involved hard work and struggle. Jacob experienced something similar in his wrestling match with God, when he was physically injured as a result. Prayer involves hard work as much as it does celebration.

Furthermore, what happens when we pray? Imagine a heavenly conversation taking place between Father, Son and Spirit. It is a conversation which never stops and which expresses all the concerns of the universe. When we pray in the name of Jesus, we are privileged to join in this heavenly conversation for a time, to participate in the cabinet meeting of the cosmos. Young people want to change the world and they want to do it now. What would be a better way to start than this? Prayer is celebration before the Lord, hard work for the Lord and participation with the Lord, in his plans for everyone.

Community service

Evangelicals used to be deeply suspicious of community service as part of church programmes. Perhaps the feeling was that if programmes of this kind were begun, they would take over the major church resources. The energies of God's people would be taken up with perfectly good endeavours to relieve human suffering while the real task of evangelism would be side-lined or forgotten. In the past, we have been rightly keen to defend the faith against error, but in doing this we have unwittingly embraced another error: not working out the faith in our communities.

Looking at the figures, it is clear that although some young people think churches are doing enough in the area of community service, others think that community service should not be a church concern. If questioned further, respondents might suggest that the task of relieving human need rests primarily with the social services and government, rather than the church. The small percentages who responded positively to the idea may indicate that community service has little appeal to young teenagers and is not the sort of thing they would feel comfortable doing.

On the other hand, I remember the response of some young people in a church of which I was part. We had a panel-type discussion, with a group of ministers as leaders. As a member of the panel I was excited, if a little nervous, about what might emerge in our discussions. Once the initial stiffness wore off, the young people began to express their feelings of alienation from the decision-making processes in the church. They had little sense of ownership of what we did each week at worship. They had scant knowledge of our thinking as ministers, and of our future strategy for the churches. In short, they told us that as ministers we were fossilized ! 'How many ministers does it take to change a light bulb?', says one. 'I don't know. How many ministers does it take to change a light bulb?' says another. 'Change?' says the first. 'You've got to be kidding . . .' The joke is told with only half a smile. The young people in my church were not stupid or irresponsible. They were full of energy and potential and wanted to serve God, but no one was allowing them to get on with it. The structures of our church were too rigid. The young needed an outlet through which they could actually accomplish something for God, but we were unwilling to let them do it.

It is true to say that young people in the 1990s are rather less impressed by the truth or consistency of the arguments of the clergy than by the relevance of what the clergy do. Doing a 'dirty hands' job for God will transform the way a person thinks—not only about the job before them, but about God. Take someone I once met called Mike, for example. Mike was a sceptic about Christianity. He was very gifted with his hands, especially when working with wood, but he found all the religious talk in church too much to take. Succeeding preachers had found to their cost that Mike considered even their best pulpit efforts to be irrelevant nonsense. But one wise leader recognized Mike's gifts and wondered how to incorporate him into the fellowship. He began by asking Mike to do one or two repair jobs, and then asked for his help in a rather larger project involving the construction of a set of storage cupboards for the youth organizations. Next, he involved Mike in a fund-raising effort for a community project and after that Mike was elected to a committee to supervise the repairs to the buildings of the church and local school. The leader who had involved him at first found that as the months went by Mike was talking about the work he was doing in a different way. He wasn't doing it for himself but for God. 'Why's that, Mike?' he was asked. Mike's response was simple but profound. 'He did it all for me, right?' Right.

Our belief systems are not merely a function of what our intellects have been able to grasp about God. They are equally a function of what we have done in our lives up till now. If a person behaves in a generous, selfless manner for long enough and for good reason, they will imbibe selfless generosity as a belief, even if they didn't have it before. People are changed when they serve, even if they start out with what we might consider to be inadequate motives.

House groups

There is little overall enthusiasm among teenagers for house groups. An exception is provided by Free Church young people, who expressed a greater interest in spending time in house groups. Anglicans and Roman Catholics were correspondingly less convinced. The fact that the vast majority of young people do not want this level of involvement may simply reflect adolescent shyness and a feeling of insecurity in relating to others of different ages within the fellowship.

The most popular meeting for young people in the church calendar week is the youth fellowship, or its equivalent, because in that meeting everyone speaks the same language and it is not necessary to break out of the circle. A house fellowship group is different, because people of any age may come including, perhaps, family relatives.

This reluctance may indicate one of the difficulties we face more today than ever before. The generations have become so isolated from each other that each age group must have a specialist to cope with its specific needs. We are encouraged to think of the ageing process as an enemy rather than a friend. Youth is worshipped by our society to such an extent that vast industries exist to pander to our insatiable desire to appear younger than we are. But doesn't the Bible suggest rather the opposite? God seems to value old age rather than youth. We are encouraged to press on to maturity rather than indulge in the vanities of the young adult. The body of Christ is inter-generational, not mono-generational, but we do not practise as such any more because it has come to take too much effort.

For adults who have newly come to faith, it may well be helpful to attend a house group. But that group will not be complete without the reluctant thirteen-to fifteen-year olds, who in turn find it so difficult to believe that it can be 'cool' to be a granny.

Looking to the future, would you want your church to give more time to attend prayer group?

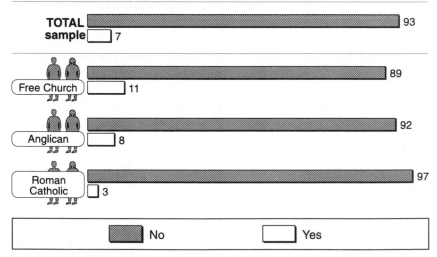

	No	Yes
TOTAL sample	93	7
Free Church	89	11
Anglican	92	8
Roman Catholic	97	3

Looking to the future, would you want your church to give more time to attend Community Service group?

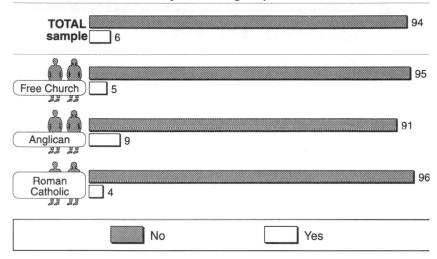

TOTAL sample
- No: 94
- Yes: 6

Free Church
- No: 95
- Yes: 5

Anglican
- No: 91
- Yes: 9

Roman Catholic
- No: 96
- Yes: 4

No ▨   Yes ☐

Looking to the future, would you want your church to give more time to attend informal house group?

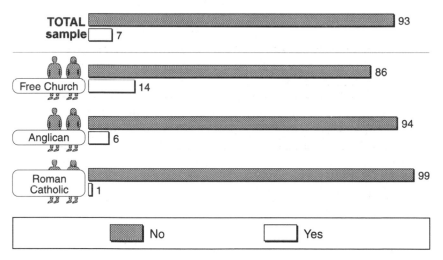

TOTAL sample
- No: 93
- Yes: 7

Free Church
- No: 86
- Yes: 14

Anglican
- No: 94
- Yes: 6

Roman Catholic
- No: 99
- Yes: 1

No ▨   Yes ☐

Source: Teenage Religion and Values Survey of 13,000 pupils in England and Wales. All figures refer to responses to the statement immediately above this diagram. The left hand column shows, at the top, the responses of the total sample which is divided, in the middle, into responses of year 9 and year 10 pupils. The right hand column deals only with the 11% of the total sample who attend church.

221

43 Nigel Hall

Rising to the Challenge

Dr Tony Campolo stated once that one of the main reasons for the church's lack of success in retaining young people was its inability to provide them with appropriate challenges. Far too often, churches in this country have failed to harness the dynamism, freshness and biblical simplicity that young Christian people can offer, and have limited their service to sponsored car washes or stacking the church chairs! It is no wonder that they see absolutely no correlation between the biblical example of empowerment of young people (such as David, Josiah and Timothy) and current church life.

A number of reasons can be offered for this:

◆ An insecurity in church leaders, who fear taking risks. It is so much easier to play safe and to restrict young people to areas of service which can never threaten the *status quo*. How would we react as ministers or youth leaders if our young people were seeing God moving in their lives far more powerfully than in our own? There might be a tendency to duck behind our structures and nurse feelings of spiritual jealousy!

◆ A lack of understanding about the need to provide the right framework for the motivation and encouragement of young people as they seek to live out their faith in a hostile post-Christian society. What was appropriate for us if we grew up in a church situation will not be appropriate for them. It has been said many times that we were never their age, and this is becoming more and more true.

◆ The lack of effective role models. We can best keep our teenagers by giving them a 'model for radical discipleship', says Andy Hickford, youth minister of Stopsley Baptist Church. Sadly, such models are few and far between.

◆ Church is still a spectator sport for most people (including young people). Faith so easily remains at the cerebral level and fails to reach the heart, let alone is worked out at the practical level by action.

◆ Superficiality—a limited understanding throughout the whole church (not just Christian youth) of commitment, discipleship and the need to outwork one's faith in order for God to use us more effectively.

All this has led to the tendency for faith to be compartmentalized with an often lack of practical application to everyday life issues. If 300 young people are leaving the church every week or are not joining at the lower age range,[1] then it is clear that we are failing to stimulate, challenge and inspire the right framework for young people to *rise to the challenge*.

Statistics from the Teenage Religion and Values Survey are illuminating:

◆ 58 per cent of all young people interviewed expressed the wish that, looking to the future, they would not only want their church to devote more time to helping people in the local neighbourhood, but that they would want to be involved. By denomination, this statistic broke down to 68 per cent from the Free Church, 60 per cent from the Anglican Church and 45 per cent from the Roman Catholic Church. This reflects a clear desire for the church to be proactive in satisfying the needs of the 'whole' person in the locality. It would be interesting to have been able to match this against a statistic of what percentage of young people felt that they had been *given* such opportunities to help!

◆ On the face of it, a more surprising statistic is in response to the question as to whether, looking to the future, the church should be giving more time to conducting evangelism. Some 56 per cent of pupils said 'No', with only 14 per cent stating 'Yes' and that they would wish to be involved! By denomination, 47 per cent from the Free Church said 'No', with 55 per cent and 64 per cent from the Anglican Church and Roman Catholic Church saying 'No' respectively. How do we reconcile this view with the previous clear desire for action in the neighbourhood? There are two alternative possibilities:

We are seeing a generation of Christian young people who place a low emphasis on evangelism.

Those surveyed saw 'evangelism' as a particular adult type of activity consisting of cold door knocking; verbal dexterity by smooth-talking, oleaginous American evangelists; or of mass appeals in draughty tents with blue-rinsed choirs singing Moody and Sankey hymns. Or perhaps they were simply worried about conducting evangelism without preparation and training.

I trust that the latter is the more likely possibility and that had the question been phrased in a different way, we may have seen a vastly different response. It seems that we may have been guilty here of tragically distorting the younger generation's perception of what evangelism is actually about! In the words of Rebecca Manley Pippert, there seems to be the view that 'evangelism is something you shouldn't do to your dog, let alone a best friend!'[2]

So what should our response be to these statistics? How can we rise to the challenge of providing short term service opportunities and projects?

Principles for stimulating involvement in service opportunities

◆ Provide the information on opportunities. An increasing number of organizations can provide details of exciting, worthwhile schemes which will challenge and stretch people's faith, and work towards them being salt and light in the community or abroad. (Examples include: Careforce, Crusaders, Christian Service Centre, Evangelical Missionary Alliance, Interserve, London City Mission, Oasis, Operation Mobilisation, Saltmine Trust, Salvation Army, Scripture Union, Tear Fund, Time For God, World Horizons, YFC and YWAM). It is so much more effective if you can link this with a young person who is able to talk about a particular project from personal experience. Daily exposure to television and radio has created a hardened shell around most people, so you need to be inventive in the way you communicate. For example, one church known to me has built up links with a key Christian in Addis Abbaba, Ethiopia; and has raised money to send a small fact-finding team out there, who then made a video to launch a fundraising programme for particular projects.

◆ Be responsible in your expectations. You know the capabilities of your young people and will be aware of what opportunities will be appropriate for them. However, do not be limited in your opinions of how God can use them!

◆ Ensure that you do what you can to allow them to discover their own gifts and potential, both natural and spiritual. So many are not motivated to be involved in opportunities because they are used to receiving overwhelmingly negative messages about youth. Responsibility breeds a sense of ownership, which breeds yet further motivated involvement. One girl who attended one of Crusaders' overseas expeditions found this; she said afterwards: 'God blessed me and changed me so much that it is almost with shame that I look back to my initial reactions'.

◆ Ensure that the young people are trained and prepared as much as possible. God will equip them spiritually for situations in a tremendous way, but this does not negate the need for training. Most organizations which offer service opportunities offer practical, biblical training as a necessary precursor to these projects.

Conclusion

A government survey entitled 'Young People in the Eighties', found that the main reasons which teenagers gave for going to church were 'meeting friends', 'an opportunity to participate' and 'doing something useful'. Those churches and groups around the country which are most successful at keeping teenagers are those which motivate by a clear challenge to involvement. However, unless we propagate a Christ-centred gospel that is outward-looking and promotes radical discipleship, then our attempts to show the need for a practical outworking of our faith in service opportunities will be doomed.

References

1. English Church Census, 1991.
2. Rebecca Manley Pippert in *Out of the Saltshaker*, IVP, 1980.

Looking to the future, would you want your church to give more time to conducting evangelism?

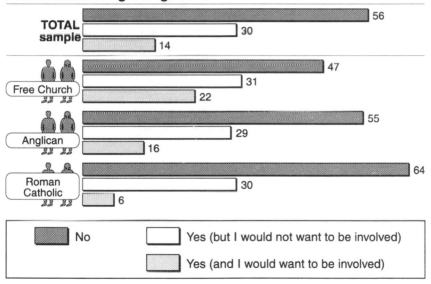

Source: Teenage Religion and Values Survey of 13,000 pupils in England and Wales. All figures refer to responses to the statement immediately above this diagram. The left hand column shows, at the top, the responses of the total sample which is divided, in the middle, into responses of year 9 and year 10 pupils. The right hand column deals only with the 11% of the total sample who attend church.

Looking to the future, would you want you church to give more time to helping people in the local neighbourhood?

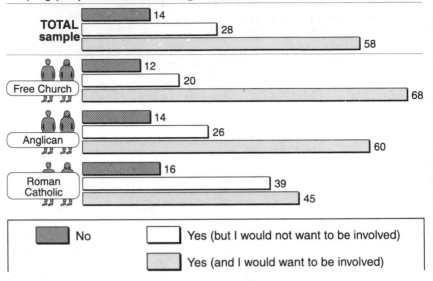

Source: Teenage Religion and Values Survey of 13,000 pupils in England and Wales. All figures refer to responses to the statement immediately above this diagram. The left hand column shows, at the top, the responses of the total sample which is divided, in the middle, into responses of year 9 and year 10 pupils. The right hand column deals only with the 11% of the total sample who attend church.

44 Russ Oliver

Youth Congregations or Youth Churches?

This question hinges a lot on the definition of terminology and, furthermore, varying church structures will place a different meaning on these groupings.

The statistics from the Teenage Religion and Values Survey show a surprising lack of youth initiatives within our churches. This was especially true within the Anglican set-up, which historically has been a leading light in providing facilities for young people. The Free Church shows an encouraging trend in youth provision. This is in keeping with their national church growth and general greater flexibility in meeting venues, communication and so on. Those churches not providing specialist youth input will find that this affects their growth, enthusiasm and the life of the congregation. Young people need a safe haven from the world they face and the metaphor of being pulled into a boat from a storm is appropriate.

Many 'new churches' are labelled youth churches, primarily because of the perceived number of young people who attend. The perception is often untrue, although new initiatives do generally attract the youth. This can be seen in the continuous changes in culture and fashion exploited by the media and retail trade.

I personally struggle with the youth church concept. By this term, I mean a homogenous group of young people with its own church government that is clearly exclusive to a defined age group. The Bible refers to no such model, but clearly promotes body ministry, inclusive church models and family. For example, Romans 12:4 and 1 Corinthians 12:12 talk of many aspects of the body making a whole. This imagery of the body, I assume, is inclusive of social class, maturity, sex, culture and so forth.

In today's society, one in three marriages are ending in divorce, with the church increasingly called upon to provide stability and parenting role models. Within my own church, we have needed to use many couples who have not considered themselves youth workers, but who have provided an excellent 'surrogate' parent role for many young people who have never experienced this unconditional love. Some young people may rebel against this model, searching for their own identity and independence. But it is vital that we leave opportunities for them to return to this environment for the love and stability they need (Luke 15:11ff.).

Exclusive groups of people often breed content, shallow roots and selfish lifestyles. The contentment comes out of the lack of need for change. Different age groups stimulate changes and challenge mind-sets, whilst providing a depth to life. If these things are not challenged, and if groups of people do not communicate or work together, this begins to restrict our effectiveness to relate. It also creates groups which are solely intent on self-pleasure.

As with all groups of people, young people have specialized needs to be addressed. This is often done best within the context of youth groups or similar set-ups, but should be set in the framework of the church, that is, all-inclusive.

Clearly, many youth congregations start out of frustration. This is primarily due to the restrictions felt by many young people in our churches. Possibility through lack of responsibility, ownership, identity and freedom in style of worship/meeting structure etc. This is a wider issue, including social class and race. Many of our churches lack flexibility and cause these groups of people to do their own thing. What does the Bible say about hospitality, family, prejudice, friendship and so on? The other problem soon to face the youth church concept is 'when are you not a youth?'!

Youth congregations

If this is a group that is part of and under a wider central leadership, it can be a very successful tool for resourcing young people. Within this model, I would anticipate that there would be opportunities to work across age and groups of people. This may be through leadership roles or through public environments such as public meetings, social action, evangelism, prayer and so on. It remains part of the 'whole', whilst benefiting from the privilege of specific programming for that age group.

Youth church

I would understand this to be a group of young people with its own governmental leadership. It may still have an apostolic input or be covered by an 'area' leadership team, although this is often not the case. The danger is that this becomes exclusive and restrictive. Many current church structures are functioning this way; not simply those relating to young people, but also those made up of a few people—often in the same social class and age bracket. This limits development, training and impact within their communities. The risks of this model were explained earlier.

Transfer

The transfer to an 'adult' church from a 'youth' church can prove very difficult for all concerned. There are massive benefits for doing so, but I do feel that it would be easier not to run with this model from the beginning, in order to alleviate the hassles. I am aware, too, that this integration raises its own problems.

The young people struggle with a loss of identity when they come into a larger, diverse group of people. Some who were in leadership can lose this role because of others already in position, maybe with greater gifts. Some are not taken seriously because of their age and there is a need to prove themselves in this new setting. They can display a lack of maturity and feel overawed by the new challenges. The need for greater responsibility causes pressure and, in the midst of losing the 'youth' tag, so many other changes can prove to be the final straw.

Nonetheless, depending on the individual, these areas of difficulty can also be beneficial. Other plus factors (depending on the churches concerned) are the increased opportunities for role models and development. With the loss of a 'youth' tag, it can mean that young people are taken more seriously, both in the church context and with regards to available social activities.

With so many pros and cons, many can find a cause to defend either corner. This is where a scriptural foundation needs to be set and questions asked, structures adapted, lifestyles changed and God heard in order successfully to find the way forward. My personal view is that, as churches, we need to face up to the challenge, providing a positive alternative to individual church groups for different social classes and ages. We are in danger of ignoring the major issue by pretending that it does not exist. Young people are serious about taking this nation; we can either help them to achieve this or be at risk of being left behind. For the benefit of God and his kingdom, let us walk the difficult path, tackle the awkward questions, possibly fall flat on our face, and see our young people equipped to be men and women of God.

Apart from church services do you belong to a church group for young people only?

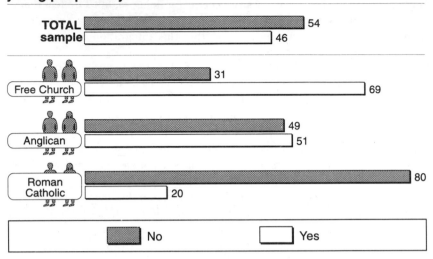

Source: Teenage Religion and Values Survey of 13,000 pupils in England and Wales. All figures refer to responses to the statement immediately above this diagram. The left hand column shows, at the top, the responses of the total sample which is divided, in the middle, into responses of year 9 and year 10 pupils. The right hand column deals only with the 11% of the total sample who attend church.

45 Colin Bennett

Equipping Youth Leaders

Education is what remains when you have forgotten everything you
have been taught.
Albert Einstein

Study the youth culture as deeply and as seriously as any missionary
preparation to an unreached nation. Most mission fields have remained
unchanged for centuries; this one changes daily.
The price for failing: a lost church.
Winkle Pratney

It was the summer of 1990, and my first day as Director of Youth Work at
Moorlands College. It was also the first day of setting up a brand new course on
youth work and, when being introduced to my fellow lecturers, a colleague in the
team joked in a friendly sort of way, 'Well, perhaps we'll next have a member of
staff training students to deal with the elderly!' As I reflected on this in my new
post, I thought quietly, 'Is there really a need to train people specifically for
working with young people?' Of course, I quickly came to what I hoped were my
senses! It did seem right and fitting, but in beginning a brand new course in
youth work I was forced to ask, 'What should such a course look like?' In this
chapter, we will be looking at various training routes for the aspiring Christian
youth worker, examining some of the options in setting up such a course.

Looking at the statistics that were raised by the Teenage Religion and Values
Survey, we can see that within the free and independent churches, 71 per cent of
young people felt that their minister was good with teenagers; in Anglican
churches, 65 per cent of young people felt their minister was good with
teenagers; and in the Roman Catholic denomination, 55 per cent felt the
same. About 20–30 per cent of young people in all of the denominations were
unsure about how good their minister was with young people; whereas 8 per cent
of Free Church respondents, 15 per cent of Anglicans, and 17 per cent of Roman
Catholics thought that their minister wasn't good with young people. We could,
perhaps, ask the question, 'Isn't that enough?' After all, why have a youth

specialist if most ministers are good with young people anyway? Should we not forget about this idea of a separate specialist worker and just allow the minister to do the work of a minister to all of his flock?

This chapter will highlight the reasons why we do need specialist youth workers, and it will also outline some of the training opportunities on offer to the emerging youth worker.

Youth workers as specialists

Paul Borthwick, in his book, *How to Choose a Youth Pastor*[1] indicates that there are three essentials for a good youth pastor: theological consistency; ability to relate to young people and to mobilize and care for a youth team; and the development of a strategy that is in line with local church mission. Terry Dunnell, in his book, *Mission and Young People at Risk*,[2] says, 'A youth worker is someone who is a leader of young people, an enabler to help young people do things, an adult who offers friendship and advice.'

If you go to a doctor's surgery, you would not expect to be seen by someone who had not received any medical training. The church and young people similarly deserve to be ministered to by youth workers who have been adequately trained.

Church-based youth workers are certainly specialists, but how do they differ in their specialism from the minister in the church? In addition to the requirements above identified by Borthwick and Dunnell, they also possibly require cross-cultural training. Young people today live in a world which is culturally different from that of the adult generation and which is poles apart from that of most adult church members. This produces a generation gap which, to be filled, requires a special mission focus as part of the youth worker's training. A church leadership team with a variety of specialists is essential, as it is impossible for ministers to be trained in every single area of ministry in a church to the depth that is necessary. This is particularly true in the area of youth work.

It is clear that the youth worker's task is not only to stand in the gap between one generation and the next, but also to support the emerging group of new disciples—the young people—by helping them to fit into the main body of the church. The product is a church that is on the move—a church which has not become fixed in a cultural time-warp, but which has grown fresh ideas that continually challenge the church, its position and its impact on society. In this way, the youth worker becomes a conciliator between the generations and contributes to maintaining the unity and growth of the local church.

What type of training?

One major dilemma in youth work training is: should a potential Christian youth worker choose a course with or without an overt Christian content? This has been a major sticking point for many aspiring Christian youth workers through the years. Certainly, there are many good youth work courses run by a variety of colleges which specialize in training youth workers irrespective of their religious beliefs. Notable examples in the United Kingdom are to be found at the YMCA College in London, West Hill College in Birmingham, St Martin's College in Lancaster, St Mark's and St John's in Plymouth, and Brunel University in Egham. Such courses are 'sympathetic' to Christianity and have a 'broad educational premise'. However, the purpose of this chapter is to consider the sort of youth work course which may be more acceptable to the average church.

The question is: should youth workers receive from a training course an educational basis for youth work and pick up their theology in a less structured way, or should the worker be trained in systematic and consistent theology and perhaps pick up youth work skills in a less structured way? Certainly, it is a brave course which attempts success in both these different disciplines. The purposes of this chapter is to consider youth work training which is overtly Christian in content and makes claims to develop youth work skills through a theological framework.

Anton Baumohl in his book, *Grow Your Own Leaders*,[3] categorizes three types of training which are applicable to the Christian youth worker, all of which will be considered here in turn:

on-the-job training;
off-the-job training;
distance-learning.

The following are just a few examples.

On-the-job training

On-the-job training is just that—working in a supervised or apprenticed way with someone who is tackling a youth work project and enabling the apprentice to gain skills through a variety of tasks.

On-the-job training certainly has many advantages as it both gets a job done and equips a youth worker with training that should meet individual and church work needs. In addition to churches training their own people, a large number of organizations provide one-off or consultative help, providing short courses and conferences.

Examples of such organizations are: Youth for Christ, Frontier Youth Trust, Crusaders, YMCA, Scripture Union, Youth with a Mission, Cypher, the Spectrum and Kaleidoscope initiatives, Covenanters, Campaigners and many others. Similarly, in some parts of the country, networks of youth workers have been formed for mutual support and training. These networks often include a cross-section of people, from full-time youth ministers to those who run weekly youth fellowships. In a comparable way, denominational youth officers try to support and train church-based youth workers, often using packages such as the *Spectrum* training pack.

On-the-job training is also available from local authorities, if the church-based youth work is affiliated; local authority training courses may also be free. Conferences and one-off events are also an additional part of on-the-job training. Brainstormers, Frontier Youth Trust, Covenanters, and Campaigners hold conferences which aim to give youth workers a boost, encouraging them to continue their work at church as well as giving them precious training.

As we have seen, the advantages of on-the-job training mean that it can be very specifically geared to the needs of a particular church, and the worker can be adventurous and innovative. Disadvantages include a potential lack of structure and breadth of learning experiences. In this type of training, there may also be a lack of consistency in the theological and youth skills taught. Fundamentally, who will structure the emerging youth worker's on-the-job training?

Off-the-job training

Off-the-job training courses are predominantly residential, but provide a student with opportunities to train and develop within churches, para-church organizations and other innovative Christian projects. They are designed to challenge and stimulate thought in order to tackle youth work from a variety of perspectives. A recent edition of *Youthwork* magazine[4] summarized some of the key youth-orientated, full-time, theological and practical youth work opportunities available in the United Kingdom.

Examples include Oasis Trust's Christian Youth Ministry Course, the Moorlands College Youth and Community Work Course, and Oxford Youth Works' Diploma in Youth Ministry. There are also other Bible College courses which offer some degree of youth training. Another significant scheme is Youth for Christ's 'Operation Gideon' (now offering an NVQ-style award in youth work). Oasis' Frontline Teams also offer one-year options in church work: NFI's Frontier Teams, TIE Teams and Time for God Teams, and YWAM's training schools do much good work in beginning to address some of the gaps in 'hands-on' youth work training. There are obvious advantages to off-the-job training; the main disadvantages are that the training may sometimes be remote from normal work, and it can be expensive and time-consuming.

Distance learning

Distance-learning includes a whole range of structured material—from text-books and audio tapes to self-help books and organized distance-tuition. The advantages of distance-learning are that it can be inexpensive, and easy to 'dip into' for those who are motivated to work alone. The main disadvantage is that without support and application from others, the work may lack appropriate direction, and the worker may lose motivation. Most courses are supported in a variety of ways, with the YMCA's Informal Education Course being the main validated course of this type. The Open Theological College is also hoping to extend its distance-learning opportunities for Christian youth workers.

Summary

In the Teenage Religion and Values Survey, half of those surveyed see the minister as being a good person with whom to relate. That may be a good start, but there is today a real need in our complex society for all of us to remain effective and up-to-date in our knowledge, skill and understanding of the gifts and ministries that God has uniquely given to each one of us to work with young people. The question which has been posed here is: which way of training is most appropriate to each of us now in the roles in which we are placed? Are we best aided by on-the-job training, off-the-job training or distance-learning? Should theology or educationally-based youth work be the main emphasis?

Whatever method of training the potential youth worker chooses, the best advice is to make sure to obtain *something*! In a society in which youth culture and young people change faster than ever before, those who aspire to be Christian youth workers need to be one step ahead—prepared, so that God can use them more effectively to reach a generation that desperately needs to change direction and live for God. As a writer on another topic once said, 'I don't care how you get it, just make sure you get it!'

Bibliography

1. P. Borthwick, *How to Choose a Youth Pastor*, Nelson Word, 1993.
2. T. Dunnell, *Mission and Young People at Risk* (second edition), Frontier Youth Trust, July 1993.
3. A Baumohl, *Grow Your Own Leaders*, 1987.
4. *Youthwork* (April–May 1993), Elm House Christian Communications.

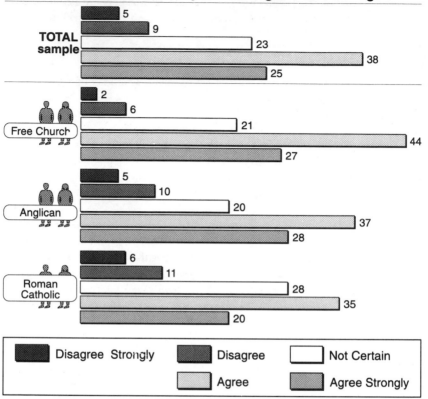

The vicar/minister/priest of my church is good with teenagers

TOTAL sample
- 5
- 9
- 23
- 38
- 25

Free Church
- 2
- 6
- 21
- 44
- 27

Anglican
- 5
- 10
- 20
- 37
- 28

Roman Catholic
- 6
- 11
- 28
- 35
- 20

| Disagree Strongly | Disagree | Not Certain |
| Agree | Agree Strongly | |

Source: Teenage Religion and Values Survey of 13,000 pupils in England and Wales. All figures refer to responses to the statement immediately above this diagram. The left hand column shows, at the top, the responses of the total sample which is divided, in the middle, into responses of year 9 and year 10 pupils. The right hand column deals only with the 11% of the total sample who attend church.

Section Seven: Storm

46

Phil Wall

This Is My World

Many young people today feel passionately about the environment. The results of the Teenage Religion and Values Survey demonstrated not only the strength of this feeling, but also that the influence of a Christian philosophy or world-view seemed to heighten people's sensitivity to this important issue. Thankfully, many churches have been moving away from an unbiblical separation of the sacred and secular. Most Christians now see the importance of a discipleship that cares for the environment.

From Francis of Assisi through John Wesley to Tony Compolo, many Christian thinkers have consistently stated that concern for the environment is wrapped up in a cultural mandate given to Adam and Eve in the Garden of Eden (Genesis 1:28–30). This mandate to care for, develop and protect the environment has never been withdrawn. Scripture tell us that the whole of God's creation— man, animal, fish and plant—waits in painful anticipation for Christ to return (Romans 8:19). Before we turn to the important question of how we express this concern, let us just briefly remind ourselves of the urgency and desperation of the situation.

The context

In the last few decades we have experienced unprecedented environmental catastrophe and abuse. Devastating oil spills have occurred, such as those following the Gulf War, or the break-up of the tanker ship, the *Exxon Valdez*, in Prince William Sound. Many animal species are being driven to extinction. The destruction of rain forests has risen to 20 million acres a year. Global warming is increasing in relatively 'microwave' proportions. Deforestation and desertification in some African countries is increasing at one kilometre per year. Ozone depletion in 1988 was three times worse than expected. Waste fill sites throughout the Western world are rapidly filling up. The United States feeds more grain to cattle to make beefburgers each year than the population of India and China eat. So-called 'natural disasters' are on the increase.

The challenge

Somebody once asked the question: What do you say to a world that says 'Elvis is alive . . . God is dead', and 'save the whale . . . kill the children'. In this crazy world, how should Christians live, particularly with regard to the environment?

The first thing to say is that 'caring for the environment' is not a new cause that Christians need to take up; it is intrinsically part of obedience to the command of Christ, part of the responsibility of being God's people. Three important stages must be worked through if the people who have the responsibility for this world are to respond appropriately.

First, we must recognize what kind of custodians we are supposed to be. Second, we need to see what kind of custodians we have become. Third we must find out how, in the midst of an environmental catastrophe, we need to change.

The dream

Exodus 19:5–6 clearly shows us God's design and role for his people. He was raising up for himself a people among the people, to be recipients and communicators of the grace of God. It is interesting that God chose to put the nation of Israel not on some remote island, where they might avoid being tainted by the world beyond. He chose to place them smack bang in the middle of the nations of the Middle East, to provide an embodied representation of God's whole society. Ethically, morally, indeed in every area, they were to reflect the heartbeat of God's kingdom. God's concern for the created order is both implicit in the creation story, and explicit in some of the directions given regarding the care of animals and agricultural land (see Deuteronomy 22:4, 6, 9).

The key to Christian thinking about the environment, then, is that Christians are supposed to live in God's way. Very often, this involves being different from the more worldly people among whom Christians are placed. But this 'being different' is important because, when other people want to know how to live or need to be challenged and shown how to live, Christians can provide a physical representation of God living among a community of people. Christians are called to be people who live in paradox. At one and the same time, we are called to be people who have no involvement in some of the practices of this world—compromise and ungodly living—yet who are totally involved as instruments of change in the heart and culture of the world. Also, we are called to be people who have no love, concern or attachment to the material world, yet who at the same time would be willing to die for the people in it. This lifestyle of paradox, living counter-culturally to the morals and ethos of sinful society, instead seeking to model God's society, is what we are called to.

The reality

We have a problem. We have a major problem. When all is said and done, the issues of the environment boil down to one single issue, and that is greed. The vast majority of environmental tragedies— oil pollution, air pollution, the destruction of animal species, the loss or our rain forests—are caused in the end by a desire for upward mobility, and driven by the combustion of greed. This greed, though not exclusively a Western trait, is largely focused around the capitalist and Western lifestyles of increased acquisition, consumerism and economic upward mobility. Tom Sine[1] calls it the Western dream in which, from their earliest days, children are taught to fulfil certain roles and live with certain expectations. These are focused around ever-increasing wealth, opportunity and the acquisition of all commodities—big houses, fancy clothes, electronic gadgets, flashy cars—leading to the fulfilment of that so-called Western dream. This materialism, children are surreptitiously led to believe, will bring ultimate happiness and satisfaction to the recipient. Besides, isn't that what the parents of so many of them are modelling? The consequence of this is that countries like the United States, which represent 5 per cent of the world's population, consume 40 per cent of all the world's disposable resources. If we are serious about addressing the issue of the environment and educating young people so that they will become eco-friendly, we must take an axe to the roots of the tree of the Western dream.

'No, heresy! You raving Commie pinko!' shouts out the dissenter. 'This is a book on youth work not a "reds under the beds" socialist manifesto!' If that is your initial reaction, first pray for common sense, then see a doctor and lastly read on! The world is heading towards an environmental Armageddon, blasting away mercilessly from the the barrels of materialism and consumerism, and the victim so much of the time is the environment. Our world just cannot survive nor even manage the present level of onslaught and destruction.

The reason why this issue is being addressed in this chapter is that so much Western Christianity itself now reflects the Western dream. It merely has religious subtitles, and a little bit of Jesus-flavouring thrown in. Far from being a counter-cultural model of God's society, with environmental concern that should have been flavoured with care, development and nurture, we have become part of a society that has raped and pillaged the planet. This has caused massive destruction and suffering for the Second and Third Worlds and, indeed, our own culture if we care to look.

To quote Sine once again, 'For anything really to change environmentally within our world we need a whole generation of people who will live to the rhythm of another dream, both economically and environmentally.' Who will begin to model an environmental lifestyle reflecting the values of the kingdom of God and redefining happiness, along the lines of the 'good life' of God?

The need

Inevitably, when someone speaks in this way, people often begin to get phobic images of travelling communities roaming the Welsh countryside (although these, perhaps, have a far greater sense of real community than the vast majority of our churches). But what we need most is people who will live the 'good life' of God *alongside* people chasing the Western dream but modelling a different life. Paul Illych, the economist and sociologist, feels our only future economically and ecologically is for people to live in 'communities of conviviality'. These, basically, are communities that will live for each other and within economic and ecological boundaries.

As youth workers and others involved in the development of young people, we need to raise up a new generation that will step away from the myths of Hollywood. We must strive to involve young people in relationships and communities which will be a model among the nations and the world around us. The big question is how? The following are just a few suggestions of how to face this challenge and begin to shape lifestyles that protect the environment.

A way forward

The first step is to identify the lies of our culture about acquisition and the so-called 'good life'. An interesting way to do this in a youth group or similar collection of young adults is to put together a collection of adverts, films, magazine articles and publicity leaflets. In a light-hearted but intelligent manner, identify the hidden and not so hidden messages selling the Western dream. For example, when I was younger I watched a certain advertisement in which a container of a certain aftershave lotion floated into view in front of a hairy chest partly-covered by a denim shirt; then, a smooth, clean pair of female hands reached inside that shirt! For many months, I tried out both the aftershave, and a similar shirt. However, the person who frequently took my shirt off (my mother) did so because it smelt so bad! The first task is to identify the underlying values of consumerism and acquisition, and the lies about worth contained within them.

These identified, Christian young people need a genuine sense of repentance for selling out, for failing to be what God originally intended. This should be rapidly followed by a commitment to seek to live differently. With particular regard to the environment, this will have a number of key consequences. It will mean sharing a great deal. How about encouraging young people to develop a clothes bank, for instance? Here they may set limits on the numbers and types of clothes they will wear as well as lend clothes to each other to share and pass on. Students tend to do this out of necessity, but it can provide a very creative means of examining value systems and it can begin to teach people to live differently.

Sharing also means making better use of what we have, both by recycling in the very creative ways suggested in a number of the books mentioned at the end of this chapter and by developing lifestyles of celebration and creation. Everyone can learn *not* to focus on the wasteful consumption of valuable resources—the unnecessary use of cars, the addiction to junk foods, the squandering of mental energy on computer games, the misspent money for unneeded shopping items.

The third key change is to educate people away from their 'hunger to have', and towards a transforming 'live to give' lifestyle. We need to develop 'budgets' of accountability that set limits on what we spend and use, and we need to be called to account by those we trust to stick to them.

Teaching intelligent giving to Second and Third world societies as well as to those of the West, will help people develop simpler lifestyles which allow more and more resources to be available for those in real need. This, more than anything, will destroy the power of the Western dream. The net result will be twofold: it will free young people from the prison of consumerism and liberate God-given resources that should be used around the world.

All this may sound both naive and grandiose. Moreover, it can only be considered in the context of a community of people committed to a common goal. But it is the only way to provide help and encouragement for young people who are struggling with accountability, and who are constantly pressurized and tempted to cop out and live the Western dream.

Why, oh why?

The very people who first need to have this change of heart are so often those of us in leadership. Young people are struggling to survive in a world that is forcing them towards the Western dream. But this dream, as well as rubbishing the environment, also rubbishes young people themselves: 'if you haven't got it, you're no good'. Young people are crawling on their emotional hands and knees under the burden of this pressure. So, they come to church to find an oasis of relief—only to find a youth leader who has, perhaps, sold out to the same dream! Young adults will only ever live differently if those they respect and love model it before them.

As leaders, we have some very big questions to ask of our own lives, the driving force behind them and the dream that we seek to live. So often, young adults do not get involved in the Christian faith because they find it no more than a reflection of a futility they already sense, with just a little bit of religious flavouring. With some honest questioning, we find that they are tragically close to the mark. 'Jesus is the answer', read one piece of graffiti on a wall. Underneath it was written, 'Who asked the question?' Many people have asked the question, but when they have looked at the lives of church members, evangelists and youth leaders they have seen people who are really little different, and Seaton they have thought they were unlikely to find any real answers.

Those questioned in the Teenage Religion and Values Survey are concerned about pollution to the environment. Both they, our environment and our God cry out for us all to live differently.

References

1. Tom Sine, *Wild Hope*, Monarch, 1991.

I am concerned about the risk of pollution to the environment

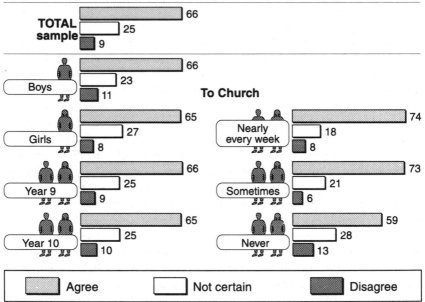

Source: Teenage Religion and Values Survey of 13,000 pupils in England and Wales. All figures refer to responses to the statement immediately above this diagram. The left hand column shows, at the top, the responses of the total sample which is divided, in the middle, into responses of year 9 and year 10 pupils. The right hand column deals only with the 11% of the total sample who attend church.

47 Towards Adult Christians

Only 15 per cent of the teenagers in the Teenage Religion and Values Survey who attend church want more preparation for adult membership or confirmation classes. Are you an optimist or a pessimist? An optimistic youth leader would read that figure and feel a warm glow of satisfaction—it must surely mean that their preparation classes are completely fulfilling the needs of 85 per cent of their teenagers! On the other hand, a pessimist might argue that 85 per cent have heard what these kind of classes are like, or experienced them firsthand, and declared that enough is enough! A realist might say that teenagers actually may want more classes, but that time constraints due to school work, for example, mean they cannot attend them.

Perhaps other recent studies can help us interpret these figures. The *Reaching and Keeping Teenagers* survey, undertaken by Peter Brierley of the Christian Research Association in 1993, paints a gloomy picture. At the end of the 1980s there were on average just four teenagers per Anglican church in the United Kingdom. During the preceding decade, the church as a whole lost nearly half of its young people as they grew from their teens to their twenties. When asked why they stopped attending church, less than one in five said serious doubts about Christianity were the reason. (For most, the key factors was boredom: with old-fashioned services, a lack of activities for young people and a serious lack of peers). A recent nine-year survey by the Diocese of Chelmsford revealed that the number of confirmation candidates under twenty-one years of age dropped significantly during the late 1980s.

When we look at the evidence, we cannot escape the fact that when it comes to joining a church—and staying in it—there is a marked reluctance on the part of many teenagers. We may not like this fact but we must accept it. It is a matter of extreme urgency that we start taking our young people very seriously.

In a recent survey,[1] more than 500 youth leaders at Greenbelt and Brainstormers said that the most important thing that churches can do to retain or gain the trust of teenagers is to involve them in the church. While counselling disaffected teenagers on Christian young people's holidays, the cry I hear time and again is for recognition in their church, both individually and corporately. Most adult churchgoers seem unaware of the huge pressure on our young people not to be part of the established church. This pressure is partly of our own making.

We all know in our heads that teenagers need elbow-room—the time and space to try out ideas independently, develop skills, explore the world around them and discover what works and what does not. But do we actually give them these opportunities within the church or do we serve up adult-organized, adult-led 'youth' programmes that are designed to fit around the rest of the church pattern? In most churches it is probably the latter. The teenagers often feel patronized, and they rebel and leave the church. This viewpoint is taken by Mike Breen in his book *Outside In*.[2] He goes on to put forward a very compelling case for dispensing with the traditional idea that Christian leaders are just providers, with the teenagers soaking up our wares as dependent clients. Instead we should consider ourselves more as servants who help teenagers to think and act for themselves in the widest sense.

Moving towards empowerment

This sounds very familiar to those involved in secular youth work where empowering young people has become one of the key initiatives of the 1990s—and a very successful one too. If we were really to involve our teenagers in the church, as suggested by the youth leaders surveyed by Crusaders, and we adopted the 'empowerment' approach, we might find ourselves with radically different young people who want to join our churches not because of what we offer them but because of what we allow them to offer us!

The first step is to educate our adult church membership. We should show them as vividly as possible what it is like to be a young person at the end of the twentieth century compared to the time in which they grew up. We must talk about the necessity to cherish all our young people because of their spiritual potential in God's eyes—and not to despise them because of their unspiritual potential in our eyes. Above all, we must teach that it is not just unrealistic, but totally unreasonable, to expect young people to conform to the adult-oriented world of the church when there is hardly any move on our part to adapt to meet their needs. This boils down to a simple principle that is not new but needs re-stating: we need to teach total and unconditional acceptance of young people, and—here comes the difficult bit—then give them a real voice within the church.

At this point, some people will urge caution. They will advise us that young people are not responsible enough to have such a voice, and remind us about a particular group of teenagers who were allowed to do such-and-such and just look at the problems that were created. They will warn us that the older folk will not like it! This is where those of us involved in youth work need to keep a cool head and spell out the options; either we change our attitudes, or the church stands to lose a whole generation of young people.

The second step is the proper training, in all aspects of leadership and responsible Christian service, of the teenagers we have managed to keep. Such crucial training cannot, and should not, be carried out by inexperienced personnel, however well-meaning they are—the trainers will need to be suitably equipped, perhaps by undergoing specialist training themselves. Perhaps all adults in contact with young people in a church should have some form of training in the understanding of youth culture, disadvantaged young people, counselling and interpersonal skills. A key element in the empowering of our young people will be the friendship and trust that is built up between them and the adults in the church. Anything we can do to foster this should be encouraged.

In his article 'Emerging Leaders',[3] Laurence Singlehurst, Director of Youth with a Mission in England, reminds us that a radical young Paul was given training and encouragement by an older mentor, Barnabas, when the latter saw Paul's potential. Later, Paul himself carried on this principle when he encouraged young Timothy into Christian leadership. The article gives examples where this principle of 'mentoring' has been used successfully today. Many organizations are now developing training courses in Christian leadership for teenagers. Crusaders, an outreach youth organization that relies heavily on volunteer leadership from local churches, has recognized the potential for leadership in many of its teenage members. The response has been to produce a unique two-year on-the-job training course for fifteen- to nineteen-year-olds. In the setting of their local Crusader group, they learn the basics of Christian youth leadership and develop their potential under the watchful eye of an experienced leader. Like other organizations, Crusaders has found that when teenagers are given such opportunities, they thrive.

Give them a break

Over the past few years I have led a number of Christian holidays for younger teenagers. Many of my staff have been so-called 'inexperienced' sixteen- to twenty-year-olds. Given suitable encouragement and guidance from a few experienced youth leaders, however, these young people have performed with a maturity that staggered some of the older people present. After one particularly exciting holiday at which we had experienced the power of God in a very real way and the young team had shared their faith by selflessly serving the youngsters non-stop, one seventeen-year-old team member was very anxious about going home. The reason? His youth group leader would not believe him capable of such responsibility. If only that leader could help release the potential of this dynamic young man who was waiting to be given the chance to serve God, instead of remembering him as the small boy who, it seemed, would never 'grow up'. How many other teenagers are stifled by similar unbelief?

What makes the story above even more painful is that these teenagers may hold a key to the problem we faced at the beginning of this section; how do we hold on to our young people until they wish to be welcomed into full church membership? Let us dream a little. Suppose we have learned to accept young people, given them a voice and begun to train them in all aspects of Christian leadership. Now we realize that they are beginning to show up our staleness, our complacency, our lack of urgency to reach the unsaved. They are starting to bring a vitality that we lack, a fresh approach to many of the things we do and a commitment to serve God that makes us re-evaluate our own priorities. Most importantly of all, they are starting to attract other young people back into our church and holding them because they are the ones in touch. Just a dream?

References

1. Crusaders, 'Trust You? Trust Who?', 1994.
2. Mike Breen, *Outside In*, Scripture Union, 1993.
3. 'Emerging Leaders' (February–March 1994), *Youthwork*, pages 24–26.

Looking to the future, would you want your church to give more time to attend adult membership/confirmation class?

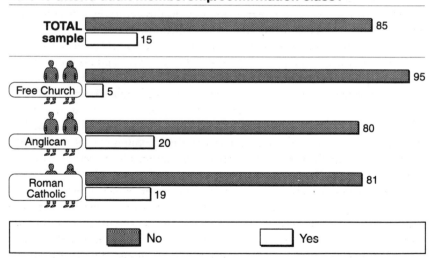

Source: Teenage Religion and Values Survey of 13,000 pupils in England and Wales. All figures refer to responses to the statement immediately above this diagram. The left hand column shows, at the top, the responses of the total sample which is divided, in the middle, into responses of year 9 and year 10 pupils. The right hand column deals only with the 11% of the total sample who attend church.

48 Dave Roberts

Compassion

Christians believe that despite humankind's rebellion against God, something of God's good grace still reaches every one of the whole human race. Jesus appears to be speaking of this when he refers to the fact that even the parents of unbelievers care for their children. It should not surprise us, therefore, when a majority of young people expresses concern over Third World poverty, with girls particularly sensitive to the needs of others (65 per cent) and churchgoing girls even more so (79 per cent).

What are we to make of those who are not certain, and the hard core who proffer unconcern? The unconcerned may either consciously or unconsciously subscribe to a survival of the fittest ethos which will characterize all their relationships. Some may even hold a racist world-view and welcome poverty and death as a means of 'keeping them under control'. This regrettable stance is not even logical. The most effective means of slowing population growth is believed by many to be economic prosperity for the Third World.

Is the uncertainty of many rooted in apathy or confusion? When one starts to scratch beneath the surface of Third World poverty, complex issues arise. Although young people may feel adequate to the task of raising some money for short-term relief, they may retreat in the face of the suggestion that the mid-1980s Ethiopian famine was caused by the Marxist government's destruction of the agricultural infrastructure. What can they do to change that situation, particularly if they do not have a well-articulated philosophy of justice? It's much easier to opt for personal peace (local and national security) and affluence (money for my needs and wants).

This does not mean that those who are 'not certain' are outside the camp of compassion, just that they haven't gone into the camp of concern. Many people remain compassionate because they are locked into a cycle of emotion-compassion-giving-detachment. They are touched by a television image, they want to help, they give money, they go back to everyday life. Money solves the problem. Bombard them with too much misery and they retreat, feeling numbed to the pain and powerless in the face of so many problems. You will only move people into the concern camp when issues begin to be framed in terms of justice. Whereas human disasters need speedy responses, long-term poverty is almost always rooted in injustice and destructive cultural patterns.

For the Christian youth worker, issues of justice will establish common ground with unchurched young people. A Christian critique of culture will further strengthen the commitment of Christian young people to bring the whole gospel to the world. The Christian doctrine of resurrection and new life is a vigorous antidote to a Hindu-based philosophy of reincarnation and Karma, with its paralysing effect: 'It's your lot in life; you can't escape your past life and your karmic punishment.'

The biblical motifs of justice and compassion are very strong. Jesus paints a picture of compassion and care as an act of worship to him; failure is rebellion, as the passage about the sheep and the goats in Matthew 25:31–46 points out. Amos pinpoints the deceit and the consequent destruction of people's dignity that characterize those who exploit the poor; and he warns us of God's punishment against those who 'sell the poor for a pair of sandals' or operate unfair scales.

We are further encouraged to active compassion and the sharing of our wealth by the story of Ruth and Boaz. It was common practice to allow the poor and destitute to pick the food gleanings from a field, and that was how this biblical couple met. All of this is underpinned by the biblical principle of 'jubilee', which sought to ensure that loans were only ever short-term (up to seven years) and that land sold by one generation would be given back to the next generation. This prevented any one person or group holding long-term control over others.

Christian history also reveals that many of its landmark figures were particularly concerned about injustice. The father of twelfth-century Protestant Christianity, Waldo the Poor, championed the poor and attracted persecution from the religious authorities of his day. Others such as Wilberforce and Shaftesbury worked for decades to undermine those who organized the slave trade and exploited children. Armed with a biblical mandate to promote both compassion and justice, the Christian is equipped for the long haul in the camp of the concerned.

A different model of compassion becomes apparent. Touched by a need and moved to compassion, the Christian is aware that helping the poor is like blessing Christ (Matthew 25:31–46). Furthermore the Christian holds his fellow brother and sister in high esteem, believing them to be made in the image of God and worthy of being treated with dignity and unconditional love, as described in 1 Corinthians 13.

Giving money and walking away is not really an option. We're not trying to salve our consciences, we're seeking to solve the problem. We don't want to give money and possibly create new dependencies and economic distortion. We are seeking to help people help themselves to break patterns of poverty and injustice.

This identification with our fellow man and woman sparks emotional relationship and empathy. Our reaction is then orientated towards involvement in promoting both compassion and justice. Involvement enables us to see tangible fruit, and allows the positive cycle of concern to continue.

Models of practical care

One of the best working role-models of this is The Christmas Cracker Trust, established in 1989. It has now raised almost 3 million for Third World aid and development causes. It does this by undertaking major fund-raising projects in December of each year and sometimes during the summer. A key to the success of these projects is the challenge and creativity involved—vital, given the supporters targeted, namely, fourteen- to twenty-one-year-olds. This has taken the form of 'Eat Less—Pay More' restaurants, 28-day radio stations and, in 1994, Really Useful Christmas Present shops. These shops seek to embody the twin principles of compassion and justice through 'Trade and Aid'. They sell Third World goods made in well-run, environmentally-sensitive factories and workshops for a fair wage. These sales help develop a nationally-run, justice-embodying economic infrastructure. Additionally the Really Useful shops sell light refreshments. The money raised is used for aid, particularly in emergency relief and development projects.

Although the central office of this charity provides a detailed resource manual, the day-to-day local management of any given project is the responsibility of the young people involved. This has several ramifications. The young person is more involved because their responsibility goes beyond putting a 1 in a box. Involvement helps create a sense of 'ownership' and commitment. The young person is empowered because their gifts and talents are being taken seriously. They are also involved in 'learning by doing'. What starts as a 'good idea to help others' becomes a process of learning, not only about practical skills, but also about the issues which underlie Third World poverty.

The fruit of this process is the emergence of more educated, sensitive and committed youth groups whose Third World concern will not wither away. Some people make a long-term personal commitment to mission. This mission will be holistic, seeking to proclaim Christ in both word and deed and to help create Christ-honouring structures in society.

The story of John Nonhebel is a case in point. John Nonhebel was a British Telecom engineer who took two weeks annual leave to work as a chef at a Christmas Cracker restaurant. During that time he watched a Cracker video about India and was so fascinated, he applied to go on a Cracker break of three weeks in Bombay. John found this such an exciting and challenging experience that he went back for a three-month programme. This in turn was so good that he then applied, and was accepted, to work with an Oasis Frontline team working for six months abroad. Inspired even further, and with the help of Oasis, he finally obtained a business visa on the basis of his engineering skills, and he now lives and works permanently in India. Nonhebel helps train Indian church leaders and youth leaders, and he administrates an Oasis programme in India; he has also become engaged to be married in India. And it all started because of his local involvement in compassionate concern.

Youth leaders will also want to bear in mind the classic maxims of care and compassion. These are 'one step at a time' and 'think globally, act locally'. 'One step at a time' in this context means having the patience to see a locality, state or nation change factory by factory, workshop by workshop, field by field. Realistic goals avoid the trauma of disappointment. In chapter 28, this book addresses the need to help young people to be realistic about sin, brokenness and evil, but idealistic about what a transformed Christian community can do, patiently and effectively bringing new life and new structures.

'Think globally, act locally' means taking lifestyle decisions that will begin to chip away at unjust economic structures. A high profile example of this is the promotion of Cafe direct. This brand of coffee is 'fairly traded' and is of significant economic benefit to the communities who produce it. Bringing fairly-traded items to the attention of householders, and perhaps trading them, too, as representatives of Traidcraft do, are part of a long-term contribution that any local church member can make to creating just economic infrastructures.

For those wrestling with issues of Third World poverty and social concern there are a myriad of resources. A channel to these can be found through:

Christmas Cracker
5 Ethel Street
Birmingham, B2 4BG
Tel: 0121-633 0873

Tear Fund Youth Officer
100 Church Road
Teddington
Middlesex TW11 8QE
Tel: 0181-977 9144

Traidcraft plc
Kingsway
Gateshead
Tyne and Wear
NE11 0NE

I am concerned about the poverty of the Third World

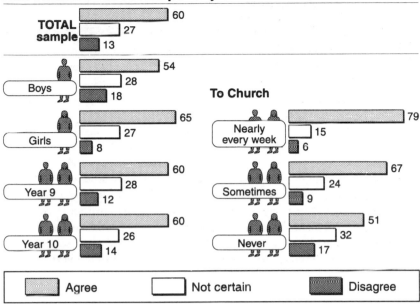

	Agree		Not certain		Disagree

Source: Teenage Religion and Values Survey of 13,000 pupils in England and Wales. All figures refer to responses to the statement immediately above this diagram. The left hand column shows, at the top, the responses of the total sample which is divided, in the middle, into responses of year 9 and year 10 pupils. The right hand column deals only with the 11% of the total sample who attend church.

49 Peter Gilbert

Youth Work

Most mutinies do not happen in the teeth of a storm. Storms either sink you or you battle through them, but you do not have mutinies in a storm. Most mutinies take place when the ship is becalmed, going nowhere: when introspection abounds. Mutinies take place when a crew feels isolated from its leaders; when a viewpoint is not even listened to, let alone acted on; when there is no opportunity for feedback; and when there is a frustrating feeling of powerlessness, often in the face of injustice.

If the above is true of mutiny at sea, it is also true of mutiny in the youth club, the classroom and the family. And the solutions are the same, too. Being 'becalmed' should be avoided. Young people around seventeen to eighteen years old are at the peak of their physical energy, and that energy needs to be harnessed and released! The attention span of many unfortunately lasts only ten minutes, so good communication should be short, sharp and snappy. In thirty minutes you may be able to make one point three different ways, at ten minutes each point.

Think of youth-orientated television programmes. Their magazine-style presentation is fast-moving, never 'becalmed'. And if going nowhere contributes to mutiny, then we had better be clear where we are going! *Aims* become important, and *goals* are vital. Finally, we need *plans* that take us to our goals. These three stages will help us to keep our ship moving, and on course.

At the end of the day, however, it is the crew that either makes the ship travel or not. Unless the crew really are a team, the journey will not happen. There are certain keys to teamwork that will unlock young people's gifts and characters, and that will empower them to make decisions that will help keep them from the destructiveness of mutiny.

We do need to be clear about this last point. We are not seeking to avoid mutiny because we want a smooth ride, and a quiet life. We all have storms to face ahead. Instead, we want to avoid mutiny partly because we do not wish to cause it and partly because the penalty for mutiny is death. God has chosen to work through leaders (Romans 13:1–6) and they are accountable to him for how they govern. But God is a God of peace and order, not of chaos (1 Corinthians 14:33). He does not want mutinous anarchy. Mutineers damage themselves, not just the ship!

The stronger the team, the less likely the mutiny. There are three vital elements to the maintenance of a good team. The team and the team leader must give attention to:

the development of the individual members of that team;
the way that team functions and relates together;
the job of the team—why it's there.

Any team or youth group that focuses solely on the job, and ignores any team problems or relational difficulties just to achieve the task, will at best only accomplish that task at the expense of it members. Mutiny lies this way. As far as God is concerned, your identity *in* him precedes your function *for* him. At Jesus' baptism, *before* he began his earthly ministry, his father called him 'my Son, whom I love; with him I am well pleased' (Matthew 3:17). Identity comes before function. Ephesians 2 and the Book of Colossians are all about how we are in Christ and how he is in us, and that our function flows from the security of identity in him. It is true for individuals, and it is true for teams and groups, too. Without a task, a purpose and a vision, the team will lose direction (Proverbs 29:18). But God is not only concerned with *what* we do, but *how* we do it: the destination and the *journey*.

How active are you in developing the individuals in your class, your group or your family? Do you have goals and faith targets for them? Do you pray for them, encourage them and listen to them? Do you give each member time and attention? Furthermore, do you pay attention to how the group communicates, how they encourage one another, how they participate, how they criticize, how their strengths and weaknesses complement each other? Do you know what their strengths and weaknesses are? Outward bound courses, weekends away and team games can be very revealing in this particular respect.

One helpful exercise is to ask your youth group what it thinks it may expect from its team leaders. Groups often benefit from a brainstorming session, to produce a list of expectations. The reverse process can be also useful: finding out what a team leader may expect of a team or youth group member. Unless expectations are voiced and adjusted, people will live with unrealistic or unreasonable demands on team leaders and on team members (mutiny lies this way, too!).

There are five component parts to moving unmotivated, press-ganged crew members away from mutiny and towards usefulness. If leaders adopt them actively, they will minimize the risks of team breakdown, of lack of volunteers and of poor commitment.

Selection

How you select both members and leaders of your team or group is important. It was important to Jesus (Matthew 4:18–22). It should involve us in prayer and fasting, and it should not allow people blindness, in which all that people see is the past and the problems rather than the potential. It is worth remembering that Jesus chose Judas Iscariot as well as the other eleven—*and* made him, a thief, treasurer for the group! No one in a group will have the same relationship with God, and everyone will need individual handling. Jesus did this with his crew of twelve. He was very close to John, close to Peter and James, fractionally less close to the other nine, friends with the seventy-two, acquainted with the 120, known by the 500, heard by the 5,000.

Demonstration

Matthew 4:23 tells us that if we would avoid mutiny, we must share our lives, time, homes, money, values and relationships with our crew. The best thing to demonstrate is our commitment to Jesus Christ in every area of our lives, along with servanthood. If you want a class to straighten their chairs then do it with them. If you want the youth group minibus cleaned, do it with them. Those whom we lead and serve will inevitably attach importance to that to which we give importance. Example is not the best way of being a leader, it is the *only* way. It is the Jesus way.

Instruction

Instruction is key to the development of young people. Aimed at both the head (Hosea 4:6) and the heart (Proverbs 29:18), biblical instruction encourages questions but answers the heart (Matthew 18:1–4). It will rebuke with love, and without fear of rejection. In Jesus, we see a team leader who did not fear losing team members, the disciples, and they knew he was committed to them. Biblical instruction makes room for both sin and mistakes (the two are quite different); it forgives the first and makes the second a learning experience. Failure of the team can, of course, reflect on the team leader and that is part of the cost of serving the group. Jesus was not infrequently attacked because of the actions of his disciples—indeed, he still is. Biblical instruction is never merely theoretical, divorced from doing. When you devise your group programmes, a good mix would be 30 per cent training, looking at the theoretical, and 70 per cent doing, working on the practical.

Impartation

Impartation—passing it on—is found in Matthew 10 with the commissioning of the disciples by Jesus. Impartation involves that which is caught as well as taught. If you have measles and teach, train, educate and preach about chicken pox, it is still measles that your group will catch. We always reproduce ourselves and need to recognize our own strengths and weaknesses as leaders if we are to avoid mutiny. If you are, at heart, resentful, rebellious, not accountable, doing your own thing in youth work, and avoid being a proper part of a good local church, do not ever expect your young people to be any different. They are followers by design and by inclination, and impartation is part of a process which decides whom and what they follow.

Delegation

This is the final and necessary part of empowering the crew and avoiding mutiny. Matthew 28:16–20 demonstrates this wonderfully. Delegation is about giving away decision-making power. It is about giving away the good jobs as well as the bad, and allowing people to do things differently—even, at first, less well than you would. In the short term, delegation is less efficient in terms of getting work done; it is, however, extremely efficient as a learning tool for those delegated to. In the long term, it is the only way to motivate the crew, increase the ownership of the team task, develop individuals, release and empower them, stave off inertia and injustice and produce individual moral responsibility. Delegation can only operate in an environment of trust (usually spelt R-I-S-K!). Trust stimulates security, mistrust stimulates stagnation, fear and condemnation.

A last word about leadership styles and young people: it is a real mistake to think that to relate to young people you must be a part of their culture or age range, becoming a kind of 'oldest hipster in town'! Young people respond most readily to those who will believe in them, trust them, joke with them, love them, and if necessary discipline them. Having God's heart for youth when working with young people is better than imitating their footwear. There is, however, no premium in ignorance, and any youth worker, leader, teacher or parent worth his or her salt will make an effort to be informed about youth culture.

Heavy authoritarianism will promote rebellion and mutiny like nothing else can. Most teenagers are trying to establish their own identity and their own authority and can react against heavy authority figures (teachers, parents, and police, for instance). Yet at the same time they are on a search for valid role models, for heroes. The mistake which society makes is in ditching all the absolutes and parameters, leaving the average teenager wondering what is and isn't permissible, and *why*. It is no longer enough to say, 'do as I say and not as I do', nor even, 'do as I say because I said it', but it is *vital* that our leadership style does set some boundaries and barriers for the young people in our care. It is equally vital that those barriers and boundaries are reasoned and explained. God is very clear about this with us in Isaiah 1:18, and we know there are certain consequences if the parameters are violated. Everyone needs to be loved and this *is* part of the nature of love (1 Corinthians 13:4–8; Hebrews 12:5–13).

Taking action on the above will mean that you have little time to worry about mutiny; you will be so busy doing the 'dos' together that you won't have time, inclination or energy to do the 'don'ts'!

Section Eight: Sailing Ahead

Alan Kerbey

50 What About the Spiritual Priorities?

We can't organize revival, but we can set our sails to catch the wind when God chooses to blow on his people again.
Campbell Morgan

It is a fact of life that few Christians involved in youth work would say that they have an easy time of it. For many, the stress is too much, with the average worker giving just two years' commitment before throwing in the towel. Within my own organization, Crusaders, we are not immune to the problem of burn-out, and this is something which should be addressed urgently and may be symptomatic of a much deeper need. If only we could capture again the excitement of working for God with young people, and see them through his eyes and not our own. If only we could make our own Christian experience so real that serving God and following Christ came an easy first and not a poor second.

The accusation of Jesus to the church at Ephesus (Revelation 2) was not for their lack of hard work. Neither was it for their inability to persevere with the task before them. The accusation was that they had lost their first love of Jesus! And for those of us who have been called to share the message of the gospel with young people this is a salutary warning. There is a distinct danger that we can become so caught up with the mechanics and methodology of youth work theory and practice, or become so concerned about the details of programme planning and execution, that we lose sight of a number of biblical principles which are the foundation of the success of the gospel in the lives of those young people with whom God has called us to work.

Scripture reminds us time and again (Genesis 28, Exodus 3, Joshua 5, Isaiah 6, Revelation 1) that a fresh vision of God is the single most important thing that will ultimately make a difference to our work as youth practitioners, because it will necessarily transform our prayer lives, renew our worship, revitalize our enthusiasm for God's work, and will increase dramatically our burden to see young people reached with the gospel, won for the kingdom, discipled, and prepared for effective leadership and Christian service. Predictably, the effect of such a supernatural intervention, either in our personal lives as believers or within the current operational framework of our churches and mission agencies would be so dramatic that we would quickly have to reevaluate our structures, programmes and priorities.

It is, of course, essential to point out that this emphasis on seeing youth workers equipped spiritually for the task to which God has called them is not to undermine or devalue the more practical aspects of current youth-work practice. Thus, the development of leadership training programmes, the emphasis on quality research which attempts to understand the nature of youth culture and how this is influenced by the society in which we live, and so on. All of these practical considerations are of paramount importance as we seek to meet the needs of young people in ways that are relevant and dynamic. However, in order for them to be used by God in the way that is most effective, we must also be prepared to acknowledge the vital importance of adopting a number of spiritual priorities to which reference has already been made. It is this further dimension of our work, so often neglected at our cost, that we must take on board, not only in our own lives as individual believers, but also in our churches, parachurch organizations and mission agencies which have a responsibility in relation to young people.

God's promise to Solomon was that 'if my people, who are called by my name, will humble themselves and pray and seek my face and turn from their wicked ways, then will I hear from heaven and will forgive their sin and will heal their land'.[1] Humility . . . repentance . . . holiness . . . sacrificial prayer. The success of the gospel as we reach out to today's young people will not depend on our physical efforts and enthusiasm alone; nor will it depend on our man-made structures and carefully designed programmes; but rather on our commitment to these fundamental principles which are rooted firmly in scripture and which have proved themselves time and time again throughout the history of the church as God's people have come to appreciate their absolute importance.

At a time when many youth leaders are struggling in their work because of physical tiredness, increasing family commitments, pressures of work, lack of support and so on; or equally because of increasing problems with discipline or having to cope with the disturbing consequences of family breakdown or abuse, such an emphasis becomes even more of a priority and must intensify if we are to see a real breakthrough for the gospel in the lives of children and young people.

But how can youth leaders begin to make progress in this vital area which is either neglected or not seen as being of great importance? John Wesley, in addressing a group of fellow preachers, helpfully pointed out part of the problem. He asked the question: 'Why are we not more holy?' The answer came back: 'Chiefly because we are enthusiasts, looking for the ends without the means. We want lively churches, thriving evangelistic programmes, glorious worship and social sensitivity, but we are often not prepared for the personal renewal which must undergird these things.'

Writing in his book *Renewal in the Furnace*, George Mallone says:

Refinement is the prerequisite of spiritual power. Reformation does not come cheaply. We cannot expect to have revival and have it cost us nothing. Indeed it will cost us everything. It will cost us our egotism, our pride, our desire for self-advancement. There must be a purging of every thought that we may merit righteousness or deserve God's renewing touch. For a new reformation in the church there must be an accent on God's cleansing activity. He longs, in the words of Malachi, to purify the sons of Levi and refine them like gold and precious silver, till they present their offerings to the Lord.[2]

This is true consecration for the believer, and it must be considered a major priority in our lives before we can even contemplate, using the title of this section of the book, 'Sailing Ahead', with our programmes, strategies and so on. This is the one thing which, ultimately, will have the most significant impact on our work with young people, and the only pathway that will lead us to it is the pathway of broken-ness of heart, deep spiritual hunger and earnest prayer.

If the glory of the Lord is to fill our churches week by week; if each youth meeting place is to be holy ground where our young people can encounter the living God in a powerful and exciting way; if our camp-sites and holiday programmes are to become temples upon which the fire of God can fall in a mighty way, then we have to understand afresh what it means to consecrate our lives day by day. Only then will we fully realize the incredible power of intercessory prayer!

. . . *'Not by might nor by power, but by my Spirit,' says the Lord Almighty.[3]*

References

1. 2 Chronicles 7:14.
2. George Mallone, *The Furnace of Renewal*, Kingsway Publications, 1981.
3. Zechariah 4:6.

51 Andy Hickford

How Should Churches Respond?

Last night at about 8.45 p.m. there was a huge explosion above our house. It was so loud that it sounded as if someone was hammering down the door. Yet my only response was to go to the window and watch. You see, I like thunder storms and this was a corker!

However, fifty years ago the same experience would have caused a very different reaction. Britain was at war, the blitz was on, and sounds of explosions had everyone in the street running as fast as they could for the nearest air-raid shelter. Our response to an experience is dictated by its context. Spill a glass of water in the kitchen and you just mop it up; spill a glass of water in the desert and you desperately try to save the smallest drop. We behave differently in a crisis.

That is what makes all current research on young people and the church important. It is not so much the research itself, but rather the context in which it comes, that demands a response. Young people have always been fairly ambivalent about 'the establishment'. Authority is not generally popular during the adolescent years and so in some ways it should not surprise us when teenagers sound fairly negative about 'the church'. It is the context, though, in which these views are expressed that is alarming.

In 1989, 13 per cent of teenagers in the United Kingdom had some form of contact with organized Christianity. That was frighteningly low when you consider the nominal relationship that this phrasing allowed. But worse was to come. By 1991 only 9 per cent of British teenagers had anything to do with the church and now some estimates at the time of writing put that as low as 7 per cent.

But it is not just the church that is facing a crisis with its young. There is plenty of evidence to suggest that there is a problem facing the whole of society. In May 1993, the National Opinion Poll conducted a survey for the BBC of 500 British sixteen- to twenty-six-year-olds. The results were stark. One in four would be prepared to commit a credit card fraud if they could get away with it, and one in eight would commit a violent crime if it was guaranteed that they would not be caught.

Many more examples of the crises of the young could be cited, from family breakdown to the problems of school discipline. The point is this: if it is perceived that the only issue which faces the church is simply how to stop young people leaving its doors, then we have missed the real issue entirely. The wider context is that we have a generation of teenagers spiritually blinded by scepticism and morally deafened by relativism. We are beginning to reap what society has sown. The headlines we read in our newspapers are not the problem, they are the symptom. The real problem is the spiritual vacuum at the heart of our communities. The church is God's vehicle to address that emptiness and yet this in itself is what makes the situation so alarming. We can communicate truth all we like, but fewer and fewer people are listening.

What, then, should the church's response be when many fellowships are acting as if nothing is wrong? How do we sail ahead? First, there must be a recognition of the state of things. In the words of Eddie Vass, 'The church of Jesus Christ is called to be a lifeboat station and yet it plays at being a yacht club'. We turn a lifesaving activity into a pleasurable pursuit and when we do, society picks up the pieces. We have to acknowledge that there is a crisis, because only then will we begin to respond appropriately.

Second, we must act decisively. In Vice-President Gore's book on environmental issues, *Earth in the Balance*, he talks of a global 'timidity of vision' in world leaders. Everyone is dealing with the issues piecemeal instead of being brave enough to grasp the nettle and start paying the price today for a secure tomorrow. Surely it is that challenge that faces the church? Instead of church leaders doing that which is politically expedient, there has to be a bolder vision. Reformation is fine when you have time, but surely crisis demands a revolution?

Third, we all have to take part in a 'conspiracy of the insignificant'. Local churches cannot wash their hands of their responsibility. The maxim borrowed from the Green movement is true: we have to think globally and act locally. It is precisely in the seemingly irrelevant chapels and churches up and down the country where change must first take hold. It is a change which will allow the needs of our not-yet-Christian culture to dictate the agenda, and which will make both our message and its medium relevant. To do that is not to sell out on the gospel, it is to recapture the heart of it, to hold on resolutely to our destination, and to plot a new course for getting there.

To what extent can we work together in this task? How do Christians from all the various denominations cooperate and encourage one another to rise to the challenge?

Let us consider how it must not be done! It is a natural human reaction to seek support in a crisis and over the years of declining numbers, local church activities have often reflected this tendency. Tremendous amounts of time, energy and personnel have been side-tracked into drawing churches together. These ecumenical initiatives are understandable, after all, when numbers in individual congregations are dropping and many evening services no longer take place. It would appear, superficially at least, sensible to pool resources. But such moves miss the point entirely. They are still essentially looking inward not outward. They have more to do with preserving a relic of the past, albeit a redefined relic, than with serving the community of the future. Surely we must ask the question: cooperate about what? Pool resources—for what task? If we are failing so obviously as individual churches in the evangelistic task, how will working corporately fare any better? Working out the intricacies of an inter-church process does nothing to halt the church's slide to the periphery of community life. Ecumenism in this form is a cul-de-sac of irrelevance, a road to nowhere for a church in crisis.

However, there is a form of togetherness and cooperation which is advantageous at times such as this. It is a togetherness which is focused primarily on purpose not process, on task not structure. It is a togetherness which sees fellowship as a by-product of kingdom activity and sees cooperation as a means to an end, not an end in itself. It is informal and liberating, not structured and restrictive. It is hardly ever 'launched'; more often it simply emerges as individual churches explore what it means to be part of God's initiative and then share those discoveries together. This cross-fertilization of ideas happens more often on the phone or over a quick coffee than in a formal committee. When each individual church takes the mandate for mission seriously, it is not necessary to manufacture momentum. It is rather in the resourcing and shaping of that momentum that this togetherness plays its part. It is a togetherness which does not seek to blur the distinctiveness of denominational settings (which we must see as an advantage of free choice), but rather affirms our differences and seeks to learn from a variety of approaches.

Above all, it is a togetherness which is led by a generation of Christians who are primarily focused on the kingdom, not a denomination. It is in these informal networks of vibrant faith that hope for the church's future lies.

Finally, we must remember that there is a big difference between a crisis and a disaster. Two thousand years ago the cross was a crisis, but it certainly was not a disaster! Since time began, God has been in the process of turning our weakness into his opportunity, and this has been proved time and time again in the history of the church. As G. K. Chesterton put it, 'Several times the church has appeared to be going to the dogs and each time it has been the dogs that have died!'

Our response to this crisis must be to pray and to work unceasingly for change, to share our resources unreservedly with those of a like mind and trust unswervingly in a God, whose victory is revealed through crisis.

52

Phil Moon

Church Demographics

The church is a strange kind of organization. Looked at from a human perspective, it is often weak, disorganized and, to be honest, often pretty hopeless. It seems irrelevant to most people, and for many it forms an all too effective barrier between them and any form of worthwhile faith.

But that's not how God sees it. For God, the church is utterly important, and any model of youth work which is going to have God's 'seal of approval' must take the church as seriously as God does. At the moment, though, we are not taking the church sufficiently seriously, and the following statistics reveal some worrying trends in the effectiveness of the church to reach and keep teenagers.

Certain figures[1] illustrate this fact. They show the actual drop in church attendance, both in absolute figures and in percentage terms, between 1979 and 1989, and they follow a particular age group through so that, for example, the 940,000 who came to church as nought- to nine-year-olds in 1979, become the 760,000 who come to church as ten- to nineteen-year-olds in 1989. We see, therefore, that the same group of people has suffered a 180,000 drop in church attendance over this ten-year period, which constitutes a 19 per cent drop in numbers coming to church.

The more worrying percentage drop is in the next age band, where the figure of 960,000 ten- to nineteen-year-olds who came to church is 1979 has now dropped to 490,000 twenty- to twenty-nine-year-olds in 1989, a 49 per cent drop; and an overall figure of 470,000 ex-teenagers who no longer come to church. There are further statistics in *Christian England* which was the original statistical report giving rise to the *Reaching and Keeping Teenagers* investigation.

If we combine the above statistics with those lower down the table, we see that we have an ageing church. The 550,000 churchgoers in the fifty- to fifty-nine-year-old age group in 1979 had grown to 580,000 in the sixty- to sixty-nine-year-old age group in 1989, a 5 per cent increase; and there was an identical percentage increase for those in the sixty- to sixty-nine-year-old age group in 1979 who had become the seventy-and-over age group in 1989.

We have an ageing church, and one that is probably becoming less and less attractive to young people every year. Moreover, the pool from which we will draw many of our church leaders in the future (in other words, current young members of the church) is shrinking at an alarming rate.

One natural reaction to this is to say that the young are not really part of the church yet, so we needn't worry too much about them. Another reaction is at the opposite extreme: forget the existing church, and start again, with a youth church. But both these are thoroughly unbiblical approaches to the problem. The solutions now must take the church even more seriously than we have taken it so far. We must see Christian young people as part of the church. The ideal that God is working for is to have God's people in God's place under God's rule, and so he pays a lot of attention to how the people of God live, work and worship together.

The Old Testament is the story of how the Old Testament people of God (the people of Israel) were to live in God's place (the promised land) under God's law (the first five books of the Bible). In New Testament times (from the time of Jesus up to, and including, the twentieth century), the people of God are the church. God's place is heaven, for which we are preparing ourselves, and the rule of God is that revealed to us in the Bible.

The church is very important to God, and he intends normally to work through the church to accomplish his purposes on earth. That means that God is likely to work through the church to reach and keep teenagers today, and so we must pay very close attention to the church to make it the sort of people through whom God will work, and to make it the sort of place where teenagers will feel welcome.

How, therefore, should we respond? Here are three practical steps that all churches could take, to raise the profile of young people in the church, to stop the ageing profile, and to help the church to have a long-term future.

First, we must make youth work a priority. We need to make it a priority in terms of our resources, our staffing, our budgeting, and our time. This means that other areas of church life are going to have to come down the list of priorities and may therefore suffer from neglect. If that is the result of a clearly thought-through and agreed strategy, then that will have to be something that local churches will have to cope with. Perhaps house groups will have to be less well-financed and supported in order to help the youth work in our churches. Perhaps refurbishment will have to be curtailed. Or there may be other important areas of church life which will have to be pruned in order to redirect important resources into the area of youth work.

Nor is it just a matter of where we spend our church budget. It is also a matter of which leaders get appointed first. If young people are a priority, then the appointment of youth leaders and their training must take priority over the appointment of leaders to work in other areas of church ministry. For the future health of the church we need to invest in our young people now.

Second, we need to make sure that we teach both the older church members and the younger church members a robust theology of the church, which sees both young and old as members of the same body. Young people need to see that they are part of this body, and the old need to see that the young are as much a part of the body as they are. What is more, if the young and the more immature (physically and spiritually) are to be included as part of the church, this is likely to involve give and take on both sides. The older church members are more likely to have to do more of the giving, because they will be spiritually more mature and therefore have more understanding of what the church is.

This all needs to be worked out in practice. Church leaders need to be convinced of the importance of teaching about the church to everyone in the church. Much individual work will need to be done with older church members to convince them that, if they lead in making concessions for the sake of the younger members, concessions are likely to come from the young as well.

Third, we have traditionally looked at the need to integrate young people into the life of the church by looking at services. Church services are important, but if we just work at changing these, we are not likely to arrive at a unified and integrated church, attractive to young people, and one which keeps, teaches and trains them. The solution to the Sunday problem lies elsewhere in the week.

We need to nurture the church family, and that means getting together on other occasions during the week to allow church family relationships to develop. As we get to know each other, so the friendships will build up between older and younger people in the church and our young people will gradually become far more part of the church. At the same time, church services will begin to sort themselves out, as the younger people will want to help the older people to worship God in their way, and the older will want to help the younger to worship God in their way.

If the church is going to be a healthy spiritual organization in twenty, thirty or forty years' time, in line with the demographics of the local population, then individual local churches need to place a far greater emphasis on the care of young people and on the life of the church family than many are doing at the moment.

And it will work. It will work because the church is not merely a human institution. If the long-term future of the church was solely in our hands, it would indeed look bleak. But thankfully we are God's people, a holy nation belonging to God, and we must have confidence that God has the future of his people in his hands. That, of course, does not absolve us from responsibility. It actually places more responsibility on our shoulders, because we are dealing with a divine institution, and with matters very close to the divine heart.

But we may indeed have confidence in the future of the church. It is God's church, and we will not sit back and do nothing. We have a divine mandate—to act for the present and for the future of God's people.

References

1. Peter Brierley, *Reaching and Keeping Teenagers*, MARC, 1993, table 20, page 90.

Conclusion: Look Out

53 Michael Eastman

Conclusion

Water in turbulent motion is untidy. It ebbs and flows. Waves build and clash. Cross-currents tug and push. The preceding chapters chart the restless change which characterizes work with and among young people. These fifty-two essays from twenty-seven contributors are an untidy, at times contradictory, kaleidoscope which, when shaken and turned, provides different perspectives. What you see and discern depends on who you are and what you look for. Church leaders, policy makers and strategists have much to ponder from this collected experience, especially those responsible for ministerial education and training. Parents have much to learn from those who have invested their lives in Christ's service among the young. The accumulated wisdom and passionate concern in these pages is a treasure trove for Christian youth workers.

The eddies and breakers on the surface described here point to deeper flows and undertows, shaping contemporary culture and society. These underlying forces form the experience of adolescence in the modern world and impact on the mission of the Christian community. Together, they affect Christian youth ministry. While making the lengthening journey from the dependency of childhood to the interdependency and responsibilities of mature adulthood, the young are a sensitive barometer, reflecting as no other section of the population the changes of pressure in our society. These chapters are a commentary on the anomy of Western culture at the end of the twentieth century. Here is exposed the hollowness of 'anarchic materialism' (Allan) with its emphasis on consumption, profit and greed. Changes in the law, family life and education and their effects are tellingly described. Ethical confusion, pluralism and relativism makes an unthinking existentialism (Wall) the only practical way of coping with uncertainty. The confident attitudes of the Enlightenment have been superseded by the fragmentation and dislocation of our world, forcing a retreat into little individual and private worlds of our own. Here, too, we encounter the idolatry of our time. The sharp realities of abortion, drug abuse, poverty, injustice, exploitation and the threat of ecological disaster jostle alongside family dislocation and sexual ambiguity.

The electronic media both reflect and reinforce these deep currents. We live in a post-literary (Hogg) era. Image replaces substance. Truth is up for grabs. Esoteric do-it-yourself religion (Allan) flourishes, while secularism removes the religious from our public life. Those who analyse contemporary culture will recognize all this and much more as making for our 'post-modern' world in all its uncertainties.

Several contributors note the role of the men of Issachar in Israel who were able 'to discern the times'. Christian youth workers, as all contemporary missionaries, are required to be 'good social anthropologists' or be relegated to the sidelines of history. Retreat into the safe womb of mother church is not an option for us. These deep-seated forces turn up in the lives of young people. With passion and compassion, various writers highlight the powerlessness, anxieties, disillusion and cynicism of the young, whose ideals and aspirations are blocked and blunted. Confused about identity, including sexual identity, faced with a bewildering range of role models, the young seek worth, significance and entry into adulthood. Many feel disenfranchised, alienated and helpless, relegated to the margins of society and the churches. They experience unemployment or under-employment. Violence is a worry, including bullying in the playground. Racism is a concern. They are exploited commercially and are wary of adults. They see and feel the need for peace and justice. The big questions—Who am I? Where am I from? Where am I going?—receive myriad different answers. So why not eat, drink and be merry while we can? The young ache for others who understand enough to support them as they negotiate their personal transitional journeys.

This primary task of the Christian youth worker is illustrated and illuminated in each chapter. These pages contain a disturbing critique of the contemporary Western church. Contributors write as committed members who do not disown God's church, but who wish wholeheartedly for it to change, better to engage in its God-given mission. The persistent and, to date, inexorable decline over the past fifty years in the numbers of young people linked to Christian faith communities provides the backdrop. Less than 10 per cent of the nation's young people nowadays are numbered in the churches. The Christian story is no longer known in contemporary Britain, let alone lived by. The church's defensiveness, inwardness and irrelevance is noted. We are the casualties of rapid social change, marooned on a sandbank as the streams of history rush on.

With few exceptions, comments on the Teenage Religion and Values Survey statistics note surprisingly little difference between the attitudes of young people in the churches and their contemporaries. Styles of communication, forms of worship, ways of learning, methods of teaching, all come in for comment. So does our concern for orthodoxy (belief) rather than orthopraxis (behaviour). All too often the church is not a counter-culture, but is captive to the very values of modernity which God's good news in Christ confronts.

Our class captivity is also exposed. Herein is a heartfelt plea that we Christians together shift from a maintenance strategy to engage in mission. God's mission is not centred in the church with the agenda set by our faith. It centres in the kingdom, with the agenda set by the context. For these writers, this is the plethora of youth subcultures of our day. Primary cross-cultural mission issues in primary church planting. Having learnt how to contextualize God's good news, we now need to contextualize church. New wine requires new wine skins. Christian youth workers are painfully caught between the old and the new.

Featured here also are questions of support for parents of teenagers; training and retraining of clergy and ministers; a mentoring approach to discipling; partnership between the church in its local congregational form and its mobile 'parachurch' form; and much else. As they wrestle with these realities, Christian youth workers find themselves at the cutting edge of the struggle to refocus the church's strategy. They find common cause with others who are addressing these issues in church growth and church planting movements, and who are variously engaged in pioneering contemporary means of evangelism and nurture, as well as new ways of being the church. Christian youth workers live constantly with a puzzling paradox.

As different contributors make clear, the current generation of the young express in a variety of ways an awareness of the spiritual dimensions of being human. 'Spiritual development' features as a significant component of the youth work curriculum outside and beyond the churches. Religious education has returned prominently to the school curriculum, albeit in a multi-faith form. The dried-up wells of contemporary culture are unable to quench the desires of modern men and women. Yet at this point, most young people regard the company which bears the name of Jesus Messiah to be the last place on earth to go to for life-giving water!

Various contributors wrestle with this perplexing reality and in so doing set out some essential elements of effective youth ministry. First, incarnation is at the heart of God's mission in Christ. God's good news is to be embodied, seen, touched and felt in the many and varied contexts and subcultures in which the young are at home. Relationships are primary. God's love is experienced face to face. This kind of ministry is long-term, intensive, small, consistent and committed. It is costly.

Second, the realities of life as it is known and experienced by particular young people in specific contexts are to be faced, felt and understood. The young value those who are able and willing to journey with them and who are able to show that Christ's way makes a practical difference as well as giving worth, purpose and meaning to life. Living in Christ is living as it was intended to be in all its richness and possibilities. Christian truth is personal rather than propositional.

Third, constant caring action and the struggle for social justice are as much the expression of God's good news as telling the story of Jesus and passing on his teaching. Words, works and wonders belong together. Conversion is a process.

Fourth, the call to discipleship is for us to become one with all those who embody God's upside kingdom and who seek through self-sacrificial love the radical transformation of individuals and their families, every community and neighbourhood, each nation and the whole created order. It is an all-embracing cause worth living, struggling and dying for, the demands of which give purpose and meaning to life.

Fifth, we learn best by doing in active partnership with others. This is a two-way process. The gifts that the young bring enhance and enable the whole. Together we are to be creators rather than consumers.

Sixth, Christian youth workers are called to be servants and enablers rather than providers. The hopes, fears, interests, anxieties and questions of the young are our concern. So too is their need for challenge, achievement, significance and security. The content of the informal curriculum of Christian youth ministry is embedded in these pages; tried and tested approaches are also described.

Seventh, there is to be no unbiblical split between sacred and secular. The whole of life is God's concern. Prayer and worship bring heaven and earth together. Spirituality is grounded in the hard realities of everyday experience, in all its joys and sadnesses, possibilities and disappointments, triumphs and failures. The richness of human creativity and the darkness of human depravity are of a piece. In effective Christian youth work, God's heart, mind and intentions, as made known in the Jesus of the scriptures and the faith community, connect with the here and now.

Several consequences flow from these central thrusts of contemporary Christian youth ministry:

◆ Christian youth work is at the cutting edge of today's mission. It is a ministry that calls for our best resources and long-term commitment. It is a life-long calling, not a ministry lightly taken up for a few years and left behind for 'greater' things.

◆ Those who undertake such tasks, whether full-time or part-time, or in a paid or voluntary capacity, need appropriate and skilled training (Bennett). Such training should itself embody and model the styles and approaches which are of its essence. We need the best of the considerable knowledge and experience available through the fields of education, social work, community youth work, and from those who research and study young people and their subcultures, including educationalists, psychologists and sociologists. This is to be integrated with a thoroughgoing practical theology and training in missiology. Those so trained ought to at least come up to the minimum standards set for accredited youth workers. We expect no less for Christian teachers, doctors and other 'professionals'.

◆ Church youth workers, both paid and voluntary, should be recognized. The move towards orders of ministry alongside those called to be pastors or evangelists is a welcome step in this direction. With such should go adequate means of support and supervision.

◆ The spiritual roots of Christian youth workers and teams (Gilbert) need nurture in communities of faith and the Spirit (Kerbey). To work with others at risk is to be at risk ourselves. Living water flows from those tapped into the fountain.

◆ We need to learn better how to form flexible and adaptable networks, alliances and coalitions (Fogwill) which bring together those engaging with young people in a variety of contexts. School-based/church-based partnership is one example. In our mobile, changing society many contexts are transient, particularly for the young who leave school behind (Wilkins) and usually, eventually, leave home. Who is called to ride with the bikers; to hang out on the streets; to house the homeless; to visit in prison; to act as chaplain of Colleges of Further Education? A survey several years ago of the contexts in which professional training youth workers were employed listed well in excess of 200 and stopped counting!

◆ The 'boat' metaphor needs to be enlarged. We need whole fleets. If the young beyond the present forms of church are to see, touch, feel and follow Jesus Messiah, communities are needed of Jesus people distinctively designed for the myriad locales inhabited by young people. Some means of interchange and communication between these fleets, their boats and their crews exist; others will need to be forged. Events such as Greenbelt is where many can and do meet. At present, such networks rarely connect with the church in its historic and institutional forms, to the loss of both.

◆ Prophetic voices are raised in these pages. Christian youth workers deal with the effects of deeper-seated causes in church and nation. Their voices join with others who share similar concerns. This takes Christian youth workers into political arenas. High levels of youth unemployment are destructive, often to thousands of young people. So is homelessness. Different contributors expose areas of our public, corporate and private live which impact negatively on the young. Those given the power and charged with the responsibility of ordering our national life, our institutions and corporate resources need to hear these voices. So do those in church leadership. Persuasive advocacy grounded in rigorous analysis is required. All too easily we can blame and hector others. Let us, rather, empower the young so that they, with us, act as agents of change and become their own best advocates.

Alongside this testing agenda lie equally daunting theological tasks. Christian truth claims are not self-evident. Various contributors wrestle with some of the issues with which contemporary Christian apologetics needs to engage. These include:

Who or what is 'God' in the face of do-it-yourself religions and vibrant aggressive ancient faiths?
Can 'true for me' be 'true for anyone else'? Why should it be?
What absolutes, if any, exist? Does this matter?
Where is 'authority' to be located? What is its nature?

Christian ethics is equally problematic as we face the complexities of the modern world. Touched upon here are hot issues.

What is responsible sexual behaviour when the gap between earlier onset of puberty and delayed marriage extends?
Where is the place of sex in human affairs when human multiplication threatens the survival of planet Earth?
How do we cope with the changes wrought by technology, particularly in electronic media and biological sciences, which out-flank our legal frameworks and raise possibilities we have not imagined?

Issues, of hunger, poverty, race, abortion and AIDS are featured. Trite answers to complex questions do not satisfy the sceptical young. Our Christian understanding is stretched on matters such as:

Humanness in the light of modern knowledge of our origins, history, psychology, biology, anthropology and sociology.
Evil in its corporate, global and institutional forms, as well as in its personal and individual expression.
How are the 'principalities and powers' evident and active in the world?
The radical nature and magnitude of God's good news and his salvation which is co-extensive with evil in all its forms.
God's kingdom of justice, shalom, joy and love in action.
The church, its nature, purpose and mission.

And so on!

Tough questions arise about the biblical roots of our faith. Our commentators note that we are called to engage with a pre-Christian, post-literary generation. How is scripture to be understood and interpreted by a generation for whom history has little or no significance, and who do not learn from books? How does God make himself known? Is he knowable? Who is to be trusted?

Christian youth ministry takes us beyond our comfort zones. It is not a soft option. The insight and experience brought together in this book has been forged by strenuous engagement in the arena. Answers do not come cheap. So, in the light of it all, what lies ahead? Choppy seas and a stormy passage!

One scenario is yet further retreat by the Christian community into a self-preserving remnant, heaved to, battened down, seeking to stay afloat in a secular sea battered by contrary gales and tides, doing its best to hang on to its own. Survival is paramount. We opt out. Another is to run before the wind, swept along and tossed by the tides flowing round us. Shipwreck lies ahead. We give up. A third is to hoist sail to catch the new winds of the Spirit and, risking our necks, stake everything on the Lord of the waves and tides of history. We plunge ahead.

There will be those who opt for one or another of these strategies. Our writers and those they represent are in no doubt! Come on board! Cut the anchors! Hoist sail! Face into the seas. There is nothing to lose. Christ is already ahead. His destiny is ours.

YOUTHWORK
AND HOW TO DO IT

The Oxford Youth Works Guide to
Working with Young People

Pete Ward, Sam Adams,
Judith Levermore

A self-help resource for anyone involved in youthwork—part-time or full-time. Oxford Youth Works is one of the most respected training groups in the field: their expertise is now available in this practical book, which can be used by individuals or groups.

Paperback, £8.00 (Pack of six £39.00)
ISBN 0 7459 2879 X

Also on youthwork, 2 multi—contributor title for publishing in July 1995:

What is Youth Ministry?
Worship and Youth Ministry